A SUNSATIONAL ENCORE

FROM THE

Junior League of Greater Orlando

Another great cookbook from the producers of SUNSATIONAL

The Junior League of Greater Orlando, Florida, Inc.
is an organization of women committed to promoting volunteerism,
developing the potential of women, and to improving the community
through the effective action and leadership of trained volunteers.
Its purpose is exclusively educational and charitable.

All proceeds from the sale of A SUNSATIONAL ENCORE will benefit
our community through our trainings and programs.

This cookbook is a collection of favorite recipes,
which are not necessarily original recipes.
Published by Junior League of Greater Orlando, Florida, Inc.

A Sunsational Encore
Copyright © 1999 by
Junior League of Greater Orlando, Florida, Inc.

To order additional copies,
please use the order form in the back of this book, or contact:

Junior League of Greater Orlando
125 North Lucerne Circle, East
Orlando, Florida 32801
407-422-5918

Library of Congress Catalog Number: 98-066410
ISBN: 0-9609426-1-0

Edited, Designed, and Manufactured by Favorite Recipes® Press
an imprint of
FRP.
P.O. Box 305142, Nashville, Tennessee 37230
800-358-0560

Manufactured in the United States of America
First Printing: 1999 15,000 copies

Cover illustration is by Rick Fruisen of Savannah, Georgia,
and depicts Lake Eola, the centerpiece of downtown Orlando.
In the center of the lake is the Centennial Fountain, dedicated in 1957
for the 100th anniversary of Orlando. Lake Eola Park is the site of many
of Orlando's outdoor community events such as Fiesta in the Park
and the Orlando-UCF Shakespeare Festival.

A Sunsational Encore
Committee

Chairmen
Lynn Luzadder, 1995-97
Kelly Acree, 1996-98
Marianne Vanness, 1997-98

Marketing Chairman
Mary Catharine Kolbert

Business Manager
Cynthia Nants

Recipe Chairman
Carrie Gill

Committee Members

Joy Ashlock
Sally Blake
Cindy Brodie
Pamela Buckley
Laura Burst
Shelly Carter
Stephanie Earley
Vera Farmen
Julie Folmar
Cheree Foreman
Theresa Feuger
Laura Goeb
Inevett Hahn
Julee Harris
Rebecca Hathaway-Casey
Tricia Hensley
Ann Kelly
Penney Lawrence
Debbie Leider
Ruth Littleford-Hanson

Karen Manglardi
Nancy Mele
Sheila Musante
Marcea Owen
Lisle Pallin
Holli Parker
Cindy Phelps-Shirley
Paula Pratt
Lauren Quackenbush
Ann Reisch
Yvette Rhode
Anna Tschetter
Kristine Vorpagel-Shields
Jodie Wexelberg
Diana Wicks

Sustaining Advisors
Kathy Emmons
Shannon Gridley
Missy Guentz

The committee of *A Sunsational Encore* would like to thank the following for their generous financial support:

Section Sponsors
A. Duda and Sons, Inc.
Downeast Orvis Winter Park
Missy and John Guentz
Holiday Inn International Drive and
    Holiday Inn Select
Hyatt Regency Grand Cypress
Kelly's Cakes
Middleton Pest Control, Inc.
Omni Rosen Hotel
Bill and Sara Raley—Servpro of Greater
    Orlando, Inc.
State of Florida Department of Citrus

Other Sponsors
Crane Rental
First Orlando Development
Junior League of Greater Orlando
    Board of Directors, 1997-98
Lincoln Property Company
Michael Wicks
Mr. and Mrs. Michael Hand
Vanderweil Engineers, Inc.
Whispering Heaven Tea Room

We gratefully thank the following for contributing citrus labels:
Jerry Chicone, Jr. (Shine, Crane, Kiss-Me, Fairvilla and Flame Vine)
Dr. Rufus Holloway, Jr. (Sunnyside, Pledge)
The Caruso Family (Blue Bird)
The Duda Family (Dandy)
The Musante Family (Pineapple)

We also thank the following for sharing their expertise:
Sara Van Arsdel and Hayley Fensch of the Orange County Historical Museum
State of Florida Department of Citrus
Christine Van Dyk, Copywriter
Edie Hall Smith, Copywriter
Laura Pooser, Copywriter and Graphic Designer

and

Junior League of Greater Orlando Board of Directors for their unfailing support

CONTENTS

History of the
Junior League of Greater Orlando, Florida, Inc. 8
Introduction 9

SUNNY SIDES

SUN BAKED

SUN DRIED

SUNFISH

SUN SEASONED

SUN SWEETS

HISTORY OF THE JUNIOR LEAGUE OF GREATER ORLANDO, FLORIDA, INC.

• • •

Celebrating Fifty Years of Community Commitment

The Junior League of Greater Orlando was founded in 1931 as the Junior Welfare Association. It joined the Association of Junior Leagues International in 1947 and became one of 293 Junior Leagues in the United States, Canada, Mexico, and England. In 1975, the Junior Service League of Winter Park, with its own 17-year history, merged with the Junior League of Orlando.

Since its inception, the Junior League of Greater Orlando has been on the front line of addressing the needs of children and families in Central Florida. Throughout its history, League members have given generously of their time, talent, and resources to improve the lives of countless members of the community. Some of the signature programs initiated by the Junior League include the following: ADDitions, an Orange County School System school-based volunteer program; Orlando Youth Center, known as Rock Haven, which provides a safe, drug-free and alcohol-free environment for middle school dances; Crisis Nursery, a short-term residential facility for children whose parents are in or near crisis; and Family Support & Visitation Center, a facility which offers children who have been placed in foster care a safe, homelike setting to visit with their biological parents, as well as parenting classes and other resources.

The Bargain Box, a thrift store, is a League fundraiser that offers high-quality, low-cost merchandise. As the longest running community program, it donates thousands of dollars of merchandise annually to social service agencies throughout Central Florida.

INTRODUCTION

• • •

Orlando, *The City Beautiful,* is more than just theme parks and sunshine. Those of us fortunate enough to call Central Florida home—from the few natives to the many transplants— enjoy beautiful lake vistas, lovely parks, fragrant orange groves, and summer weather from April through October.

This cookbook celebrates the Orlando lifestyle. Our balmy climate provides the perfect setting for outdoor dining. Picnics during a jazz festival, tailgate parties at the Citrus Bowl, and poolside barbecues all epitomize Orlando living at its casual best. We like to eat outside on beach blankets and picnic tables, and we've raised outdoor cooking to a competitive sport. While there is great debate over gas versus charcoal, all agree that grilling is a must.

Not long ago, citrus was king in Central Florida. Along with oranges and sunshine, tourist attractions included Gatorland, Cypress Gardens, and the Citrus Tower, to name a few. Mom-and-pop produce stands sold five watermelons for a dollar, buckets of bright red tomatoes, juicy Silver Queen corn, and citrus by the crate, gathered by hand from groves that spread as far as the eye could see. Wooden crates were used from the late 1880s through World War II, when cardboard boxes began slowly replacing the old standard. The crate labels themselves were spectacular works of art, as well as advertising for the grower and our great state. The artwork in this book pays homage to the history depicted by these labels and to the citrus industry which developed the region.

Orlando has successfully blended its humble beginnings with its dynamic presence today as an international business and tourist destination. In recent times, newcomers have influenced our palates with a delightful variety of foods, spices, and preparation techniques. Today, Orlando is home to a plethora of award-winning restaurants and "at-home" cooks serving a variety of delectable dishes from ethnic to southern, gourmet to casual.

To a sunny past and a zesty future, we dedicate *A Sunsational Encore.*

Citrus crate labels showcase the history of early advertising for Florida citrus. The artwork carried many themes, including family members, birds, animals, and flowers. Sunshine was used in many labels. This label took its name from the nickname of its owner, Shine Hardman. The former West Robinson Fruit Company is now a state office building in Orlando.

SUNRISE

Brunches and Breads

•   •

• • •

Section sponsored by
State of Florida Department of Citrus

Grapefruit in Rosemary Syrup

1¼ cups sugar
½ cup water
¼ cup honey
3 sprigs of fresh rosemary
6 large grapefruit
⅔ cup maraschino cherries with stems

Combine the sugar, water, honey and rosemary in a saucepan. Bring to a boil over medium heat. Boil for 5 minutes. Remove from the heat and cool completely. Remove and discard the rosemary. Peel and section the grapefruit over a serving bowl to catch the juice, discarding the seeds. Add the grapefruit sections to the bowl. Spoon the rosemary syrup over the grapefruit. Add the cherries. Chill, covered, until serving time. Garnish with additional sprigs of rosemary.

YIELD: 10 SERVINGS

Baked Grapefruit

1 grapefruit
Honey
2 teaspoons butter
Cinnamon-sugar to taste

Cut the grapefruit into halves. Cut around the sections with a grapefruit spoon. Cut a small hole in the center of each half. Fill the center cavities with honey. Place 1 teaspoon butter over the honey in each cavity. Sprinkle with cinnamon-sugar. Place on a broiler rack. Broil until the tops turn light brown.

YIELD: 2 SERVINGS

Sour Cream Oranges

6 large seedless oranges
1 tablespoon brown sugar
1 cup sour cream
½ teaspoon ground cinnamon
2 tablespoons grated orange peel

Peel and slice the oranges horizontally ¼ inch thick. Place in a shallow serving dish and sprinkle with the brown sugar. Spread the sour cream over the top. Sprinkle with the cinnamon and orange peel.

YIELD: 8 TO 10 SERVINGS

Spiced Oranges

2	**Royal oranges**
1	**lemon**
⅔	**cup water**
¼	**cup sugar**
1	**cinnamon stick, broken into halves**
4	**whole cloves**

Cut 2 long strips of peel from 1 orange and from the lemon. Remove and discard the remaining peel and pith from both oranges. Squeeze 1 tablespoon juice from the lemon; set aside. Cut the oranges crosswise into ½-inch slices. Arrange the slices in a shallow dish. Combine the water, sugar, cinnamon stick and cloves in a heavy saucepan. Bring to a boil over medium heat, stirring until the sugar dissolves. Simmer for 3 minutes. Add the reserved lemon juice, orange peel and lemon peel. Remove and discard the cinnamon stick and cloves. Spoon the hot syrup over the orange slices. Chill, covered, until serving time, turning the slices occasionally.

YIELD: 2 SERVINGS

Creamy Cheese Grits

6	**cups water**
1½	**cups grits**
¾	**cup margarine**
1	**pound Velveeta cheese, cut into pieces**
3	**eggs, beaten**
1	**tablespoon Accent**
2	**teaspoons salt**
	Dash of Tabasco sauce

Bring the water to a boil in a large saucepan or Dutch oven. Add the grits and reduce the heat. Cook for 7 to 10 minutes or until the grits reach the desired consistency. Add the margarine and cheese and mix well. Cool completely. Add the eggs, Accent, salt and Tabasco sauce and mix well. Spoon into a greased casserole. Bake at 250 to 300 degrees for 1 hour. Freezes well.

YIELD: 8 TO 10 SERVINGS

For Candied Bacon, cut 8 ounces sliced bacon horizontally into halves and let stand until at room temperature. Mix ½ cup packed brown sugar and 1 teaspoon ground cinnamon together. Coat each bacon slice with the brown sugar mixture. Twist the coated bacon slices and place in a shallow baking pan. Bake at 350 degrees for 15 to 20 minutes or until crisp. Drain the bacon and place on foil to cool.

Huevos y Chorizo

1 pound ground beef
1 pound chorizo
1 onion, chopped
4 cloves of garlic, minced
¼ cup chili powder
6 tablespoons vinegar
½ teaspoon pepper
½ teaspoon ground cloves
1 teaspoon cinnamon
2 teaspoons oregano
  Dash of salt
8 eggs, beaten
  Small flour tortillas

Combine the ground beef, sausage, onion, garlic, chili powder, vinegar, pepper, cloves, cinnamon, oregano and salt in a large bowl and mix well. Chill, covered, for 4 hours. Remove and reserve 1 cup of the sausage mixture. Freeze the remaining sausage mixture in 1-cup portions for future use. Heat the reserved sausage mixture in a skillet over low heat. Cook over medium heat until the sausage and ground beef are cooked through, stirring frequently; drain well. Add the eggs to the sausage mixture in the skillet. Scramble gently until the eggs are set. Wrap in warm tortillas to serve.

Note: May add shredded Cheddar cheese, salsa or sour cream.

YIELD: 4 SERVINGS

Three-Pepper Frittata

3 cloves of garlic, minced
1 large purple onion, sliced
1 red bell pepper, cut into thin strips
1 yellow bell pepper, cut into thin strips
1 orange bell pepper, cut into thin strips
2 tablespoons olive oil
2 yellow squash, thinly sliced
2 zucchini, thinly sliced
1 tablespoon olive oil
1 (8-ounce) package fresh mushrooms, sliced
1 tablespoon olive oil
6 eggs
¼ cup whipping cream
2½ to 3 teaspoons salt
2 teaspoons freshly ground pepper
8 slices sandwich bread, cut into cubes
8 ounces cream cheese, softened, cut into cubes
2 cups shredded Swiss cheese

Sauté the garlic, onion and bell peppers in 2 tablespoons olive oil in a large skillet until tender; drain well. Remove the garlic mixture and set aside. Sauté the squash and zucchini in 1 tablespoon olive oil in the skillet until tender; drain well. Remove the squash mixture and set aside. Sauté the mushrooms in 1 tablespoon olive oil in the skillet until tender; drain well. Remove the mushrooms and set aside. Whisk the eggs, whipping cream, salt and pepper in a large bowl. Stir in all the sautéed ingredients, half the bread cubes, cream cheese and Swiss cheese. Press the remaining bread cubes into a lightly greased 10-inch springform pan. Place on a baking sheet. Spoon the vegetable mixture over the bread in the pan. Bake at 325 degrees for 45 minutes. Remove from the oven and cover with foil. Bake for 15 minutes longer. Serve warm.

YIELD: 8 SERVINGS

Ham and Broccoli Strata

12 slices white bread, crusts trimmed
1   cup shredded Cheddar cheese
1   (10-ounce) package frozen chopped broccoli,
    partially cooked, drained
2   cups chopped cooked ham
2   teaspoons finely chopped onion
6   eggs, lightly beaten
3½ cups milk
½   teaspoon salt
¼   to ½ teaspoon dry mustard

Cut each slice of bread with a biscuit cutter. Fit the bread scraps into a greased 9x13-inch baking dish. Layer the cheese, broccoli and ham over the bread scraps. Sprinkle with the onion. Arrange the bread circles over the top. Mix the eggs, milk, salt and mustard in a large bowl. Spoon over the bread circles. Chill, covered, for 6 hours to overnight. Bake at 325 degrees for 1 hour or until a knife inserted near the center comes out clean. Let stand for 10 minutes before serving.

Note: May substitute one 10-ounce can of asparagus for the broccoli.

YIELD: 12 SERVINGS

Ham Strudel

1   sheet puff pastry, thawed
8   ounces baked country ham or other dry ham,
    chopped
8   ounces Swiss cheese, thinly sliced
2   tablespoons Dijon mustard
1   tomato, peeled, seeded, chopped
1   egg
1   tablespoon water

Roll the puff pastry into a 9x15-inch rectangle. Place across a baking sheet sprayed with nonstick cooking spray so that the long edges hang over the sides. Arrange the ham down the center of the pastry. Top with the cheese. Spread the mustard over the cheese. Cover with the tomato. Fold 1 side of the pastry over the filling. Beat the egg with the water in a bowl. Brush some of the egg mixture over the folded surface. Fold over the other side of the dough so that it overlaps. Brush the folded surface and the edges with the remaining egg mixture. Crimp the edges with a fork to seal. Bake at 350 degrees for 20 to 25 minutes or until the pastry is golden brown.

YIELD: 8 SERVINGS

Country Brunch Pie

4	slices bacon, cut into halves
2	cups frozen hash brown potatoes
¼	cup chopped green bell pepper
¼	cup chopped onion
6	eggs, lightly beaten
¼	cup milk
½	teaspoon salt
⅛	teaspoon pepper
1	cup shredded Cheddar cheese

Place the bacon in a 9-inch pie plate; cover with paper towels. Microwave on High for 3 to 4 minutes or until crisp. Remove and crumble the bacon. Reserve the drippings in the pie plate. Spread the potatoes, green pepper and onion in the pie plate. Microwave, uncovered, for 6 to 7 minutes or until tender-crisp. Mix the eggs, milk, salt and pepper in a bowl. Spoon over the potatoes. Microwave, covered, with heavy-duty plastic wrap, for 3 minutes. Turn ¼ turn. Microwave, covered, for 3 to 4 minutes or until the eggs begin to set. Sprinkle with the cheese and bacon. Microwave, covered, for 1 to 2 minutes or until the cheese begins to melt. Let stand for 5 minutes. Cut into wedges.

Note: May substitute frozen hash brown potatoes with onions and green peppers for the hash brown potatoes, green pepper and onion.

YIELD: 6 TO 8 SERVINGS

Tomato Pie

2¼	cups biscuit mix
⅔	cup milk
2	very large tomatoes, sliced
	Salt and pepper to taste
2	stems fresh basil, chopped
½	cup mayonnaise
	Lemon juice
1	cup shredded Cheddar cheese

Mix the biscuit mix and milk in a bowl. Spoon into a lightly greased 9-inch pie plate. Press over the bottom and up the side of the pie plate to form a shell. Arrange half the tomato slices in the pie plate. Sprinkle with salt, pepper and basil. Mix the mayonnaise with enough lemon juice to be of a thin but not runny consistency. Spoon over the tomato slices in the pie plate and spread evenly. Sprinkle with half the cheese. Top with the remaining tomato slices. Sprinkle with salt and pepper. Top with the remaining cheese. Bake at 450 degrees for 15 minutes or until the crust is golden brown.

YIELD: 4 SERVINGS

Quiche-Me-Quick

- 6 slices bacon
- 1 cup chopped onion
- ¾ cup sour cream
- 2½ cups shredded Swiss cheese
- 2 eggs, beaten
- ½ teaspoon salt
     Dash of pepper
- 1 unbaked (9-inch) pie shell

Fry the bacon in a skillet until crisp. Remove and crumble the bacon. Sauté the onion in the drippings in the skillet. Combine the onion, sour cream, cheese, eggs, bacon, salt and pepper in a bowl and mix well. Spoon into the pie shell. Bake at 375 degrees for 20 to 30 minutes or until a knife inserted near the center comes out clean.

YIELD: 6 SERVINGS

To fashion Kumquat Posies from fresh kumquats, make 4 petals in each kumquat by cutting the peel only into fourths from the blossom end almost to the stem end. Curl downward. Place the posies in ice water. The fruit remains uncut, forming the center of the flower. To use preserved kumquats, curve the petals in and place a cherry in the center of each.

Corn and Cheddar Quiche

- 1 cup flour
- ½ cup yellow cornmeal
- 1¼ teaspoons salt
- ¼ cup cold margarine, cut into small pieces
- ¼ cup milk
- 1 egg
- 1¼ cups half-and-half
- 3 eggs
- 1½ teaspoons dry mustard
- ¼ teaspoon crushed red pepper
- 1 cup shredded Cheddar cheese
- 1 (16-ounce) can whole kernel corn, drained
- ½ cup sliced scallions

Combine the flour, cornmeal, ½ teaspoon of the salt and margarine in a food processor container. Pulse 10 times or until coarse crumbs form. Add the milk and 1 egg, processing constantly just until the dough leaves the side of the container. Press the dough into a 10-inch quiche dish. Freeze for 10 minutes. Press a square of foil directly on the dough surface and all the way up the side. Bake at 425 degrees for 12 to 15 minutes or until the edge of the crust is very light brown and the crust is just set. Remove from the oven and discard the foil. Decrease the oven temperature to 350 degrees. Beat the half-and-half, 3 eggs, dry mustard, remaining salt and red pepper in a bowl until blended. Sprinkle the cheese and corn evenly over the bottom of the crust. Spoon the egg mixture over the cheese and corn. Sprinkle with the scallions. Bake for 45 to 50 minutes or until the top is light golden brown at the edge and a wooden pick inserted near the center comes out clean.

Note: The cornmeal crust may be prepared by hand. Mix the flour, cornmeal and ½ teaspoon salt in a bowl. Cut in the margarine with a pastry blender until crumbly. Stir in the milk and 1 egg until a dough forms. Pat into a 1-inch-thick disk.

YIELD: 8 SERVINGS

Fresh Mushroom Quiche

- 1½ cups wheat cracker crumbs
- ½ cup melted butter
- 2½ pounds fresh mushrooms, sliced
- 7 green onions, chopped
- ½ cup butter
- 1 clove of garlic, minced
- 1 tablespoon oregano
- 1 tablespoon basil
- 1 teaspoon salt
- 1¼ teaspoons marjoram
- ¾ teaspoon thyme
- ¾ teaspoon dry mustard
- 1 tablespoon lemon juice
- 7 eggs
- 1⅓ cups evaporated milk
- ½ teaspoon white pepper
- 1⅓ cups mayonnaise
- ½ cup evaporated milk
- 2 teaspoons dried dillweed

Mix the cracker crumbs and melted butter in a bowl. Press firmly into a 10-inch quiche pan sprayed with nonstick cooking spray. Sauté the mushrooms and green onions in ½ cup butter in a stockpot for 10 minutes or until tender. Add the garlic, oregano, basil, ½ teaspoon of the salt, marjoram, thyme and dry mustard. Simmer for 10 minutes. Remove from the heat and drain. Let stand until cool. Stir in the lemon juice. Process the eggs, 1⅓ cups evaporated milk, the remaining salt and white pepper in a blender until well beaten. Spoon the mushroom mixture into the quiche pan. Pour in the egg mixture. Bake at 350 degrees for 1 hour or until set. Remove from the oven. Spread a mixture of the mayonnaise, ½ cup evaporated milk and dillweed over the quiche. Bake for 20 minutes or until the topping is golden brown. Cool for 15 minutes before serving.

YIELD: 8 SERVINGS

Spinach Quiche

- 1½ cups grated sharp Cheddar cheese
- 1 cup flour
- ½ teaspoon salt
- ¼ teaspoon dry mustard
- ½ cup melted butter
- 1 (10-ounce) package frozen chopped spinach
- ½ cup milk
- ½ cup half-and-half
- 1 teaspoon salt
- ½ teaspoon nutmeg
- 3 eggs, beaten

Combine the cheese, flour, salt, mustard and butter in a bowl and knead together with your hands. Press over the bottom and up the side of a pie plate. Remove the wrapper from the spinach package. Microwave the spinach in the package on High for 5 minutes. Drain on paper towels and let stand until cool. Squeeze the remaining moisture from the spinach. Combine the milk, half-and-half, salt and nutmeg in a saucepan. Bring almost to a boil. Stir in the eggs and spinach. Spoon into the prepared pie plate. Bake at 400 degrees for 15 minutes. Reduce the oven temperature to 325 degrees. Bake for 20 minutes longer or until set.

YIELD: 6 SERVINGS

Blueberry Coffee Cake

- 1½ cups flour
- 1 tablespoon poppy seeds
- ½ teaspoon baking soda
- ¼ teaspoon salt
- ⅔ cup sugar
- ½ cup butter, softened
- 2 teaspoons grated lemon peel
- 1 egg
- ½ cup sour cream
- 2 cups fresh blueberries, rinsed, drained
- ⅓ cup sugar
- 2 teaspoons flour
- ¼ teaspoon nutmeg
- ⅓ cup confectioners' sugar, sifted
- 1 to 2 teaspoons milk

Grease and flour the bottom and side of a 9- or 10-inch springform pan. Mix 1½ cups flour, poppy seeds, baking soda and salt together and set aside. Cream ⅔ cup sugar and butter in a mixer bowl until light and fluffy. Add the lemon peel and egg. Beat for 2 minutes. Add the flour mixture and sour cream alternately, beating well after each addition. Spread over the bottom and 1 inch up the side of the prepared pan. Mix the blueberries, ⅓ cup sugar, 2 teaspoons flour and nutmeg in a bowl. Spoon over the batter in the pan. Bake at 350 degrees for 45 to 55 minutes or until golden brown. Remove from the oven. Drizzle with a mixture of the confectioners' sugar and milk.

YIELD: 12 SERVINGS

Sour Cream Coffee Cake

- 2 cups flour
- ½ teaspoon salt
- ½ teaspoon baking soda
- 1½ teaspoons baking powder
- 1 cup butter, softened
- 1¼ cups sugar
- 2 eggs
- 1 cup sour cream
- 1 teaspoon vanilla extract
- ¾ cup ground pecans
- 2 tablespoons sugar
- 1 tablespoon cinnamon

Sift the flour, salt, baking soda and baking powder together and set aside. Cream the butter, 1¼ cups sugar and eggs in a mixer bowl until light and fluffy. Blend in the sour cream. Add the flour mixture and vanilla alternately, beating well after each addition. Spoon half the batter into a greased 9x15-inch baking pan. Mix the pecans, 2 tablespoons sugar and cinnamon in a small bowl. Sprinkle half the mixture over the batter in the pan. Layer the remaining batter and cinnamon mixture over the layers. Bake at 350 degrees for 40 minutes.

YIELD: 15 TO 18 SERVINGS

Cranberry Cinnamon Coffee Cake

1½ cups flour
2   teaspoons baking powder
1   teaspoon salt
½   cup sugar
1   egg
⅔   cup milk
3   tablespoons vegetable oil
½   cup whole cranberry sauce
3   tablespoons sugar
3   tablespoons flour
2   teaspoons cinnamon
3   tablespoons butter

Sift 1½ cups flour, baking powder, salt and ½ cup sugar into a bowl. Add the egg, milk and oil and mix well. Spread in a greased 8-inch round baking pan. Spoon the cranberry sauce over the batter 1 teaspoonful at a time. Mix 3 tablespoons sugar, 3 tablespoons flour and cinnamon in a bowl. Cut in the butter until crumbly. Sprinkle over the cranberry sauce. Bake at 350 degrees for 35 to 40 minutes or until the coffee cake tests done.

YIELD: 12 TO 15 SERVINGS

Orange-Glazed Coffee Cake

1   envelope dry yeast
¼   cup warm (105 to 115 degrees) water
½   cup warm (105 to 115 degrees) milk
½   cup fresh orange juice
½   cup sugar
½   cup ricotta cheese
1   tablespoon grated orange zest
½   teaspoon salt
1   egg, lightly beaten
3½ to 4 cups flour
1   egg, lightly beaten
1   cup confectioners' sugar
1½ to 2 tablespoons fresh orange juice

Dissolve the yeast in the warm water in a large mixer bowl. Let stand for 5 to 10 minutes or until foamy. Stir in the warm milk, ½ cup orange juice, sugar, ricotta cheese, orange zest, salt and 1 egg. Fit a heavy-duty mixer with a paddle attachment. Beat 2 cups of the flour into the yeast mixture at low speed until a sticky dough forms. Beat in enough of the remaining flour ½ cup at a time to form a stiff dough. Knead on a lightly floured surface for 5 to 10 minutes or until smooth and elastic, adding additional flour if needed. Place in a large greased bowl, turning to coat the surface. Let rise, covered with a damp cloth, in a warm place for 1½ hours or until doubled in bulk. Knead on a lightly floured surface for 1 to 2 minutes or until smooth. Divide into 3 equal portions. Roll each portion into a 20-inch-long rope. Braid the ropes together. Coil the braided dough in a greased 10-inch springform pan, tucking the ends under. Let rise, covered with a damp cloth, in a warm place for 30 minutes or until almost doubled. Brush with 1 egg. Bake at 425 degrees for 25 to 30 minutes or until golden brown. Remove to a wire rack to cool slightly. Blend the confectioners' sugar with 1½ to 2 tablespoons orange juice in a small bowl. Spread over the warm coffee cake. Serve warm.

YIELD: 12 SERVINGS

Treasure-Filled Coffee Ring

¾ cup sugar
1 tablespoon grated orange peel (optional)
¼ cup chopped pecans
2 (3-ounce) bricks cream cheese, softened
2 (10-count) cans large flaky refrigerator biscuits
½ cup melted margarine or butter

Mix the sugar, orange peel and pecans in a bowl and set aside. Cut each brick of cream cheese into halves lengthwise; cut each brick crosswise at 5 equal intervals, forming 10 equal pieces. Separate each biscuit into halves. Place 1 piece of cream cheese between 2 biscuit halves; seal the edges. Repeat with the remaining biscuit halves and cream cheese pieces. Dip each biscuit into the margarine, then into the sugar mixture. Stand each biscuit on its edge in a greased bundt pan, overlapping slightly. Sprinkle with any remaining sugar mixture; drizzle with any remaining margarine. Bake at 350 degrees for 30 to 35 minutes or until golden brown. Cool in the pan for 1 minute. Remove to a serving plate. Cool slightly.

YIELD: 10 SERVINGS

Apple Butter Muffins

1⅔ cups sugar
2 teaspoons baking soda
¾ teaspoon baking powder
3½ cups flour
2 teaspoons cinnamon
1 (16-ounce) jar apple butter
1¼ cups sour cream
4 eggs, lightly beaten
¾ cup vegetable oil
1 small Red Delicious apple, shredded

Mix the sugar, baking soda, baking powder, flour and cinnamon in a large bowl. Stir in the apple butter. Combine the sour cream, eggs, oil and apple in a medium bowl and mix well. Add to the flour mixture and mix well. Spoon into paper-lined or greased muffin cups. Bake at 350 degrees for 20 minutes or until the muffins test done.

Note: May add ½ cup chopped nuts to the batter.

YIELD: 15 SERVINGS

For Orange Frappé, combine 4 cups fresh orange juice, juice of 1 lemon, 1 large banana, 6 fresh strawberries, ¼ cup whipping cream and 6 ice cubes in a blender container. Process at high speed for 1 minute. Serve in frosted, stemmed goblets. Garnish with fresh mint leaves.

Banana Praline Muffins

6	tablespoons brown sugar
2	tablespoons sour cream
1	cup pecan pieces
1¼	cups flour
2	teaspoons baking powder
¼	teaspoon salt
3	ripe bananas
1	egg
½	cup sugar
¼	cup vegetable oil

Mix the brown sugar and sour cream in a small bowl. Stir in the pecans. Mix the flour, baking powder and salt together. Mash the bananas in a large bowl. Add the egg, sugar and oil and beat well. Add the flour mixture and stir just until moistened. Spoon into greased muffin cups. Top each with a spoonful of the brown sugar mixture. Bake at 400 degrees for 15 minutes or until golden brown. Serve warm.

YIELD: 1 DOZEN

Skyline Apple Muffins

HONORABLE LINDA W. CHAPIN,
ORANGE COUNTY CHAIRMAN

1½	cups packed brown sugar
⅔	cup vegetable oil
1	egg
1	cup buttermilk
1	teaspoon baking soda
1	teaspoon salt
1	teaspoon vanilla extract
2½	cups flour
1½	cups chopped apples
½	cup chopped pecans
⅓	cup sugar
1	teaspoon melted butter

Mix the brown sugar, oil and egg in a large bowl. Mix the buttermilk, baking soda, salt and vanilla in a medium bowl. Add the buttermilk mixture and flour alternately to the brown sugar mixture, beating well after each addition. Fold in the apples and pecans. Spoon into nonstick muffin cups. Sprinkle with the sugar, then the melted butter. Bake at 325 degrees for 30 minutes.

YIELD: 12 TO 18 SERVINGS

To make Orange Kumquat Butter, combine 3 cups sliced, seeded kumquats and 2¼ cups orange juice in a heavy saucepan. Let stand for 2 hours. Boil until the kumquat peel is tender. Add 1½ cups sugar and cook until the mixture is thickened and the kumquat is translucent. Ladle into hot sterilized jars, leaving ½ inch headspace; seal with 2-piece lids. Process in a boiling water bath for 10 minutes.

Bacon and Cheese Muffins

5   **slices bacon**
2   **cups flour**
2   **teaspoons sugar**
2   **teaspoons baking powder**
½   **teaspoon salt**
2   **tablespoons grated Cheddar cheese**
1   **cup milk**
1   **egg**
2   **tablespoons grated Cheddar cheese**

Fry the bacon in a skillet until crisp; drain well, reserving the drippings. Remove and crumble the bacon. Mix the flour, sugar, baking powder and salt in a medium bowl. Add 2 tablespoons cheese and crumbled bacon. Mix the milk, egg and reserved bacon drippings in a small bowl. Stir into the flour mixture for 15 to 20 seconds or until mixed but still slightly lumpy. Spoon into each of 6 buttered muffin cups. Sprinkle with 2 tablespoons cheese. Bake at 400 degrees for 20 to 25 minutes or until lightly browned.

YIELD: 6 SERVINGS

Tasty Bran Muffins

1   **cup boiling water**
1   **cup all-bran cereal**
½   **cup vegetable oil**
2½   **cups flour**
2½   **teaspoons baking soda**
1   **teaspoon salt**
2   **eggs, beaten**
1½   **cups sugar**
2   **cups buttermilk**
2   **cups all-bran cereal**
1   **(12-ounce) jar apple butter**
1   **cup chopped walnuts**

Pour the boiling water over 1 cup cereal in a large bowl. Add the oil and mix well. Set aside. Sift the flour, baking soda and salt together. Mix the eggs, sugar, buttermilk and 2 cups cereal in a medium bowl. Add the flour mixture and sugar mixture to the cereal mixture and mix well. Stir in the apple butter and walnuts. Spoon into greased muffin cups. Bake at 400 degrees for 15 to 20 minutes or until the muffins test done.

YIELD: 36 SERVINGS

French Puffs

1½ cups flour
1½ teaspoons baking powder
½ teaspoon salt
¼ teaspoon nutmeg
⅓ cup melted butter or margarine
½ cup sugar
1 egg, lightly beaten
½ cup milk
3 tablespoons melted butter or margarine
½ cup sugar
1 teaspoon cinnamon

Mix the flour, baking powder, salt and nutmeg together. Beat ⅓ cup butter, ½ cup sugar and egg at medium speed in a mixer bowl until light and fluffy. Add the flour mixture and milk alternately, beginning and ending with the flour mixture and beating at low speed after each addition. Fill greased miniature muffin cups ⅔ full with batter. Bake at 350 degrees for 14 to 16 minutes or until the muffins test done. Remove from the muffin cups immediately. Dip the tops of the muffins into the 3 tablespoons melted butter, then into a mixture of ½ cup sugar and cinnamon.

Note: Muffins may be baked in standard muffin cups for 20 to 25 minutes.

YIELD: 28 SERVINGS

Blueberry Breakfast

6 slices sourdough French bread, cut into 1-inch "fingers"
4 eggs
1 cup half-and-half
¼ teaspoon baking powder
1 teaspoon vanilla extract
½ cup sugar
1 teaspoon cinnamon
¼ teaspoon allspice
1½ teaspoons cornstarch
2 cups blueberries
¼ cup melted butter

Place the bread pieces on a baking sheet with sides. Beat the eggs, half-and-half, baking powder and vanilla in a medium bowl. Spoon over the bread, coating the bread completely. Cover with plastic wrap and chill overnight. Combine the sugar, cinnamon, allspice and cornstarch in a bowl. Add the blueberries and mix well. Spread the berry mixture in a greased 9x12-inch baking dish. Cover with the bread pieces. Drizzle with the butter. Bake at 450 degrees for 30 minutes. Let stand for 10 minutes. Cut into squares. Spoon the blueberry sauce over the squares.

YIELD: 6 TO 8 SERVINGS

Oven French Toast

1   **loaf French bread, cut into 1-inch slices**
6   **eggs**
1½ **cups milk**
1½ **cups half-and-half**
1   **teaspoon vanilla extract**
⅛ **teaspoon nutmeg**
⅛ **teaspoon cinnamon**
½ **cup margarine, softened**
1   **cup chopped pecans**
1   **cup packed brown sugar**
2   **tablespoons dark corn syrup or maple syrup**

Arrange the bread slices in a greased 9x13-inch baking dish. Mix the eggs, milk, half-and-half, vanilla, nutmeg and cinnamon in a bowl. Spoon over the bread slices. Chill, covered, for 12 to 24 hours. Mix the margarine, pecans, brown sugar and corn syrup in a bowl. Spread over the bread slices. Bake at 350 degrees for 40 minutes or until puffed and browned.

YIELD: 8 TO 10 SERVINGS

Stuffed French Toast

1   **egg**
¼ **cup milk**
1   **teaspoon vanilla extract**
    Softened cream cheese
4   **slices bread**
1   **banana, sliced**
    Brown sugar
    Cinnamon
2   **tablespoons butter**

Beat the egg in a shallow bowl. Add the milk and vanilla and mix well. Spread cream cheese on 2 of the bread slices. Top with banana slices. Sprinkle with brown sugar and cinnamon. Top with the remaining bread slices. Melt the butter in a hot skillet. Add a small amount of brown sugar to the butter if desired. Dip the sandwiches into the egg mixture. Place the sandwiches in the skillet. Cook until browned on both sides. Serve with syrup or fruit.

Note: Also good with peaches or strawberries.

YIELD: 2 SERVINGS

For Spiked Strawberries, beat 2 cups sour cream, ½ cup cream cheese, ½ cup packed brown sugar and 2 tablespoons Grand Marnier in a mixer bowl until smooth. Cover and chill until serving time. Serve with 1½ to 2 quarts fresh strawberries.

Apple Puffed Pancake with Orange Syrup

6	eggs
1½	cups milk
1	cup flour
3	tablespoons sugar
1	teaspoon vanilla extract
½	teaspoon salt
¼	teaspoon cinnamon
½	cup butter
2	apples, peeled, thinly sliced
2	tablespoons brown sugar
1	cup packed brown sugar
½	cup orange juice
2	tablespoons grated orange peel

Combine the eggs, milk, flour, sugar, vanilla, salt and cinnamon in a mixer bowl, blender container or food processor container and mix well. Melt the butter in a 9x13-inch glass baking dish. Layer the apples in the baking dish. Bake at 425 degrees until the butter is sizzling but not browned. Remove from the oven. Spoon the egg mixture over the apples. Sprinkle with the 2 tablespoons brown sugar. Bake for 20 minutes or until puffed and golden brown. Combine 1 cup brown sugar, orange juice and orange peel in a small saucepan. Simmer over low heat for 5 minutes. Serve the syrup with the pancake.

YIELD: 6 SERVINGS

Banana Pancakes with Cinnamon Syrup

2	cups sugar
1	cup light corn syrup or honey
½	cup water
1	teaspoon cinnamon
1	cup whipping cream
2	cups flour
2	tablespoons sugar
½	teaspoon salt
1	teaspoon baking soda
2	cups buttermilk
2	eggs
2	tablespoons vegetable oil
2	bananas, mashed

Combine 2 cups sugar, corn syrup, water and cinnamon in a saucepan. Bring to a boil over medium heat, stirring constantly. Boil for 2 minutes. Remove from the heat. Stir in the whipping cream. Cool for 30 minutes. The syrup will thicken as it cools. Sift the flour, 2 tablespoons sugar, salt and baking soda together. Combine the buttermilk, eggs and oil in a bowl, stirring just until mixed. Add the bananas. Add the flour mixture gradually, mixing well after each addition. Drop by ¼ cupfuls onto a hot griddle. Bake until the edges of the pancakes are dry; turn. Bake until browned. Serve with the syrup.

Note: The syrup will keep for several months in the refrigerator.

YIELD: 4 TO 6 SERVINGS

Football Weekend Buttermilk Pancakes

1 cup (or more) buttermilk
1 cup flour
1 egg
1 teaspoon baking powder
1 teaspoon baking soda
⅛ teaspoon salt
1 tablespoon vegetable oil or melted butter

Whisk the buttermilk, flour, egg, baking powder, baking soda, salt and oil in a bowl until blended. The batter should be fairly thick. Ladle by silver-dollar-size spoonfuls into a lightly oiled or buttered nonstick skillet. Bake until the edges begin to bubble; turn. Bake until browned. Serve with butter and syrup.

YIELD: 5 OR 6 SERVINGS

Cinnamon Waffles

4 Granny Smith apples, sliced
¼ to ½ cup packed brown sugar
   Cinnamon to taste
2½ cups flour
1 tablespoon baking powder
½ teaspoon salt
2 tablespoons cinnamon
3 tablespoons sugar
2 cups milk
4 egg yolks
⅓ cup vegetable oil
4 egg whites, stiffly beaten

Arrange the apple slices in a glass baking dish. Sprinkle with the brown sugar and cinnamon to taste. Microwave on High for 7 to 10 minutes or until tender-crisp. Mix the flour, baking powder, salt, 2 tablespoons cinnamon, sugar, milk, egg yolks and oil in a large bowl. Fold in the egg whites. The batter should be fairly thin. Add more milk if needed to thin batter. Spoon onto a hot greased waffle iron. Bake until golden brown. Serve the apples over the waffles or on the side.

YIELD: 8 SERVINGS

Lemon Waffles with Lemon Cream

- 5 egg yolks
- ½ cup sugar
- 1 cup scalded milk
- 5 tablespoons fresh lemon juice
- 4 egg yolks
- 3 tablespoons sugar
- ½ teaspoon salt
- 1 cup milk
- 2 teaspoons fresh lemon juice
- 2 tablespoons grated lemon peel
- ¼ cup cooled melted butter
- 1 cup flour
- 4 egg whites, stiffly beaten but not dry
- ½ cup whipping cream, whipped

Combine 5 egg yolks and ½ cup sugar in a double boiler and beat until thick and pale yellow. Blend in the scalded milk. Cook over simmering water for 8 minutes or until the mixture thickens and coats a spoon, stirring constantly. Remove to a medium glass or porcelain bowl. Stir in 5 tablespoons lemon juice. Chill, covered, for 3 hours or longer. Beat 4 egg yolks, 3 tablespoons sugar and salt in a medium bowl. Blend in the milk, 2 teaspoons lemon juice, lemon peel and melted butter. Sift in the flour. Fold in the egg whites. Spoon onto a hot greased waffle iron. Bake until golden brown. Fold the whipped cream into the chilled mixture. Serve immediately with the waffles.

YIELD: 4 OR 5 SERVINGS

Orange Pecan Waffles

- 2 cups flour
- 2 teaspoons baking powder
- 1 teaspoon baking soda
- ½ teaspoon salt
- 1 tablespoon wheat germ
- 2 eggs
  Grated peel and juice of 2 oranges
- 1½ cups milk
- 6 tablespoons melted butter
- ¼ cup chopped pecans

Sift the flour, baking powder, baking soda and salt into a medium bowl. Stir in the wheat germ. Whisk the eggs, orange peel, orange juice, milk and butter in a small bowl. Stir into the flour mixture. Fold in the pecans. Spoon onto a hot greased waffle iron. Bake until golden brown. Serve hot with orange butter and orange syrup.

YIELD: 4 SERVINGS

For Orange Butter, whip ½ cup softened butter, ½ cup orange juice and 3 tablespoons confectioners' sugar in a bowl. Chill thoroughly. To prepare Orange Syrup, cook ½ cup orange juice, 1 cup sugar and 1 tablespoon grated orange peel in a small saucepan over low heat, stirring until the sugar is dissolved. Cook for 5 minutes, stirring occasionally. Serve over waffles, pancakes or toast, or use to baste ham, pork roasts and chops.

Cheesy Citrus Pastries

2   oranges
1¼ cups packed brown sugar
1   cup whipping cream
½   cup butter or margarine
1   cup chopped pecans, toasted
8   ounces cream cheese, softened
3   tablespoons confectioners' sugar
2   tablespoons butter or margarine, softened
½   cup flaked coconut
2   (10-count) cans flaky refrigerator biscuits

Grate 1 tablespoon peel from the oranges; set aside. Squeeze ½ cup juice from the oranges. Combine the orange juice, brown sugar, whipping cream and ½ cup butter in a saucepan. Bring to a boil over medium heat. Boil for 3½ minutes. Remove from the heat and cool slightly. Spoon into a greased 9x13-inch baking dish. Sprinkle with the pecans; set aside. Combine the reserved orange peel, cream cheese, confectioners' sugar and 2 tablespoons butter in a small mixer bowl. Beat at medium speed just until blended. Stir in the coconut. Separate each can of biscuit dough into 10 pieces. Roll each piece into a 4-inch circle on a lightly floured surface. Spread 1 tablespoon of the cream cheese mixture on the center of each circle. Roll up as for jelly rolls. Arrange the biscuits seam side down in 2 long rows in the prepared baking dish. Bake on the lowest oven rack at 350 degrees for 32 minutes or until browned. Let cool in the baking dish for 5 minutes. Remove carefully to a large serving platter. Top with any remaining brown sugar mixture.

YIELD: 20 SERVINGS

Cinnamon Scones with Strawberry Butter

1   cup self-rising flour
1   tablespoon cinnamon
½   teaspoon salt
6   tablespoons butter
1   egg
¼   cup milk
3   tablespoons sugar
1   cup butter, softened
1   cup strawberry jam
2   tablespoons fresh lemon juice

Sift the flour, cinnamon and salt into a large bowl. Cut in 6 tablespoons butter. Beat the egg and milk in a medium bowl. Add the sugar. Add to the flour mixture, mixing until a soft but not sticky dough forms. Knead on a lightly floured surface until smooth. Roll ½ inch thick. Cut into 12 rounds with a 1-inch biscuit cutter. Place on a greased baking sheet. Bake at 400 degrees for 10 to 15 minutes or until golden brown. Cool on a wire rack. Beat 1 cup butter, jam and lemon juice in a mixer bowl for 15 to 20 minutes or until very light and fluffy. Serve at room temperature with the scones.

YIELD: 12 SERVINGS

Fruited Scones

2   **cups flour**
1   **tablespoon baking powder**
¼   **teaspoon salt**
¼   **cup sugar**
½   **cup golden raisins**
½   **cup dried mixed fruit, such as blueberries,
     cherries, apricots and cranberries**
1¼ cups whipping cream

Combine the flour, baking powder, salt and sugar in a large bowl. Add the raisins and dried mixed fruit and mix well. Add most of the whipping cream, stirring just until mixed; do not overmix. Knead 5 times on a floured surface, shaping the dough into a ball. Flatten into a ½-inch-thick circle. Cut into wedges. Place the wedges on a baking sheet sprayed with nonstick cooking spray. Brush the top of the wedges with the remaining whipping cream. Sprinkle with additional sugar. Bake at 400 degrees for 15 minutes or until golden brown. Cool on the baking sheet for 5 minutes. Serve warm.

YIELD: 10 TO 12 SERVINGS

Orange Scones

2   **cups flour**
2   **teaspoons baking powder**
½   **teaspoon baking soda**
½   **teaspoon salt**
⅓   **cup sugar**
½   **cup butter, cut into small pieces**
⅓   **cup milk**
2   **tablespoons grated orange peel**
⅓   **cup orange juice**
½   **teaspoon grated orange peel**
2   **tablespoons orange juice**
½   **cup confectioners' sugar**

Combine the flour, baking powder, baking soda, salt and sugar in a large bowl. Cut in the butter with a fork or pastry blender until crumbly. Combine the milk, 2 tablespoons orange peel and ⅓ cup orange juice in a medium bowl. Add to the flour mixture, stirring just until moistened. Drop by spoonfuls into 8 mounds 1 inch apart on a lightly greased baking sheet. Bake at 375 degrees for 8 to 10 minutes or until golden brown. Let cool. Mix ½ teaspoon orange peel, 2 tablespoons orange juice and confectioners' sugar in a bowl. Drizzle over the scones.

YIELD: 8 SERVINGS

Orange Cranberry Bread

2	cups flour
1½	teaspoons baking powder
½	teaspoon baking soda
½	teaspoon salt
1	cup sugar
2	tablespoons melted butter
¾	cup orange juice
1	egg, beaten
½	teaspoon almond extract
1	tablespoon grated orange peel
1½	cups coarsely chopped cranberries

Combine the flour, baking powder, baking soda, salt and sugar in a medium bowl. Combine the butter, orange juice, egg and almond extract in a small bowl and mix well. Add to the flour mixture, stirring just until moistened. Fold in the orange peel and cranberries. Spoon into a greased and floured 4x8-inch loaf pan. Bake at 350 degrees for 1 hour or until a wooden pick inserted near the center comes out clean.

Note: May double the recipe, increasing the cranberries to one 12-ounce package.

YIELD: 12 SERVINGS

To prepare Florida Conserve, simmer the peel of 1 coarsely chopped orange with 1 cup water in a saucepan for 10 minutes. Cover and set aside to cool; drain well. Combine the orange peel, 2 cups grapefruit pulp and 2 cups orange pulp in a saucepan and simmer for 20 minutes, stirring occasionally to prevent sticking. Add 2 cups sugar and stir until dissolved. Add ½ cup grated canned pineapple and cook until thickened and syrupy. Add ¾ cup chopped nuts and ½ cup raisins and boil for 2 minutes. Ladle into hot sterilized jars, leaving ½ inch headspace; seal with 2-piece lids. Process in a boiling water bath for 10 minutes.

Zucchini Cranberry Bread

3 **tablespoons butter, softened**
1 **cup sugar**
2 **eggs**
1 **tablespoon grated orange peel**
1 **(16-ounce) can whole cranberry sauce**
1½ **cups whole wheat flour**
1½ **cups all-purpose flour**
1 **teaspoon baking soda**
1 **teaspoon baking powder**
1½ **cups coarsely grated zucchini**
1 **cup coarsely chopped walnuts**

Cream the butter, sugar and eggs in a mixer bowl until light and fluffy. Stir in the orange peel and cranberry sauce. Add the whole wheat flour, all-purpose flour, baking soda and baking powder, stirring gently just until mixed. Fold in the zucchini and walnuts. Spoon into a greased and floured 5x9-inch loaf pan. Bake at 350 degrees for 1 to 1¼ hours or until the loaf tests done.

Note: May be baked in 2 greased and floured 4x8-inch loaf pans.

YIELD: 12 TO 15 SERVINGS

Eggnog Bread

2¼ **cups flour**
2 **teaspoons baking powder**
1 **teaspoon salt**
2 **eggs**
¾ **cup sugar**
¼ **cup melted butter or margarine**
1 **cup eggnog**
½ **cup chopped candied cherries**
½ **cup raisins**
½ **cup chopped pecans**

Mix the flour, baking powder and salt together and set aside. Combine the eggs, sugar and butter in a large mixer bowl and beat well. Add the flour mixture and eggnog alternately, beating well after each addition. Stir in the candied cherries, raisins and pecans. Spoon into a greased and floured 4x8-inch loaf pan. Bake at 350 degrees for 1 hour or until a wooden pick inserted near the center comes out clean. Cool in the pan for 10 minutes. Remove to a wire rack to cool completely.

Note: May be baked in smaller loaf pans; baking time may need to be adjusted. Freezes well.

YIELD: 12 SERVINGS

Orange Fritters

2 cups flour
2 teaspoons baking powder
½ teaspoon salt
2 eggs
½ cup sugar
2 tablespoons melted butter
1 tablespoon grated orange peel
½ cup orange juice
   Shortening for frying
   Sifted confectioners' sugar

Sift the flour, baking powder and salt together and set aside. Beat the eggs in a bowl. Beat in the sugar gradually. Stir in the butter and orange peel. Add the flour mixture and orange juice alternately, mixing well after each addition. Let the batter stand for 15 minutes. Heat the shortening in a skillet to 350 degrees. Drop the batter by teaspoonfuls into the hot shortening. Fry until golden brown. Drain on paper towels. Sprinkle with confectioners' sugar.

YIELD: 36 SERVINGS

Orange peel is a great flavoring that can liven up many recipes. Before eating or juicing oranges, peel them with a sharp knife, vegetable peeler, or zester, cutting away only the orange part of the peel. Chop the peel and place in a sealable plastic bag or plastic freezer container. Whenever a recipe calls for orange peel, you can just scoop out the amount you need.

Orange Coconut Rolls

1 envelope dry yeast
¼ cup warm water
¼ cup sugar
1 teaspoon salt
2 eggs
¼ cup sour cream
6 tablespoons melted butter
2¾ to 3 cups flour
¾ cup sugar
¾ cup shredded coconut
2 tablespoons grated orange peel
2 tablespoons melted butter
¾ cup sugar
½ cup sour cream
2 tablespoons orange juice
¼ cup butter
¼ cup shredded coconut

Dissolve the yeast in the warm water in a bowl. Stir in ¼ cup sugar, salt, eggs, ¼ cup sour cream and 6 tablespoons butter. Add the flour gradually, mixing well after each addition. Let rise, covered, for 2 hours or until doubled in bulk. Mix ¾ cup sugar, ¾ cup coconut and orange peel in a small bowl. Knead the dough 15 times on a lightly floured surface. Divide the dough into 2 equal portions. Roll 1 portion into a 12-inch circle. Brush with 1 tablespoon of the butter. Sprinkle with half the coconut mixture. Cut into 12 wedges. Roll up, starting with the wide end and rolling to a point. Repeat with the remaining dough, coconut mixture and 1 tablespoon butter. Arrange the rolls point side down in 3 rows in a greased 9x13-inch baking pan. Let rise, covered, in a warm place for 1 hour. Bake at 350 degrees for 25 minutes. Combine ¾ cup sugar, ½ cup sour cream, orange juice and ¼ cup butter in a saucepan. Boil for 3 minutes, stirring constantly. Spoon over the hot rolls. Sprinkle with remaining coconut.

YIELD: 24 SERVINGS

Refrigerator Rolls

½ cup shortening
½ cup margarine, softened
¾ cup sugar
1 cup boiling water
2 envelopes dry yeast
1 cup lukewarm water
2 eggs, lightly beaten
6 cups flour
1 tablespoon salt
½ cup melted margarine

Combine the shortening, softened margarine, sugar and boiling water in a large bowl. Let stand until completely cool. Dissolve the yeast in the lukewarm water in a small bowl. Add to the sugar mixture. Add the eggs, flour and salt and mix until a sticky dough forms. Let rise, covered tightly with plastic wrap, in the refrigerator for 8 hours or until doubled in bulk. Punch the dough down. Roll on a floured surface. Cut with desired cutter. Dip each roll into the melted margarine. Place the rolls on a greased baking sheet. Cover with a tea towel or waxed paper sprayed with nonstick cooking spray to prevent sticking. Let rise for 2 to 4 hours or until almost doubled in bulk. Remove the tea towel. Bake at 400 to 425 degrees for 10 minutes or until browned.

YIELD: 48 SERVINGS

Beau Monde Bread

1 loaf Italian bread
8 ounces Swiss cheese, cut into ¼-inch slices
1 cup butter or margarine, softened
2 tablespoons grated onion or onion flakes
1 tablespoon prepared mustard
½ teaspoon Beau Monde seasoning
2 tablespoons lemon juice
1 tablespoon poppy seeds

Trim the crust from the bread. Cut ¾ of the way through the bread in a diagonal pattern across the top. Cut in the same manner in the opposite direction across the top to form an X pattern. Stuff the cuts with Swiss cheese. Place the bread on a large piece of foil. Beat the butter, onion, mustard, Beau Monde seasoning, lemon juice and poppy seeds in a bowl until smooth. Spread over the top and sides of the stuffed bread. Wrap in the foil. Bake at 350 degrees for 30 minutes.

YIELD: 12 SERVINGS

The Best Hush Puppies

1　cup self-rising cornmeal
½　cup self-rising flour
1　tablespoon sugar
1　egg, beaten
½　cup milk or beer, or ¼ cup milk and
　　¼ cup beer
½　cup chopped onion
½　cup chopped green bell pepper
1　jalapeño, finely chopped
　　Vegetable oil for frying

Combine the cornmeal, flour and sugar in a large bowl. Make a well in the center of the mixture. Beat the egg and milk in a medium bowl. Add to the flour mixture, stirring just until moistened. Stir in the green pepper and jalapeño. Drop by teaspoonfuls into hot oil in a skillet. Fry for 2 minutes per side or until browned.

YIELD: 4 SERVINGS

Clayton Corn Bread

1　cup butter or margarine, softened
1　cup sugar
4　eggs
1　(15-ounce) can cream-style corn
½　cup shredded Monterey Jack cheese
½　cup shredded Cheddar cheese
1　cup flour
1　cup cornmeal
¼　teaspoon salt
4　teaspoons baking powder

Cream the butter and sugar in a mixer bowl until light and fluffy. Beat in the eggs 1 at a time. Add the corn, Monterey Jack cheese, Cheddar cheese, flour, cornmeal, salt and baking powder and mix well. Spoon into a lightly greased 9x13-inch baking pan. Bake at 300 degrees for 1 hour.

YIELD: 24 SERVINGS

To prepare Lime Jelly, mix 1 cup lime juice, one 2-ounce package powdered fruit pectin and 2 cups water in a stockpot. Cook over high heat for 5 minutes or until bubbles form around the edge, stirring constantly. Stir in 2¾ cups sugar. Cook for 2 minutes or just until the sugar dissolves, stirring constantly; do not boil. Remove from the heat. Stir in several drops each of green and yellow food coloring. Skim away any foam. Ladle into hot sterilized jars, leaving ½ inch headspace; seal with 2-piece lids. Process in a boiling water bath for 10 minutes.

CRANE
BRAND

CITRUS GROWERS ASSN.
WINTER GARDEN, FLA.

IN SOUTH LAKE APOPKA SECTION

Crate labels were used to distinguish one grower from another and
one fruit variety from another. Many showcased Florida's native bird species.
In the 1920s, Crane was one of the nation's top brands.

SUNSET

Appetizers and Beverages

• •

Section sponsored by

Bill and Sara Raley—Servpro of Greater Orlando, Inc.

Bacon-Wrapped Scallops with Orange Honey Sauce

1	small onion, chopped
2	cloves of garlic, minced
½	cup olive oil
½	teaspoon sugar
½	teaspoon ground red pepper
¼	teaspoon oregano
2	pounds sea scallops
12	bacon slices, cut into halves
	Orange Honey Sauce

Combine the onion, garlic, olive oil, sugar, red pepper and oregano in a large sealable food storage bag. Add the scallops and seal the bag. Marinate in the refrigerator for 30 minutes. Drain and discard the marinade. Place the bacon on a rack in a broiler pan. Broil 6 inches from the heat source for 2 minutes. Wrap bacon around scallops, securing with a wooden pick. Broil for 7 minutes. Turn the scallops over. Broil for 3 minutes or until the bacon is crisp and the scallops are tender. Serve with Orange Honey Sauce.

Orange Honey Sauce

¾	cup chicken broth
1	tablespoon cornstarch
⅓	cup orange juice concentrate
¼	cup honey
2	tablespoons apple cider vinegar
1	tablespoon Dijon mustard
½	teaspoon tarragon

Mix the broth and cornstarch in a bowl until smooth. Combine the orange juice concentrate, honey, vinegar, mustard and tarragon in a saucepan. Bring to a boil over medium heat, stirring constantly. Stir in the broth mixture. Return to a boil. Boil for 1 minute or until thickened, stirring constantly.

YIELD: 24 SERVINGS

Christmas Crab Meat

32	ounces cream cheese, softened
1	pound deluxe steamed crab meat
1	(9-ounce) jar horseradish sauce
1	tablespoon lemon juice
½	cup slivered almonds

Beat the cream cheese in a mixer bowl until smooth. Add the crab meat, horseradish sauce and lemon juice and mix well. Spoon into a greased 1½-quart glass baking dish. Sprinkle with the almonds. Bake at 300 degrees for 30 minutes or until bubbly. Let stand until slightly cool. Serve with assorted butter crackers.

YIELD: 24 TO 30 SERVINGS

Grilled Jumbo Shrimp with Prosciutto and Basil

1   cup dry white wine
1   cup olive oil
¼   cup lemon juice
2   tablespoons Dijon mustard
½   cup chopped fresh basil
    Freshly cracked peppercorns to taste
24 fresh jumbo shrimp
24 fresh basil leaves
24 thin prosciutto slices, trimmed

Combine the wine, olive oil, lemon juice, mustard, chopped basil and peppercorns in a bowl and mix well. Peel and devein the shrimp, leaving the tails intact. Add the shrimp to the marinade. Marinate, covered, in the refrigerator for 3 hours or longer. Remove the shrimp, reserving the marinade. Bring the reserved marinade to a boil in a small saucepan. Boil for several minutes and remove from the heat. Wrap a basil leaf and slice of prosciutto around the middle of each shrimp and thread onto skewers. Place on a preheated grill rack. Grill for several minutes on each side or until the shrimp turn pink, basting with the reserved marinade.

YIELD: 24 SERVINGS

Coconut Shrimp with Orange Dipping Sauce

2   pounds medium fresh shrimp
1½   cups flour
1   (12-ounce) can beer
½   teaspoon baking powder
½   teaspoon paprika
½   teaspoon curry powder
½   teaspoon salt
¼   teaspoon ground red pepper
½   cup flour
1   (14-ounce) package flaked coconut
     Vegetable oil for frying
     Orange Dipping Sauce

Peel and devein the shrimp, leaving the tails intact. Combine 1½ cups flour, beer, baking powder, paprika, curry powder, salt and red pepper in a bowl and mix well. Dredge the shrimp in ½ cup flour. Dip in the batter and roll in the coconut. Preheat the vegetable oil to 350 degrees in a deep skillet. Add the shrimp. Fry until golden brown. Remove shrimp to a platter lined with paper towels to drain. Serve with Orange Dipping Sauce.

Orange Dipping Sauce

1   (10-ounce) jar orange marmalade
3   tablespoons prepared horseradish
3   tablespoons Creole mustard

Combine the orange marmalade, horseradish and mustard in a bowl and mix well.

YIELD: 6 SERVINGS

Citrus Meatballs

2	pounds ground beef
½	teaspoon salt
¼	teaspoon pepper
½	cup beef broth
½	cup bread crumbs
¼	cup orange juice
2	teaspoons grated orange peel
2	teaspoons lime juice
1	teaspoon grated lime peel
	Flour
	Spicy Orange Sauce

Combine ground beef, salt, pepper and beef broth in a bowl and mix well. Add bread crumbs, orange juice, orange peel, lime juice and lime peel and mix well. Shape into 1-inch balls and sprinkle with flour. Place on a baking sheet sprayed with nonstick cooking spray. Bake at 350 degrees for 15 to 20 minutes or until the meatballs are cooked through. Serve with Spicy Orange Sauce.

Note: For hamburgers, shape ground beef mixture into patties and grill until cooked through. Serve with Spicy Orange Sauce.

Spicy Orange Sauce

½	cup orange marmalade
½	cup catsup
2	teaspoons prepared horseradish

Melt the marmalade in a small saucepan. Stir in the catsup and horseradish. Simmer for 2 minutes. Let stand until cool.

YIELD: 6 TO 8 SERVINGS

Roast Beef Crostini

2	(6-ounce) jars marinated artichoke hearts, drained
1	clove of garlic
¼	cup white wine vinegar
½	cup olive oil
	Salt and pepper to taste
2	loaves Italian bread
2	heads romaine lettuce, rinsed, separated into leaves
2½	pounds filet of beef, thinly sliced
36	slices provolone cheese

Process the artichoke hearts, garlic, white wine vinegar, olive oil and salt and pepper in a food processor until smooth. Cover and chill in the refrigerator. Cut the bread diagonally into 36 slices ½ inch thick. Spread with the artichoke mixture. Layer the lettuce, beef and cheese on top of each slice.

YIELD: 36 SERVINGS

When buying oranges, look for ones that are firm and heavy. The heaviest oranges are the juiciest. Avoid oranges with soft spots.

Italian Cheese Terrine

8   **ounces cream cheese, softened**
2   **tablespoons butter or margarine, softened**
½   **cup grated Parmesan cheese**
2   **tablespoons pesto**
9   **(1-ounce) slices Muenster cheese**
    Basil Tomato Sauce

Beat cream cheese and butter at medium speed in a mixer bowl until smooth. Add Parmesan cheese and pesto and beat well. Cut 5 slices of the Muenster cheese diagonally into halves to form triangles. Cut the remaining 4 slices Muenster cheese into halves to form rectangles. Line a 3-cup mold or bowl with plastic wrap, allowing edges to hang over the side of the mold by 6 to 7 inches. Arrange the cheese triangles in the mold pinwheel fashion, slightly overlapping to line the mold. Layer the cream cheese mixture, Basil Tomato Sauce and cheese rectangles ½ at a time in the prepared mold. Fold the plastic wrap over the layers, sealing securely; place a heavy object on top to compact layers. Chill for 8 hours or up to 3 days. Invert terrine onto a cheese board; remove plastic wrap. Garnish with an herb sprig. Serve with crackers or baguette slices.

Basil Tomato Sauce

1   **(14-ounce) can whole tomatoes**
¾   **cup chopped onion**
1   **tablespoon minced fresh garlic**
2   **tablespoons olive oil**
2   **bay leaves**
½   **teaspoon sugar**
1   **teaspoon chopped fresh basil**
1   **(7-ounce) jar oil-packed sun-dried tomatoes, drained, chopped**

Drain the whole tomatoes, reserving ¼ cup juice. Chop the tomatoes. Sauté the onion and garlic in olive oil in a large skillet over medium heat until tender. Stir in the chopped tomatoes, reserved tomato juice, bay leaves, sugar and basil. Bring to a boil and reduce heat. Simmer for 3 to 5 minutes or until thickened, stirring frequently; remove from heat. Discard the bay leaves. Stir in the sun-dried tomatoes. Chill, covered, for 2 hours or longer.

YIELD: 3 CUPS

Turkey-Filled Orange Rosemary Muffins with Cranberry Chutney

2   cups unbleached flour
1   teaspoon baking soda
½   teaspoon salt
½   cup unsalted butter, softened
1   cup sugar
2   eggs
1   cup sour cream or buttermilk
1   cup golden raisins
    Zest of 1 large orange
1   tablespoon dried rosemary
    Juice of 1 large orange
    Honey mustard
2   pounds sliced turkey breast
    Cranberry Chutney

Sift the flour, baking soda and salt together. Beat the butter and sugar in a mixer bowl until smooth and creamy. Beat in the eggs 1 at a time. Continue to beat until light and fluffy. Add the flour mixture and sour cream alternately, beating well after each addition. Process the raisins, orange zest and rosemary in a food processor fitted with a steel blade until finely minced. Stir into the batter. Spoon into lightly greased miniature muffin cups. Bake at 375 degrees for 10 to 12 minutes or until golden brown. Brush the tops lightly with orange juice. Invert onto a wire rack. Let stand until cool. Split each muffin into halves. Spread the bottom with honey mustard. Fold a slice of turkey in half and place over the mustard. Replace the tops. Arrange on a serving platter. Serve with Cranberry Chutney.

Cranberry Chutney

1½   cups sugar
½   cup fresh orange juice
¼   cup water
1   tablespoon grated orange peel
½   teaspoon ground ginger
4   cups fresh cranberries
½   cup toasted pecans, chopped

Combine the sugar, orange juice, water, orange peel and ginger in a heavy medium saucepan. Heat until the sugar dissolves. Add the cranberries. Cook over medium-high heat for 7 to 8 minutes or until the cranberries pop and become slightly mushy. Stir in the pecans. Remove from heat. Let stand until cool. Chutney will thicken as it cools. Store, covered, in the refrigerator.

YIELD: 5 DOZEN

Smoked Salmon Canapés

3 ounces cream cheese, softened
3 tablespoons whipping cream
¾ to 1 teaspoon curry powder
2 teaspoons chopped onion
6 thin slices smoked salmon
24 thin slices scored unpeeled cucumber
24 rounds toasted crackers
24 slices pimento-stuffed olives

Beat the cream cheese and whipping cream in a bowl until smooth. Add the curry powder and onion and mix well. Spread over the salmon slices to the edge and roll up as for a jelly roll. Chill for several hours to overnight. Cut into ⅛-inch slices. Layer a cucumber slice and salmon slice on each cracker. Top each with a stuffed olive slice. Serve immediately.

YIELD: 24 SERVINGS

Artichoke Pesto Toasts

6 slices French bread, diagonally sliced
1 (7-ounce) can artichoke hearts
2 tablespoons prepared pesto sauce
1 tablespoon mayonnaise
Pinch of crushed red pepper flakes
3 tablespoons pine nuts, toasted

Place the bread on a baking sheet. Broil for 1 to 2 minutes or until slightly toasted. Drain the artichoke hearts and pat dry. Chop the artichoke hearts and place in a bowl. Add the prepared pesto, mayonnaise and red pepper flakes and mix well. Spread on the toasted bread. Sprinkle with the pine nuts. Broil for 2 to 3 minutes or until the tops are brown and bubbly.

YIELD: 6 SERVINGS

Artichoke Fritters with Greek Scallion Dip

2 cups mashed drained artichoke hearts
¼ cup Dijon mustard
2 tablespoons Cavender's Greek seasoning
2 eggs
1 cup flour
Vegetable oil for deep-frying
Greek Scallion Dip

Combine the artichoke hearts, Dijon mustard, seasoning, eggs and flour in a bowl and mix well. Drop by spoonfuls into hot vegetable oil in a deep fryer. Deep-fry until golden brown. Serve with Greek Scallion Dip.

Greek Scallion Dip

2 cups mayonnaise
1 cup sour cream
Juice of 1 lemon
2 tablespoons Cavender's Greek seasoning
1 tablespoon Dijon mustard
1 bunch scallions, finely chopped

Combine the mayonnaise, sour cream, lemon juice, seasoning and Dijon mustard in a bowl and mix until smooth. Stir in the scallions. Chill, covered, until serving time.

YIELD: 25 SERVINGS

Southwestern Sushi

8	ounces cream cheese, softened
4	ounces boursin cheese
2	tablespoons chopped roasted red peppers
1	package large flour tortillas
1	red bell pepper, thinly sliced
1	yellow bell pepper, thinly sliced
1	tomato, thinly sliced
1	cucumber, seeded, thinly sliced
1	red onion, thinly sliced
1	head romaine lettuce, thinly sliced
2	cups sliced smoked chicken or beef
1	avocado, thinly sliced

Process the cream cheese, boursin cheese and roasted red peppers in a food processor until smooth. Place each tortilla on a large piece of plastic wrap. Spread a thin layer of the cheese mixture on each tortilla. Sprinkle with the vegetables, chicken and avocado. Roll each tortilla up tightly and wrap in the plastic wrap. Freeze for 2 hours. Remove from the freezer 10 minutes before serving. Cut into slices and serve.

YIELD: 12 SERVINGS

Crab Meat and Brie Appetizer

1	(8-ounce) round Brie cheese
½	cup butter or margarine
2	tablespoons minced fresh parsley
1	clove of garlic or to taste
¼	teaspoon basil leaves
8	ounces crab meat
1	(14- to 16-inch) loaf French bread

Remove the rind from the cheese and cut into chunks. Melt the butter in a medium saucepan over medium heat. Add the cheese, parsley, garlic and basil. Cook until blended, stirring frequently. Fold in the crab meat. Remove from heat. Cut the bread into halves lengthwise. Spread with the crab meat mixture. Place on a baking sheet lined with foil. Broil 6 inches from the heat source for 5 minutes or until the tops are bubbly. Cut into 1-inch pieces and serve immediately.

Note: May prepare up to 24 hours in advance before broiling. May also use garlic or sun-dried tomato bread for additional flavor.

YIELD: 2 TO 2 ½ DOZEN

Savory Phyllo-Wrapped Brie

1½ cups sliced fresh mushrooms
2 tablespoons butter or margarine
2 tablespoons dry sherry
2 teaspoons Worcestershire sauce
¼ teaspoon thyme
   Dash of pepper
2 tablespoons fine dry bread crumbs
4 sheets (14x18 inches) frozen phyllo dough, thawed
3 tablespoons melted butter or margarine
1 (4½-ounce) round Brie cheese

Sauté the mushrooms in 2 tablespoons butter in a medium skillet until tender. Stir in the sherry, Worcestershire sauce, thyme and pepper. Cook for 1 minute or until the liquid evaporates. Remove from heat. Stir in the bread crumbs. Let stand until cool. Place the phyllo dough in a stack 1 sheet at a time, brushing each layer with some of the 3 tablespoons butter and keeping the phyllo covered with a damp cloth to prevent drying out. Cut a 9½- to 10-inch circle from the phyllo stack, discarding the trimmings. Cut the cheese into halves horizontally. Layer the cheese and mushroom mixture ½ at a time on the phyllo circle. Bring the edges of the phyllo up to cover the layers, pleating the phyllo as needed. Brush with the remaining butter. Place pleated side up in a shallow baking pan. Bake at 400 degrees for 20 minutes or until golden brown. Serve immediately with fresh fruit.

YIELD: 6 SERVINGS

Fresh Tomato Bruschetta

6 red or yellow tomatoes, peeled, seeded
1 cup chopped red onion
3 cloves of garlic, minced
¼ cup balsamic vinegar
½ cup extra-virgin olive oil
1 large bunch fresh basil, chopped
2 teaspoons kosher salt
2 teaspoons pepper
1 loaf French baguette
   Olive oil to taste
   Minced garlic to taste

Chop the tomatoes into ½-inch pieces. Combine the tomatoes, onion, 3 cloves of garlic, balsamic vinegar, ½ cup olive oil, basil, kosher salt and pepper in a plastic, glass or stainless steel bowl and mix well. Let stand at room temperature for 1 hour. Chill, covered, in the refrigerator. Cut the baguette diagonally into 2-inch-thick slices. Brush with olive oil and garlic to taste. Place on a grill rack. Grill until crisp. Serve with the chilled tomatoes.

Note: Bread may be heated in a 350-degree oven until crisp, not brown.

YIELD: 8 SERVINGS

Herbed Vegetable Tarts

1 (17-ounce) package frozen puff pastry
½ cup chopped onion
½ cup chopped fresh basil leaves
1½ cups (⅛-inch-thick) yellow squash slices
1½ cups (⅛-inch-thick) zucchini slices
1 cup chopped green bell pepper
4 plum tomatoes, thinly sliced
8 ounces shredded mozzarella cheese
2 tablespoons olive oil

Thaw the pastry at room temperature for 30 minutes. Unfold the pastry on a lightly floured surface. Roll each pastry sheet into a 12x13-inch rectangle. Cut each rectangle into halves crosswise. Fold edges over ½ inch on each side, forming a border and sealing with water. Place on a baking sheet and prick thoroughly with a fork. Bake at 400 degrees for 10 minutes. Layer the onion, basil, squash, zucchini, green pepper, tomatoes and cheese on the prebaked pastries. Bake for 15 minutes. Drizzle with olive oil. Garnish with additional fresh basil leaves and plum tomato slices. Serve immediately.

YIELD: 4 SERVINGS

Mushroom Quesadillas

6 large shiitake mushrooms
1 tablespoon olive oil
Salt and freshly ground pepper to taste
2 tablespoons unsalted butter
12 corn tortillas
1 cup shredded Monterey Jack cheese
½ cup small red onion, thinly sliced
2 ripe plum tomatoes, cut into ¼-inch pieces
1 jalapeño, seeded, minced

Discard the mushroom stems and wipe the caps to clean. Brush the mushroom caps with olive oil on both sides. Season with salt and pepper. Place a cast-iron griddle over low heat for 5 minutes. Add the butter. Heat until melted. Increase the heat to medium-high. Place the mushroom caps smooth side down on the griddle. Cook for 3 to 4 minutes or until brown and crisp. Reduce the heat to medium. Turn over the mushroom caps. Cook for 3 to 4 minutes. Remove to a plate. Wipe the griddle clean and reduce the heat to low. Add 1 tortilla. Sprinkle with 2 heaping tablespoons of the cheese, some of the red onion, tomatoes and jalapeño. Add 1 mushroom cap. Top with 1 tortilla and press together to seal. Heat until the cheese is melted. Remove to a cutting board and cut into wedges. Repeat the process 6 times. Serve immediately.

YIELD: 24 SERVINGS

Salmon Quesadillas

1	pound salmon, cooked
¼	cup chopped green bell pepper
¼	cup chopped celery
1	cup chopped Spanish onion
1	tablespoon chopped garlic
1	tablespoon cumin
1	tablespoon fajita seasoning
2	jalapeños, seeded, chopped
1	bunch fresh cilantro, chopped
2	bunches scallions, chopped
⅔	cup grated Cheddar cheese
	Salt and pepper to taste
8	(10-inch) flour tortillas
1	tablespoon butter

Flake the salmon in a bowl, discarding the skin and bones. Add the green pepper, celery, onion and garlic and mix gently. Stir in cumin and fajita seasoning and drain. Add the jalapeños, cilantro and scallions and mix well. Stir in the cheese. Season with salt and pepper to taste. Fill each tortilla with ¼ cup of the salmon mixture. Fold each tortilla in half. Melt the butter in a skillet over medium heat. Add the filled tortillas. Cook until the cheese melts and the tortillas are toasted. Serve with salsa and sour cream.

Note: May make fajita seasoning by mixing equal amounts of celery salt, black pepper, paprika and cayenne together.

YIELD: 8 SERVINGS

Spanakopitas

1	small onion, chopped
2	tablespoons olive oil
1	(10-ounce) package frozen chopped spinach, thawed, squeezed dry
1	egg
⅓	cup grated Parmesan cheese
⅛	teaspoon pepper
⅓	pound phyllo dough
½	cup melted butter or margarine

Sauté the onion in the olive oil in a 2-quart saucepan over medium heat until tender. Remove from the heat. Stir in the spinach, egg, Parmesan cheese and pepper. Cut the phyllo lengthwise into 2-inch-wide strips. Place the strips on waxed paper and cover with a damp towel. Brush the top of 1 phyllo strip with butter. Place 1 teaspoonful of the spinach filling at one end of the strip. Fold 1 corner of the strip diagonally over the filling so the short edge meets the long edge, forming a right angle. Continue folding over at right angles until the end of the strip is reached, forming a triangular package. Repeat with the remaining phyllo and spinach filling. Place the packages seam side down in a 10x15-inch baking pan. Brush with remaining butter. Bake at 425 degrees for 15 minutes or until golden brown. Serve immediately.

YIELD: 42 SERVINGS

Strawberry Flowers

40 medium strawberries
16 ounces cream cheese, softened
3 tablespoons confectioners' sugar
¼ teaspoon almond extract
¼ teaspoon vanilla extract

Cut a thin slice from the stem end of each strawberry to enable the strawberries to stand upright. Place the strawberries cut side down on a serving platter. Cut each strawberry into 4 wedges cutting to but not through the bottom. Fan the wedges slightly. Beat the cream cheese, confectioners' sugar and flavorings at medium speed in a mixer bowl until light and fluffy. Spoon into a decorating bag fitted with a large star tip. Pipe into the center of each strawberry. Chill, covered, until serving time.

YIELD: 40 SERVINGS

Apricot Brandied Brie

1 (16-ounce) round Brie cheese, rind removed
1 cup apricot preserves
½ cup apricot brandy
2 French baguettes, cut into ½-inch slices

Let the cheese stand at room temperature for 1 hour. Pierce with a fork in several places. Place on a lettuce-lined serving plate. Heat the preserves and brandy in a medium saucepan, stirring frequently. Pour over the cheese. Garnish with seedless grapes, dried apricots or strawberries. Serve with baguette slices.

YIELD: 12 TO 15 SERVINGS

Raspberry Brie in Rye

2 (7-inch) round loaves rye bread
1 (15-ounce) round Brie cheese
½ cup seedless raspberry jam
¼ cup sliced almonds

Cut a ½-inch slice from the top of 1 of the bread loaves, reserving the top. Place the cheese on top of the loaf. Trace around the cheese edge with a serrated knife. Remove the cheese. Cut the bread 2 inches deep using the traced mark as a guide. Remove the bread from the center, leaving a 2-inch cavity 5 inches in diameter. Cut the reserved bread top, bread trimmings and remaining loaf of bread into 1- to 1½-inch cubes. Remove the rind from the top of the cheese. Place the cheese in the bread cavity. Spread the top with the jam and sprinkle with almonds. Bake at 325 degrees for 15 to 20 minutes or just until soft. Serve immediately with the bread cubes.

YIELD: 12 TO 15 SERVINGS

Beer Cheese Spread

8 ounces shredded Colby and Monterey Jack cheese, softened
8 ounces shredded sharp Cheddar cheese, softened
½ cup beer
1 teaspoon garlic powder
½ teaspoon dry mustard
⅛ teaspoon salt
2 teaspoons Worcestershire sauce
¼ teaspoon hot sauce

Combine the cheeses, beer, garlic powder, dry mustard, salt, Worcestershire sauce and hot sauce in a heavy-duty sealable plastic bag. Push out all the air and seal. Knead the plastic bag until the mixture is blended and of a spreading consistency. Spoon into a serving bowl. Serve with bagel chips.

Note: Prepare the spread just before serving and do not refrigerate.

YIELD: 8 SERVINGS

Spicy Shrimp Dip

32 ounces cream cheese, softened
1 large onion, chopped
1 clove of garlic, chopped
1 (12-ounce) jar banana peppers, drained, chopped
1 jalapeño, chopped, or to taste
1 (12-ounce) package frozen salad shrimp, thawed, rinsed, drained
2 large tomatoes, chopped

Combine the cream cheese, onion, garlic, banana peppers, jalapeño, shrimp and tomatoes in a microwave-safe bowl and mix well. Microwave on High for 3 to 5 minutes or until heated through, but not bubbly. Serve immediately or at room temperature with corn chips.

YIELD: 25 TO 30 SERVINGS

Mushroom Pâté

2   tablespoons unsalted butter, softened
8   ounces mushrooms, finely chopped
¼   cup finely chopped scallions
1½   teaspoons finely chopped garlic
⅓   cup chicken stock
4   ounces cream cheese, softened
2   tablespoons unsalted butter, softened
2   tablespoons minced fresh chives
     Salt and pepper to taste

Melt 2 tablespoons butter in a medium skillet. Add the mushrooms. Sauté for 2 to 3 minutes. Add the scallions and garlic. Sauté for 1 minute. Add the chicken stock. Cook over high heat for 4 to 5 minutes or until all the liquid has evaporated. Remove from heat and cool to room temperature. Combine the cream cheese and remaining 2 tablespoons butter in a mixer bowl and mix well. Add the mushroom mixture, chives, salt and pepper and mix well. Spoon into a serving bowl. Chill, covered, in the refrigerator. Garnish with additional chopped chives before serving. Serve with toast points, crackers or Belgian endive leaves.

YIELD: 8 TO 10 SERVINGS

Pecan-Crusted Artichoke Spread

3   tablespoons butter or margarine
1   medium onion, chopped
2   cloves of garlic, minced
4   cups coarsely chopped spinach
1   (13-ounce) can artichoke hearts, drained,
     chopped
8   ounces cream cheese, chopped
½   cup mayonnaise
2   cups grated Parmesan cheese
4   ounces Cheddar cheese, shredded
4   ounces mozzarella cheese, shredded
1   tablespoon butter or margarine, softened
⅔   cup chopped pecans
½   cup herb stuffing mix

Melt 3 tablespoons butter in a large skillet. Add the onion and garlic. Sauté until tender. Add the spinach. Cook over medium heat for 3 minutes, stirring frequently. Add the artichoke hearts, cream cheese, mayonnaise, Parmesan cheese, Cheddar cheese and mozzarella cheese. Cook until the cheeses are melted. Spoon into a greased 2-quart baking dish. Bake at 350 degrees for 20 minutes. Combine the butter, pecans and stuffing mix in a bowl and toss to blend well. Sprinkle over the spinach mixture. Bake for 15 minutes. Serve with pita chips or sliced French bread.

YIELD: 15 TO 20 SERVINGS

Caponata

1	**pound eggplant**
	Salt
½	**cup olive oil**
1	**cup finely chopped celery**
½	**cup finely chopped onion**
¾	**cup tomato purée**
¼	**cup tomato paste**
½	**cup water or wine vinegar**
1	**teaspoon salt**
⅛	**teaspoon pepper**
1½	**teaspoons sugar**
½	**cup thinly sliced green olives**
1	**tablespoon capers**
1	**tablespoon sweet basil**
1	**tablespoon oregano**
1	**clove of garlic, minced**

Peel the eggplant and cut into ½-inch cubes into a colander. Sprinkle generously with salt. Let drain for 30 minutes and pat dry. Sauté the eggplant in 4 tablespoons olive oil in a skillet for 8 to 10 minutes. Remove the eggplant to a platter. Add the remaining 4 tablespoons olive oil to the skillet. Add the celery. Sauté for 2 to 3 minutes or until tender-crisp. Add the onions. Sauté for 8 to 10 minutes or until transparent. Add the eggplant, tomato purée, tomato paste, water, 1 teaspoon salt, pepper, sugar, olives, capers, basil, oregano and garlic. Simmer for 20 to 30 minutes or until thickened, stirring frequently. Adjust the seasonings. Serve warm or chill, covered, in the refrigerator and serve on crackers.

Note: May store in the refrigerator for 1 to 2 weeks.

YIELD: 4 CUPS

Gorgonzola Camembert Butter

½	**cup unsalted butter, softened**
8	**ounces Gorgonzola cheese, softened**
4	**ounces Camembert cheese, softened**
¼	**cup brandy**
1	**to 2 cloves of garlic, minced**

Combine the butter, Gorgonzola cheese, Camembert cheese and brandy in a bowl and mix well until smooth. Stir in the garlic. Pack into a 1½-cup crock. Chill, covered, in the refrigerator. Bring to room temperature before serving. Serve with rye bread or crackers.

Note: May store for up to 2 weeks in the refrigerator.

YIELD: 1 ½ CUPS

To make a Butterfly Garnish, place 2 sections from an orange or a grapefruit back to back to form wings. Arrange thin green bell pepper strips at the top for antennae.

Orange Sugared Nuts

2   pounds English walnuts or pecans
1½ cups sugar
½   cup orange juice
1   teaspoon grated orange peel

Crack and remove the shells from the walnuts, leaving the walnuts whole or in halves. Place in a large bowl. Combine the sugar and orange juice in a small heavy saucepan. Cook over medium heat to 234 to 240 degrees on a candy thermometer, soft-ball stage. Remove from the heat. Stir in the orange peel. Pour over the walnuts. Stir using a wooden spoon until all the walnuts are coated with the glaze. Spread in 1 layer on a lightly greased baking sheet. Let stand until dry. Store in an airtight container.

YIELD: 3 CUPS

Spiced Pecans

1   cup sugar
¼   teaspoon salt
2   teaspoons cinnamon
½   teaspoon nutmeg
½   teaspoon ground cloves
½   cup water
2   cups pecan halves

Combine the sugar, salt, cinnamon, nutmeg, cloves and water in a heavy saucepan. Cook to 236 degrees on a candy thermometer, soft-ball stage. Remove from the heat. Add the pecans and stir until the sugar mixture is creamy. Spoon onto waxed paper. Separate the pecan halves using 2 forks. Store in an airtight container.

YIELD: 2 CUPS

Parmesan Walnuts

1½ to 2 cups walnut halves
1   tablespoon melted butter
¼   teaspoon seasoned salt
¼   teaspoon salt
¼   cup shredded Parmesan cheese

Spread the walnuts in a single layer in a 9x13-inch baking pan. Bake at 350 degrees for 10 minutes. Combine the butter, seasoned salt and salt in a bowl and mix well. Pour over the walnuts and toss to coat. Sprinkle with the Parmesan cheese and toss to coat. Spread the mixture in a single layer in the pan. Bake for 3 to 4 minutes or until the Parmesan cheese is melted. Spoon immediately onto waxed paper and spread in a single layer. Let stand until cool. Store in an airtight container; do not refrigerate.

YIELD: 2 CUPS

For Citrus Sugar Cubes, scrape 1 side of each cube over the outside of a clean orange or lemon until the color of the peel is visible on the sugar cube.

Frozen Cappuccinos

- 1 cup freshly brewed espresso or very strong coffee, cooled to room temperature
- 2 cups ice cubes
- ¼ cup half-and-half or whole milk
- 3 tablespoons sugar, or to taste
- ¼ teaspoon cinnamon
- ¼ cup Kahlúa or other coffee-flavored liqueur
  Cinnamon to taste

Combine the espresso, ice cubes, half-and-half, sugar, ¼ teaspoon cinnamon and Kahlúa in a blender container. Process until smooth and thick. Pour into tall glasses and sprinkle with cinnamon.

YIELD: 2 SERVINGS

Orange Spiced Cider

- 5 cups apple cider
- 2 cups orange juice
- ½ cup packed light brown sugar
- 8 whole allspice
- 5 (3-inch) cinnamon sticks
- ¾ teaspoon whole cloves
  Pinch of salt

Bring the apple cider, orange juice, brown sugar, allspice, cinnamon sticks, cloves and salt to a boil in a saucepan, stirring until sugar is dissolved. Reduce the heat. Simmer for 15 minutes. Remove from the heat and let stand until cool. Chill, covered, for several hours. Strain into a punch bowl. Ladle into punch cups and garnish each with an orange slice.

Note: May reheat the cider and serve hot.

YIELD: 14 SERVINGS

Chocolate Almond Café au Lait

- 2 cups chocolate milk
- 2 teaspoons sugar
- 2 tablespoons almond-flavored liqueur, or 1 teaspoon almond extract
- 2 cups freshly brewed coffee
- ½ cup whipping cream
- 1 tablespoon confectioners' sugar
- ½ teaspoon vanilla extract
  Chocolate curls

Heat the chocolate milk in a small saucepan over medium heat for 5 minutes or until tiny bubbles form around the edge; do not boil. Stir in the sugar and almond liqueur. Remove from the heat. Pour into a heatproof pitcher. Add the coffee and stir to blend well. Beat the whipping cream, confectioners' sugar and vanilla in a mixer bowl until soft peaks form. Pour the coffee mixture into mugs. Dollop with the whipped cream and sprinkle with chocolate curls.

YIELD: 4 TO 6 SERVINGS

Citrus Margaritas

Ice cubes
4½ ounces tequila
2 ounces Triple Sec
2 ounces Grand Marnier
4 ounces orange juice concentrate
2 ounces limeade concentrate
Juice of 1 lime

Fill a blender container with ice cubes. Add the tequila, liqueurs, orange juice concentrate, limeade concentrate and lime juice. Process until blended to the desired consistency. Pour into chilled glasses. Garnish each with a slice of fresh lime.

YIELD: 4 SERVINGS

Mango Daiquiris

1 cup (about) undrained chopped mango
½ (6-ounce) can lemonade concentrate
½ cup rum, or to taste
Ice cubes
Sugar or lemon juice to taste

Purée the mango in a blender. Add the lemonade concentrate, rum and enough ice cubes to finish filling the container. Process until the ice is crushed, adding water if needed to ease the blending process. Add sugar or lemon juice to taste. Pour into glasses.

YIELD: 2 SERVINGS

Peach Smoothies

1½ cups sliced peaches
½ cup dark rum
½ cup peach schnapps
1 (6-ounce) can frozen limeade concentrate
2 cups ice cubes

Combine the peaches, rum, schnapps, limeade concentrate and ice cubes in a blender container. Process until smooth. Pour into glasses. Garnish with a sprig of fresh mint and a peach slice.

YIELD: 4 SERVINGS

Citrus Cooler

3 cups pink grapefruit juice
1 cup pineapple juice
¼ cup thawed frozen orange juice concentrate
1 cup chilled lime-flavored sparkling mineral water

Pour 1 cup of the grapefruit juice into an ice cube tray. Freeze until firm. Combine the remaining grapefruit juice, pineapple juice and orange juice concentrate in a pitcher. Chill, covered, for 3 to 4 hours. Stir in the mineral water just before serving. Place 3 frozen grapefruit juice cubes in each of 4 glasses. Fill each glass evenly with the fruit juice mixture. Garnish with lime slices. Serve immediately.

YIELD: 4 CUPS

Summer Cooler

1 **cup water**
¾ **cup sugar**
1 **cup lightly packed fresh mint leaves**
 Juice of 6 lemons
 Juice of 3 oranges
 Floral Ice Cubes
 Ginger ale or sparkling wine

Bring the water and sugar to a boil in a small saucepan and reduce the heat. Simmer for 5 minutes. Pour over the mint leaves in a large glass bowl. Let stand for 1 hour or until cool. Strain into a pitcher, discarding the mint leaves. Stir in the lemon juice and orange juice. Pour ¼ cup juice mixture into each of twelve 8-ounce glasses. Add the Floral Ice Cubes. Add enough ginger ale to fill each glass. Garnish with sprigs of mint.

Floral Ice Cubes

Water
Blossoms or petals from edible flowers, such as violets, borage, dianthus, roses, marigolds, forget-me-nots, bee balm and calendula

Fill ice cube trays half full with water. Place several edible flower blossoms or petals on water in each section. Freeze until firm. Add enough water to completely fill the trays. Freeze until firm.

YIELD: 12 SERVINGS

Lemon Chillers

1½ **cups sugar**
1 **cup water**
 Grated peel of 2 lemons
1½ **cups fresh lemon juice**
 Crushed ice
20 **to 24 thin lemon slices**
 Ice water

Bring the sugar, water and lemon peel to a boil in a small saucepan and reduce the heat. Simmer for 5 minutes. Strain into a jar with a tightfitting lid. Chill, tightly covered, in the refrigerator. Stir in the lemon juice. Chill, tightly covered, until serving time. Fill tall glasses with crushed ice and add 2 lemon slices to each. Add ¼ cup of the lemon mixture to each glass. Add enough ice water to fill each glass and mix gently. Garnish each with a mint sprig and a maraschino cherry.

YIELD: 10 TO 12 SERVINGS

To juice citrus, gently roll the fruit on a flat surface, using the palm of your hand to soften the pulp. Cut the fruit into halves horizontally and extract the juice by using a handheld reamer, a citrus juicer, or an electric juicer.

Orange Blush

1   (12-ounce) can frozen orange juice concentrate, thawed
2   cups cranberry juice
½   cup sugar
1   (32-ounce) bottle club soda or Champagne, chilled

Combine the orange juice concentrate, cranberry juice and sugar in a large pitcher. Stir until the sugar is dissolved. Chill in the refrigerator. Add the club soda just before serving and stir to blend well. Serve over crushed ice.

YIELD: 10 SERVINGS

Orange Peach Champagne

1   (12-ounce) can frozen orange juice concentrate, thawed
1½ cups peach schnapps
2   (10-ounce) bottles ginger ale
2   (10-ounce) bottles tonic water
1   bottle Champagne

Combine the orange juice concentrate and peach schnapps in a punch bowl and mix well. Stir in the ginger ale, tonic water and Champagne. Ladle into punch cups.

YIELD: 20 TO 25 SERVINGS

Whiskey Snowballs

1   cup water
1   cup sugar
1   (6-ounce) can frozen orange juice concentrate, thawed
1   (46-ounce) can pineapple juice
1   fifth bourbon
½   liter 7-Up

Bring the water to a boil in a saucepan. Add the sugar. Cook until the sugar is dissolved, stirring constantly. Remove from the heat and let stand until cool. Combine with the orange juice concentrate, pineapple juice, bourbon and 7-Up and mix well. Pour into a large freezer container. Freeze until slushy, stirring occasionally. Serve frozen.

YIELD: 10 TO 12 SERVINGS

Sparkling Strawberry Tea

1   (10-ounce) package frozen strawberries
1½ quarts boiling water
3   family-size tea bags
½   cup sugar
1   (6-ounce) can frozen lemonade concentrate, thawed
1   (2-liter) bottle Sprite

Process the strawberries in a blender until smooth. Pour the boiling water over the tea bags in a pitcher and steep for 5 minutes. Remove the tea bags. Add the sugar, lemonade concentrate and strawberry purée and mix well. Chill in the refrigerator. Stir in the Sprite just before serving. Serve over ice.

YIELD: 10 TO 15 SERVINGS

Ambrosia Punch

2½ quarts orange juice
2   cups pineapple juice
1   cup cream of coconut
3   cups vanilla ice cream
3   cups ginger ale
½   cup flaked coconut, toasted

Combine the orange juice, pineapple juice and cream of coconut in a punch bowl and blend well. Add tiny scoops of the ice cream. Pour in the ginger ale. Sprinkle with toasted coconut. Ladle into punch cups.

YIELD: 4 QUARTS

Strawberry Punch

2   cups sugar
6   cups boiling water
2½ cups orange juice
½   cup lemon juice
4   cups pineapple juice
2   (10-ounce) packages frozen strawberries, thawed
1   (64-ounce) bottle Sprite

Dissolve the sugar in boiling water in a Dutch oven. Stir in the orange juice, lemon juice, pineapple juice and undrained strawberries. Pour into a large plastic freezer container. Freeze until firm. Remove from the freezer 1 hour before serving. Place in a punch bowl and break into chunks. Add Sprite and stir until slushy. Garnish with sliced fresh strawberries and orange slices.

Note: May add the pineapple juice at serving time if freezer space is a problem.

YIELD: 15 TO 20 SERVINGS

To make Citrus Wheels, cut the citrus into slices in desired widths. Cut away a section of the rind in a straight line from each slice 6 times to form a hexagon. To make Citrus Points, cut the citrus into halves through the stem ends. Place 1 half cut side down; cut into halves again through the stem end. Turn the half sideways. Cut across the previous cut, forming perfect points. Repeat with the remaining half. To make smiles, cut citrus into halves horizontally. Cut each half into thirds. Separate the ends of the sectioned citrus from the rind for about ¼ inch, leaving the rest of the rind intact.

Growers often used different labels to attract different markets—homemakers, farmers, and auction brokers. Many used babies or children in labels designed for the "housewife" market. This brand name highlights the comical mispronunciation of the town's name, Kissimmee (kis-ím-ē), by visitors.

SUN KISSED

Salads and Dressings

•   •

• • •

Section sponsored by

Hyatt Regency Grand Cypress

Grapefruit and Crab Meat Salad

CHEF ALAN GOULD, HYATT REGENCY GRAND CYPRESS

2 grapefruit
4 ounces jumbo lump crab meat
1 tablespoon brandy
2 tablespoons mayonnaise
1 tablespoon chili sauce
1 teaspoon Worcestershire sauce
1 teaspoon chopped fresh herbs of choice
3 drops of Tabasco sauce
1 teaspoon Key lime juice
   Salt and pepper to taste
4 ounces gourmet salad mix

Peel the grapefruit and cut into sections. Combine the crab meat, brandy, mayonnaise, chili sauce, Worcestershire sauce, herbs, Tabasco sauce and Key lime juice in a bowl and mix well. Season with salt and pepper to taste. Arrange sections from 1 of the grapefruit around the edge of a salad plate. Place ½ of the salad mix in the center. Spoon ½ of the crab mixture on top of the salad mix. Repeat the process with the remaining ingredients.

YIELD: 2 SERVINGS

Scallops with Orange and Chervil Vinaigrette

2 cups orange juice
2 cups dry white wine
2½ pounds sea scallops
1 bunch scallions, sliced
⅓ cup coarsely chopped pitted niçoise olives
3 medium tomatoes, seeded, cut into ¼-inch pieces
   Finely chopped zest of 1 orange
3 tablespoons chopped fresh chervil
1 tablespoon drained capers
1 cup fruity olive oil
   Salt and freshly ground pepper to taste

Bring the orange juice, wine and scallops to a boil in a large skillet over high heat. Reduce the heat to low. Simmer for 2 to 3 minutes or until the scallops are barely cooked through. Remove the scallops to a bowl using a slotted spoon. Add the scallions, olives, tomatoes, orange zest, chervil and capers to the scallops and toss to mix well. Cook the remaining liquid in the skillet over high heat until the liquid is reduced to ½ cup. Remove from the heat. Whisk in the olive oil. Season with salt and pepper. Pour over the scallop mixture and toss to coat. Serve immediately or chill, covered, until serving time.

YIELD: 6 SERVINGS

Citrus Shrimp Salad

3   **quarts water**
4   **pounds medium fresh shrimp, unpeeled**
3   **tablespoons chopped shallots**
1   **tablespoon grated lemon peel**
½   **cup fresh lemon juice**
2   **tablespoons Dijon mustard**
1½ **teaspoons salt**
¼   **cup canola oil**
4   **cups sliced romaine lettuce**
2   **cups pink grapefruit sections**
    (about 4 large grapefruit)
2   **cups orange sections (about 5 oranges)**
¼   **cup chopped fresh chives**

Bring the water to a boil in a large saucepan. Add the shrimp. Cook for 3 to 5 minutes or until the shrimp turn pink. Drain and rinse with cold water. Peel the shrimp and devein. Chill, covered, in the refrigerator. Combine the shallots, lemon peel, lemon juice, Dijon mustard and salt in a small bowl. Add the canola oil in a steady stream, whisking constantly. Add the shrimp and toss gently. Line a large platter with the lettuce. Spoon the shrimp mixture into the center. Arrange the grapefruit and orange sections around the edge. Sprinkle with chopped chives. Garnish with sprigs of chives.

YIELD: 8 TO 10 SERVINGS

Orange Caesar Salad

1   **teaspoon anchovy paste**
2   **tablespoons Dijon mustard**
½   **tablespoon finely chopped garlic**
1   **cup orange juice**
¾   **cup olive oil**
1½   **cups grapefruit juice**
¼   **cup lime juice**
2   **cups orange juice**
1½   **tablespoons finely chopped garlic**
1   **teaspoon Old Bay seasoning**
48   **medium shrimp, peeled, deveined**
24   **cups chopped romaine lettuce leaves**
3   **cups seasoned croutons**
2   **cups orange sections**
6   **tablespoons grated Parmesan cheese**

Purée the anchovy paste, Dijon mustard and ½ tablespoon garlic in a food processor until smooth. Add 1 cup orange juice and olive oil in a fine stream, processing constantly. Chill, covered, in the refrigerator. Combine the grapefruit juice, lime juice, 2 cups orange juice, 1½ tablespoons garlic and Old Bay seasoning in a shallow dish and mix well. Place 8 shrimp on each of 6 skewers. Add to the marinade. Marinate in the refrigerator for 4 hours. Drain, discarding the marinade. Cover and chill the skewers of shrimp in the refrigerator. Grill each skewer of shrimp for 2 to 3 minutes per side or until the shrimp turn pink. Toss the romaine lettuce with the dressing in a large salad bowl. Divide among 6 salad plates. Arrange ½ cup croutons and ⅓ cup orange sections on each plate. Sprinkle each with 1 tablespoon Parmesan cheese. Top each plate with the shrimp from 1 skewer. Serve immediately.

YIELD: 6 SERVINGS

Grapefruit Salad with Shrimp and Avocado

- 3 tablespoons honey
- 2 tablespoons cider vinegar
- 2 tablespoons catsup
- 2 teaspoons water
  Dash of ground red pepper
- ½ cup thinly sliced onion
- 1 bay leaf
- 12 ounces medium shrimp, unpeeled
- 2 grapefruit, peeled, sectioned, seeded
- 1 small avocado, peeled, sliced
- 8 Boston lettuce leaves

Combine the honey, cider vinegar, catsup, water and red pepper in a small bowl and mix well. Chill, covered, in the refrigerator. Add enough water to a large skillet to measure a depth of ½ inch. Add the onion and bay leaf. Bring to a boil. Add the shrimp. Cover and reduce the heat. Simmer for 3 to 5 minutes or until the shrimp turn pink. Drain, discarding the onion and bay leaf. Rinse the shrimp with cold water. Chill, covered, in the refrigerator. Peel and devein the shrimp. Divide the shrimp, grapefruit and avocado evenly among 4 plates lined with Boston lettuce leaves. Drizzle the honey dressing over each salad. Serve with toasted French bread slices.

YIELD: 4 SERVINGS

Grapefruit is delicious just halved and eaten with a spoon, but it can be served in many different ways. Serve chilled grapefruit halves spread with crushed strawberries or a spoonful of mint jelly. Try broiling grapefruit halves sprinkled with brown sugar, spices, and other toppings. Grapefruit sections served with a sprinkling of cranberries and drizzled with grapefruit/cranberry cocktail is also delicious. For a delicious accompaniment to meat or poultry, try marinating grapefruit sections in French salad dressing.

Teriyaki Shrimp and Rice Salad Florentine

12 ounces large fresh shrimp, cooked
1 cup long grain rice
1 (8-ounce) bottle red wine vinaigrette
1 tablespoon teriyaki sauce
1 teaspoon sugar
2 cups thin fresh spinach strips
½ cup sliced celery
½ cup sliced green onions
6 slices bacon, cooked, crumbled
1 (8-ounce) can sliced water chestnuts, drained

Peel the shrimp and devein. Cut the shrimp into halves. Cook the rice using package directions. Combine the shrimp and hot rice in a large bowl and toss to mix well. Cool slightly. Mix the vinaigrette, teriyaki sauce and sugar in a bowl. Stir into the rice mixture. Chill, covered, for 8 to 10 hours. Fold in the spinach strips, celery, green onions, bacon and water chestnuts. Serve immediately.

YIELD: 6 TO 8 SERVINGS

Couscous Salad with Peppers and Feta Cheese

¼ cup medium sherry
¼ cup white vinegar
3 cloves of garlic, mashed
1 teaspoon pepper
¼ cup olive oil
¼ cup medium sherry
½ cup water
1 clove of garlic, mashed
1 cup couscous
1 large red bell pepper, cut into quarters
1 large yellow bell pepper, cut into quarters
1 large green bell pepper, cut into quarters
4 to 6 scallions, sliced
12 kalamata olives, seeded
3 ounces feta cheese, crumbled

Combine ¼ cup sherry, vinegar, 3 cloves of garlic, pepper and olive oil in a bowl and whisk well. Bring ¼ cup sherry, water and 1 clove of garlic to a boil in a saucepan. Remove from the heat. Stir in the couscous. Cover and let stand until the couscous swells. Stir with chopsticks to separate the grains. Pour ⅓ cup of the dressing over the couscous and toss to mix well. Grill the bell peppers on a grill rack over hot coals until tender, turning and basting frequently with some of the remaining dressing. Cool and cut into strips. Combine the bell pepper strips, scallions and olives in the remaining dressing in a bowl. Marinate in the refrigerator. Combine the couscous, bell pepper mixture and feta cheese in a salad bowl and toss to mix well. Serve immediately.

YIELD: 4 TO 6 SERVINGS

Citrus fruits will yield more juice if allowed to stand in boiling water for a few minutes before squeezing. If the citrus peel is going to be used, always grate or peel before placing the fruit in boiling water. The yield for citrus fruits are as follows:

- 3 medium oranges will yield 1 cup juice;
- 1 medium orange will yield 4 teaspoons grated peel;
- 1 medium orange will yield 10 to 12 sections;
- 1 medium grapefruit will yield ⅔ cup juice;
- 1 medium grapefruit will yield 10 to 12 sections;
- 6 medium lemons will yield 1 cup juice;
- 1 medium lemon will yield 1 tablespoon grated peel.

Orange Chicken Tabouli

1½ cups boiling water
¾ cup bulgur
2 oranges
1½ cups chopped cooked chicken or turkey
2 cups chopped seeded cucumber
2 tablespoons chopped fresh parsley
2 tablespoons chopped green onions
1 tablespoon chopped fresh mint, or
    1 teaspoon crushed dried mint
1 tablespoon olive oil
½ teaspoon salt
    Romaine lettuce leaves

Pour the boiling water over the bulgur in a medium bowl. Let stand for 30 minutes; drain. Shred finely enough peel from the oranges to measure 2 teaspoons. Peel the oranges. Separate into sections over a bowl to catch the juice. Measure and reserve ¼ cup of the orange juice. Chill the orange sections and remaining juice, covered, until serving time. Combine the drained bulgur, orange peel, reserved orange juice, chicken, cucumber, parsley, green onions, mint, olive oil and salt in a large bowl and mix well. Chill, covered, in the refrigerator for 4 to 24 hours, stirring occasionally. Fold in the orange sections just before serving. Spoon onto salad plates lined with romaine lettuce leaves.

YIELD: 4 SERVINGS

Black Bean Chicken Salad

2   tablespoons mayonnaise
2   teaspoons chili powder
4   boneless, skinless chicken breast halves
1   (15-ounce) can black beans, rinsed, drained
½   cup chopped red bell pepper
⅓   cup chopped tomato
¼   cup minced fresh cilantro
1   to 1½ tablespoons lime juice
     Tabasco sauce to taste
½   teaspoon cumin
     Mixed salad greens, such as torn romaine
     lettuce and arugula

Mix the mayonnaise and chili powder in a bowl. Brush on both sides of the chicken. Place on a grill rack. Grill over hot coals for 10 minutes on each side or until cooked through. Combine the black beans, red pepper, tomato, cilantro, lime juice, Tabasco sauce and cumin in a bowl and mix well. Cut the chicken into strips. Divide the salad greens among 4 salad plates. Arrange the chicken over the salad greens. Spoon the black bean mixture over the top. Serve with an oil-and-vinegar-based salad dressing.

YIELD: 4 SERVINGS

Citrus Chicken and Feta Cheese Caesar Salad

4   boneless, skinless chicken breast halves
6   cups torn romaine lettuce
6   ounces feta cheese, crumbled
½   cup thinly sliced red onion
½   orange bell pepper, cut into rings
¼   cup olive oil
3   tablespoons orange juice concentrate
1   tablespoon white wine vinegar
2   teaspoons finely chopped green onions

Place the chicken on a grill rack. Grill over hot coals until cooked through. Cut into ¼-inch strips. Combine the lettuce, chicken, cheese, onion and pepper rings in a large salad bowl and toss to mix well. Mix the olive oil, orange juice concentrate, vinegar and green onions in a bowl. Pour over the chicken mixture and toss lightly. Serve immediately.

YIELD: 6 SERVINGS

Curried Poached Pears with Coconut Orange Chicken Salad

¾ **cup slivered almonds**
¾ **cup flaked coconut**
8 **firm pears**
1 **quart water**
¼ **cup lemon juice**
2 **quarts water**
3 **tablespoons curry powder**
3 **cups chopped, cooked chicken**
1 **cup minced celery**
⅓ **cup minced green onions**
 Coconut Orange Dressing

Arrange the almonds and coconut on a baking sheet. Bake at 350 degrees for 5 to 10 minutes or until toasted, stirring frequently. Cut the pears into halves lengthwise, removing the cores. Place the pear halves in a shallow dish. Add 1 quart water and lemon juice. Let stand for 10 to 15 minutes; drain. Bring 2 quarts water and curry powder to a boil in a large saucepan. Add the pears and reduce the heat. Simmer for 6 to 8 minutes or until tender; drain. Place the pears cut side up in a 10x15-inch baking pan. Combine the almonds, coconut, chicken, celery and green onions in a large bowl and mix well. Stir in the Coconut Orange Dressing. Spoon into the pear halves. Broil 3 inches from the heat source with the oven door ajar for 2 to 3 minutes or until the tops are light brown. Serve on lettuce-lined salad plates.

Coconut Orange Dressing

¼ **cup egg substitute**
¼ **cup coconut milk**
2 **tablespoons fresh lemon juice**
1 **teaspoon grated orange peel**
¼ **teaspoon salt**
¼ **teaspoon white pepper**
½ **cup vegetable oil**

Combine the egg substitute, coconut milk, lemon juice, orange peel, salt and white pepper in a blender container. Process until smooth, stopping once to scape down the side. Add the oil in a steady stream, processing at high speed until thickened.

YIELD: 4 TO 6 SERVINGS

Orange or lemon twists are the perfect garnish for the center of a salad or fruit plate. Cut an orange or lemon horizontally into thin rounds. Cut from 1 side to the center of each round and then pull out to make a curl.

Tropical Spicy Steak Salad

3	cups grapefruit juice
6	tablespoons lime juice
6	tablespoons cream of coconut
½	tablespoon coriander
½	tablespoon crushed red pepper
1	teaspoon black pepper
2	(1½-pound) beef flank steaks, trimmed
2	tablespoons Dijon mustard
5	tablespoons olive oil
24	cups mixed salad greens
½	cup (⅛-inch) red onion slices
½	cup (¼-inch) red bell pepper slices
1½	cups cooked black beans, rinsed, drained
2	cups grapefruit sections

Combine the grapefruit juice, lime juice, cream of coconut, coriander, crushed red pepper and black pepper in a bowl and mix well. Pour ½ of the mixture over the flank steaks in a shallow dish. Marinate, covered, in the refrigerator for 24 hours. Add the mustard and olive oil to the remaining mixture, whisking constantly. Chill the dressing, covered, in the refrigerator. Drain the steaks and pat dry, discarding the marinade. Place on a grill rack. Grill on each side for 5 to 6 minutes or until the desired degree of doneness. Remove from the heat and keep warm. Cut the steaks into thin slices. Arrange the salad greens on each of 6 salad plates. Layer the onion, red bell pepper, black beans, grapefruit sections and steak slices over the salad greens. Top each salad with the dressing.

YIELD: 6 SERVINGS

Turkey Apple Salad

½	to ¾ cup mayonnaise
2	to 3 tablespoons orange juice
2	large Red Delicious apples
½	cup orange juice
4	cups cubed cooked turkey
8	ounces Gouda cheese, cut into ½-inch cubes
2	fresh pineapples
½	cup almond slices, toasted
	Pineapple slices
8	strawberries

Mix the mayonnaise with 2 to 3 tablespoons orange juice in a bowl. Cut the apples into cubes and dip in ½ cup orange juice. Combine the apples, turkey, cheese and mayonnaise mixture in a bowl and mix well. Chill, covered, for several hours. Cut the pineapple lengthwise into 4 equal quarters. Remove and discard core. Place the pineapple quarters on individual serving plates. Fill with the turkey mixture. Sprinkle with almonds. Garnish with pineapple slices and strawberries.

YIELD: 8 SERVINGS

Royal Orange Walnut Salad

2 oranges
2 small heads Bibb lettuce, torn into bite-size
    pieces
½ medium purple onion, sliced
½ cup coarsely chopped walnuts
2 teaspoons melted butter or margarine
    Sweet-and-Sour Dressing

Peel the oranges. Separate into sections in a large bowl, discarding the seeds. Add the lettuce and onion and toss gently to mix. Sauté the walnuts in the butter in a skillet until light brown. Add to the lettuce mixture. Pour the Sweet-and-Sour Dressing over the salad and toss to mix well.

Sweet-and-Sour Dressing

1 cup vegetable oil
½ cup white vinegar
½ cup sugar
1 teaspoon grated onion
1 teaspoon paprika
1 teaspoon celery seeds
1 teaspoon dry mustard
1 teaspoon salt

Combine the vegetable oil, vinegar, sugar, onion, paprika, celery seeds, dry mustard and salt in a jar with a tightfitting lid. Cover tightly and shake vigorously until the sugar is dissolved. Chill for several hours. Shake the dressing before serving.

YIELD: 6 TO 8 SERVINGS

Orange Kiwifruit Salad with Marmalade Dressing

1 head romaine lettuce, torn
3 to 4 kiwifruit, peeled, sliced
1 (11-ounce) can mandarin oranges, drained
1 large red onion, sliced
⅓ cup chopped pecans or walnuts
3 ounces bleu cheese, crumbled
    Croutons (optional)
    Marmalade Dressing

Combine the romaine lettuce, kiwifruit, mandarin oranges, red onion, pecans, bleu cheese and croutons in a large salad bowl and toss to mix well. Pour the Marmalade Dressing over the salad and toss to mix well.

Marmalade Dressing

⅓ cup fresh lime juice
3 tablespoons balsamic vinegar
6 to 7 tablespoons orange marmalade
1 teaspoon salt
1 teaspoon freshly ground pepper
½ cup extra-virgin olive oil

Process the lime juice, vinegar, orange marmalade, salt and pepper in a blender until smooth. Add the olive oil in a fine stream, processing constantly.

YIELD: 4 TO 6 SERVINGS

Pear and Bleu Cheese Salad

1   head butter lettuce
4   pears, cored, sliced
    Creamy Dijon Dressing
2   ounces bleu cheese, crumbled
½   cup chopped dates
¼   cup chopped walnuts

Rinse the lettuce and pat dry. Separate into leaves. Arrange the lettuce leaves on individual salad plates. Arrange the pear slices in wheel spoke fashion on the lettuce. Drizzle with the Creamy Dijon Dressing. Sprinkle with the bleu cheese, dates and walnuts.

Creamy Dijon Dressing

2   tablespoons red wine vinegar
1   tablespoon lemon juice
2   teaspoons Dijon mustard
2   teaspoons whipping cream
⅓   cup olive oil
⅓   cup vegetable oil
½   teaspoon salt
½   teaspoon freshly ground pepper
⅛   teaspoon sugar

Whisk the vinegar, lemon juice, mustard and whipping cream in a small bowl. Add the olive oil and vegetable oil gradually, whisking constantly. Add the salt, pepper and sugar and whisk well.

YIELD: 6 TO 8 SERVINGS

Orange Slaw

3   medium oranges
1   small cabbage, shredded
¼   onion, finely chopped
¾   cup mayonnaise or mayonnaise-type salad
    dressing
1   tablespoon fresh lemon juice
    Sugar and salt to taste

Peel the oranges and separate into sections. Cut the sections into bite-size pieces. Combine the oranges, cabbage and onion in a large serving bowl. Mix the mayonnaise, lemon juice, sugar and salt in a bowl. Pour over the cabbage mixture and mix lightly. Chill, covered, for 20 to 30 minutes before serving.

YIELD: 6 SERVINGS

For Vinaigrette, combine ⅓ cup vegetable oil, ¼ cup cider vinegar, ½ cup finely chopped green onions, ¼ cup sweet pickle relish, 1 tablespoon sugar, 1 tablespoon chopped fresh basil, 1 tablespoon chopped pimento, 2 tablespoons tarragon vinegar, ½ teaspoon Dijon mustard, ¼ teaspoon salt and ⅛ teaspoon pepper in a small bowl and stir to mix well. Cover and chill for 3 to 4 hours. Serve in a hollowed-out red bell pepper.

Raspberry and Walnut Salad

4	cups torn Boston lettuce
4	cups torn red leaf lettuce
¾	cup chopped walnuts, toasted
2	cups fresh raspberries
1	avocado, peeled, cut into pieces
2	kiwifruit, peeled, sliced
	Raspberry Salad Dressing

Combine the Boston lettuce, red leaf lettuce, walnuts, raspberries, avocado and kiwifruit in a large salad bowl and toss gently. Serve with Raspberry Salad Dressing.

Raspberry Salad Dressing

⅔	cup seedless raspberry jam
¼	cup sugar
⅓	cup raspberry vinegar
1	cup vegetable oil
1	tablespoon poppy seeds

Process the raspberry jam, sugar and vinegar in a blender for 20 seconds. Add the vegetable oil in a steady stream, processing at high speed. Stir in the poppy seeds.

YIELD: 12 SERVINGS

Fruit Salad with Honey Lemon Dressing

2	bananas, sliced
2	tablespoons fresh lemon juice
¼	cup honey
1	grapefruit, peeled, sectioned
3	oranges, peeled, sectioned
1	Red Delicious apple, cubed
1	Golden Delicious apple, cubed
	Honey Lemon Dressing
¼	cup flaked coconut, toasted

Toss the bananas in lemon juice in a bowl. Drain, reserving the lemon juice. Combine the reserved lemon juice and honey in a bowl and mix well. Layer the bananas, grapefruit, oranges and apples in a bowl. Drizzle with the honey mixture. Cover and chill for 3 hours. Spoon the fruit mixture onto lettuce-lined salad plates using a slotted spoon. Drizzle with the Honey Lemon Dressing. Sprinkle with the coconut.

Honey Lemon Dressing

3	ounces cream cheese, softened
¼	teaspoon grated lemon peel
2½	tablespoons fresh lemon juice
3	tablespoons honey
1	tablespoon water

Beat the cream cheese at medium speed in a mixer bowl until creamy. Add the lemon peel, lemon juice, honey and water and mix until blended.

YIELD: 4 TO 6 SERVINGS

Sugared Almond Salad with Citrus Vinaigrette

1   egg white
¼   cup sugar
1   cup sliced almonds
2   tablespoons melted butter or margarine
1   head Bibb lettuce, torn into bite-size pieces
1   head red leaf lettuce, torn into bite-size pieces
1   (11-ounce) can mandarin oranges, drained
1   pint fresh strawberries, thinly sliced
1   green onion, chopped
      Citrus Vinaigrette
6   slices bacon, crisp-fried, crumbled

Beat the egg white at high speed in a mixer bowl until foamy. Add the sugar 1 tablespoon at a time, beating constantly until stiff peaks form. Fold in the almonds. Pour the butter into a 9x9-inch baking pan. Spread the coated almonds in the prepared pan. Bake at 325 degrees for 20 to 25 minutes or until the almonds are dry, stirring every 5 minutes. Remove from the oven and let stand until cool. Combine the lettuce, oranges, strawberries and green onion in a large salad bowl and toss gently to mix. Add the Citrus Vinaigrette and toss gently. Arrange on individual salad plates. Sprinkle each serving with sugared almonds and crumbled bacon.

Citrus Vinaigrette

¾   cup olive oil
¼   cup red wine vinegar
1   tablespoon orange juice
1   teaspoon grated orange peel
1   teaspoon poppy seeds
¼   teaspoon salt
¼   teaspoon pepper

Combine the olive oil, vinegar, orange juice, orange peel, poppy seeds, salt and pepper in a small bowl and whisk well.

YIELD: 6 SERVINGS

To section citrus fruit, remove the peel from the fruit, holding the fruit over a bowl to catch juices. Cut between 1 fruit section and the membrane carefully, cutting to the center of the fruit. Turn the knife and slide up the other side of the section next to the membrane. Continue with the remaining sections. The result will be neat citrus sections to use in salads and desserts.

Orange Strawberry Salad

4 large oranges, peeled, sectioned
3 cups sliced fresh strawberries
¼ cup slivered almonds
  Boston lettuce leaves
  Citrus Dressing

Combine the oranges, strawberries and almonds in a bowl and toss gently to mix. Spoon onto individual salad plates lined with Boston lettuce leaves. Spoon Citrus Dressing over the top.

Citrus Dressing

½ cup sugar
¼ teaspoon cornstarch
3 tablespoons orange juice
1 egg
1 egg yolk
1 tablespoon lemon juice
1 teaspoon grated lemon peel
2 tablespoons butter

Combine the sugar, cornstarch, orange juice, egg, egg yolk, lemon juice, lemon peel and butter in a small saucepan. Cook over low heat for 4 minutes or until thickened, stirring constantly. Pour into a container with a tightfitting lid. Chill, covered, in the refrigerator.

YIELD: 4 SERVINGS

There are many different kinds of oranges. Listed below are some of the most known ones.

- **The Navel Orange** is large and thick skinned and is used for eating out-of-hand, for sections and for slices. The peel crystallizes well and makes a good marmalade.
- **The Hamlin Orange** is a thick skinned orange good for juice and marmalades.
- **The Parson Brown Orange** is a rough-skinned orange that is good for eating, for juice, and for marmalades.
- **The Temple Orange** is a bright orange with a round and thick red skin. It peels easily and is best for eating out-of-hand.
- **The Tangelo** is a bright orange with a rough and thick red skin. It peels easily and is in season December through March.
- **The Ponkan** looks like a large tangerine, peels easily, and is best used fresh out-of-hand.
- **The King** is a large orange with a thick rough skin and is easily peeled. It is sweet and delicious and is best for eating out-of-hand. It is in season March to July.
- **The Valencia** is an excellent choice for making orange juice and marmalade. It is large in size and has a good flavor. The sections freeze well.

Black-Eyed Pea Salad

1½ cups dried black-eyed peas
2 meaty ham bones
¼ teaspoon thyme
¼ teaspoon basil
1 medium onion, coarsely chopped
1 medium carrot, coarsely chopped
1 rib celery, coarsely chopped
2 Roma tomatoes, coarsely chopped
1 jalapeño, finely chopped
1 banana pepper, finely chopped
1 clove of garlic, finely chopped
4 sprigs of parsley, finely chopped
1 to 2 sprigs of basil, finely chopped
5 to 7 stems chives, finely chopped
¼ teaspoon finely chopped fresh rosemary
  Dijon Mustard Vinaigrette
  Fresh mustard greens

Rinse and sort the black-eyed peas. Combine the black-eyed peas, meaty ham bones, thyme, basil and water to cover in a large saucepan. Cook, covered, until tender. Drain, discarding the bones. Combine the black-eyed peas, onion, carrot, celery, tomatoes, jalapeño, banana pepper, garlic, parsley, basil, chives and rosemary in a large bowl and toss gently to mix. Stir in the Dijon Mustard Vinaigrette. Serve on a bed of fresh mustard greens.

Dijon Mustard Vinaigrette

1 clove of garlic, minced
2 tablespoons Dijon mustard
½ cup olive oil
¼ cup balsamic vinegar

Mix the garlic and Dijon mustard in a bowl. Add the olive oil and vinegar gradually, whisking constantly.

YIELD: 4 TO 6 SERVINGS

Vegetables Citronnade

1 large head cauliflower, cut into 1½-inch florets
1 large head broccoli, cut into 1½-inch florets
1½ pounds carrots, peeled, cut diagonally ½ inch thick
2 medium summer squash, cut ¼ inch thick
2 medium zucchini, cut ½ inch thick
1½ pounds sugar snap peas, trimmed
1 red bell pepper, cut into thin julienne strips
  Citronnade Mayonnaise
½ cup chopped fresh parsley
1 tablespoon grated orange zest

Steam the cauliflower, broccoli, carrots, squash, zucchini and snap peas in separate saucepans until tender-crisp. Rinse each under cold running water and drain. Combine the steamed vegetables and red pepper in a large bowl. Add Citronnade Mayonnaise and toss to coat. Spoon into a large serving bowl. Sprinkle with the parsley and orange zest. Cover and chill for 3 to 12 hours before serving.

Citronnade Mayonnaise

1 egg yolk
1 egg
2 tablespoons Dijon mustard
2 cloves of garlic, minced
¼ cup fresh lemon juice
1½ cups vegetable oil
1 tablespoon finely grated lemon zest
  Salt and freshly ground pepper to taste

Combine the egg yolk, egg, Dijon mustard, garlic and lemon juice in a food processor container fitted with a steel blade. Process until blended. Add the vegetable oil in a fine steady stream, processing constantly until thick. Add the lemon zest and salt and pepper and process until blended.

YIELD: 15 TO 20 SERVINGS

Confetti Corn Toss

1   (15-ounce) can black beans, drained
2   (15-ounce) cans whole kernel corn, drained
1   (14-ounce) can hearts of palm, drained, sliced
2   large tomatoes, chopped
½   cup chopped purple onion
⅓   cup minced fresh cilantro
¼   cup vegetable oil
1½ teaspoons chili powder
½   teaspoon cumin
3   tablespoons lime juice

Combine the black beans, corn, hearts of palm, tomatoes, onion and cilantro in a large bowl and mix well. Whisk the vegetable oil, chili powder, cumin and lime juice in a small bowl. Drizzle over the corn mixture and toss well. Chill, covered, for 8 to 10 hours.

YIELD: 6 TO 8 SERVINGS

Corn may be used many different ways in recipes. Use ¼ or ⅓ cobs in chowders and stews. Scrape the kernels from the cob and use in scalloped dishes, succotash, custards, fritters, relishes, or chowders. Fresh corn kernels may also be added to summer main-dish salads, scrambled eggs, fresh corn pancakes, and frittatas.

Citrus-Marinated Hearts of Palm Salad

½   cup fresh orange juice
¼   cup fresh lime juice
3   tablespoons extra-virgin olive oil
1½ tablespoons honey
1   tablespoon balsamic vinegar
1½ teaspoons Dijon mustard
1½ teaspoons pink peppercorns, lightly crushed
1   teaspoon finely chopped fresh tarragon
    Salt and freshly ground black pepper to taste
2   cups fresh thinly sliced hearts of palm
4   to 5 cups mesclun
1   tablespoon finely chopped fresh chives

Combine the orange juice, lime juice, olive oil, honey, balsamic vinegar, Dijon mustard, pink peppercorns, tarragon, salt and black pepper in a nonreactive bowl and whisk until smooth. Add the hearts of palm. Weight the hearts of palm with a saucer to keep them submerged. Marinate in the refrigerator for 4 hours. Drain, reserving the marinade. Toss the salad greens with 3 to 4 tablespoons of the reserved marinade in a salad bowl. Arrange on individual salad plates. Arrange the hearts of palm on the salad greens. Drizzle with the remaining marinade. Sprinkle with the chives.

Note: May use drained, canned hearts of palm, but marinate for only 1 hour.

YIELD: 4 SERVINGS

Sugar Snap Pea and Hearts of Palm Salad

1　cup fresh sugar snap peas, cooked, chilled
2　cups torn Boston lettuce
2　cups torn romaine lettuce
1　cup drained, sliced hearts of palm
¼　cup sliced green onions
　　Honey Orange Vinaigrette

Combine the peas, Boston lettuce, romaine lettuce, hearts of palm and green onions in a large bowl and toss to mix well. Add the Honey Orange Vinaigrette and toss gently. Serve immediately.

Note: May use frozen sugar snap peas, but thaw before using.

Honey Orange Vinaigrette

2　tablespoons balsamic vinegar
2　tablespoons orange juice
1　tablespoon honey
2　teaspoons vegetable oil
⅛　teaspoon garlic powder
⅛　teaspoon chili powder

Combine the balsamic vinegar, orange juice, honey, vegetable oil, garlic powder and chili powder in a small bowl and whisk well.

YIELD: 3 OR 4 SERVINGS

*Sweet-and-Sour Spinach Salad

1　(10-ounce) package fresh spinach
8　ounces bacon, crisp-fried, crumbled
1　small red onion, sliced, separated into rings
3　to 4 ounces slivered almonds
1　(11-ounce) can mandarin oranges, drained
　　Sweet-and-Sour Dressing

Rinse the spinach and remove the stems. Pat dry. Tear into bite-size pieces. Combine the spinach, bacon, onion rings, almonds and oranges in a bowl and toss gently to mix. Chill, covered, in the refrigerator. Add warm Sweet-and-Sour Dressing just before serving and toss gently.

Sweet-and-Sour Dressing

⅓　cup sugar
1　teaspoon lemon juice
½　teaspoon paprika
½　teaspoon dry mustard
½　teaspoon celery salt
½　cup salad oil
⅛　teaspoon salt
2½ tablespoons cider vinegar
2½ tablespoons honey

Combine the sugar, lemon juice, paprika, dry mustard, celery salt, salad oil, salt, vinegar and honey in a jar with a tightfitting lid. Cover and shake well. Store in the refrigerator. Heat slightly in a saucepan before serving.

YIELD: 6 TO 8 SERVINGS

Fruit French Dressing

1 cup salad oil
¼ cup orange juice
2½ tablespoons lemon juice
1 tablespoon vinegar
⅓ cup sugar
1 teaspoon paprika
1 teaspoon grated onion

Combine the salad oil, orange juice, lemon juice, vinegar, sugar, paprika and onion in a jar with a tightfitting lid. Cover and shake well. Serve on citrus or a combination of fresh spinach and orange sections. Garnish with toasted slivered almonds.

YIELD: 1 ¾ CUPS

Paris Salad Dressing

½ cup olive oil
½ cup salad oil or oil of choice
5 tablespoons red wine vinegar
¼ cup sour cream
1½ teaspoons salt
½ teaspoon dry mustard
2 tablespoons sugar
    Coarsely ground pepper to taste
2 teaspoons chopped parsley
2 cloves of garlic, crushed

Combine the olive oil, salad oil, red wine vinegar, sour cream, salt, dry mustard, sugar, pepper, parsley and garlic in a jar with a tightfitting lid. Cover and shake well. Store in the refrigerator.

YIELD: 1 ½ CUPS

Peanut Salad Dressing

1 teaspoon peanut butter
1 tablespoon brown sugar
1 tablespoon mixed chopped fresh herbs
    such as parsley, tarragon and chives
½ teaspoon minced garlic
½ teaspoon salt
¼ teaspoon pepper
5 tablespoons malt vinegar
¾ cup peanut oil

Combine the peanut butter, brown sugar, herbs, garlic, salt and pepper in a bowl and mix well. Add the vinegar and mix well. Add the peanut oil gradually, whisking constantly.

YIELD: 1 CUP

Honey Balsamic Vinaigrette

HEATHER MCPHERSON, *THE ORLANDO SENTINEL*

½	cup drained canned apricots
⅓	cup balsamic vinegar or red wine vinegar
¼	cup honey
2	teaspoons Dijon mustard
1	clove of garlic, minced
1	teaspoon Italian seasoning
¼	teaspoon salt
¼	teaspoon pepper
1	tablespoon olive oil

Combine the apricots, vinegar, honey, mustard, garlic, Italian seasoning, salt and pepper in a blender or food processor container and process until smooth. Add the olive oil in a fine stream, processing constantly.

YIELD: 1 CUP

Orange Vinaigrette

½	cup frozen orange juice concentrate
½	cup olive oil
½	teaspoon sesame oil
2	teaspoons Dijon mustard
2	teaspoons rice wine vinegar
	Salt and pepper to taste

Combine the orange juice concentrate, olive oil, sesame oil, mustard, vinegar, salt and pepper in a container with a tightfitting lid. Cover and shake well to mix. Serve over fresh salad greens.

YIELD: 1 CUP

To reliquify crystallized honey, place the honey container in a saucepan of warm water. Heat over low heat until the crystals dissolve. May also place the honey in a microwave-safe container and microwave on High for 2 to 3 minutes or until the crystals dissolve, stirring every 30 seconds. Store honey tightly covered at room temperature.

Citrus tended to be a family-owned enterprise.
In 1928, Rufus M. Holloway and his three brothers moved to Leesburg
from Georgia and founded the Leesburg Fruit Company. The company
specialized in citrus and watermelons and is still family-owned.

SUN SHOWERS

Soups and Sandwiches

...

Section sponsored by

Middleton Pest Control, Inc.

Tempting Tomato Sandwiches

MIDDLETON PEST CONTROL, INC.

- 1 loaf sliced white bread
- 4 ounces cream cheese, softened
- 1 cup finely chopped pecans
- ¾ cup mayonnaise
- 2 dashes of Worcestershire sauce
- 1½ tablespoons onion juice
  Garlic salt to taste
- 10 ripe plum tomatoes, thinly sliced
  Chopped parsley

Trim the crusts from the bread. Cut 3 to 4 circles from each bread slice using a small biscuit cutter. Combine the cream cheese, pecans, mayonnaise, Worcestershire sauce, onion juice and garlic salt in a food processor container. Process until well blended. Adjust the seasonings to taste. Spread over each bread round. Place a thin tomato slice on top. Sprinkle with parsley.

Note: The spread may be made 1 day ahead and chilled in the refrigerator.

YIELD: 6 DOZEN

Orange Fruit Soup

- 2 tablespoons quick-cooking tapioca
- 2½ cups orange juice
- 2 tablespoons sugar
  Dash of salt
- 2 sticks cinnamon
- 1½ cups undrained orange sections
- 1 (12-ounce) package frozen peach slices, thawed
- 1 banana, sliced
  Sour cream

Mix the tapioca, orange juice, sugar and salt in a saucepan. Let stand for 5 minutes. Add the cinnamon sticks. Bring to a boil over medium heat. Remove from the heat. Cool for 10 minutes. Add the undrained orange sections, peaches and banana. Cook until heated through. Serve with a dollop of sour cream.

YIELD: 8 SERVINGS

All citrus must ripen on the tree. Citrus does not ripen once removed from the tree.

Fruit Minestrone

2	cups tomato juice
2	cups watermelon juice
¼	cup pineapple juice
	Juice of 2 lemons
	Juice of 3 oranges
	Honey to taste
½	cup diced watermelon
½	cup diced cantaloupe
½	cup diced mango
½	cup diced papaya
½	cup diced pineapple
½	cup diced peach
¼	cup diced carrot, blanched
¼	cup diced celery
1	cup ditalini, cooked al dente
½	cup chopped mint

Mix the tomato juice, watermelon juice, pineapple juice, lemon juice and orange juice in a bowl. Stir in the honey. Chill, covered, for 2 hours. Combine the watermelon, cantaloupe, mango, papaya, pineapple, peach, carrot, celery, pasta and mint in a large bowl and toss gently to mix well. Ladle the chilled juice mixture into individual shallow soup bowls. Stir in the fruit mixture.

YIELD: 4 SERVINGS

Banana and Raspberry Bisque

1	cup fresh raspberries
½	cup half-and-half
½	cup whipping cream
3	tablespoons confectioners' sugar
4	cups half-and-half
4	bananas, sliced, frozen
	Angel food cake cubes or pound cake cubes

Process the raspberries, ½ cup half-and-half, whipping cream and confectioners' sugar in a blender until smooth. Strain into a large bowl and discard the seeds. Chill, covered, in the refrigerator. Process 4 cups half-and-half and bananas ½ at a time in a blender until smooth. Pour into small serving bowls. Drizzle with the raspberry mixture. Run a wooden pick through the raspberry mixture to make desired design. Sprinkle with cake cubes.

YIELD: 6 SERVINGS

Gazpacho

1	large tomato, finely chopped
½	small onion, finely chopped
½	cucumber, finely chopped
½	green bell pepper, finely chopped
1	rib celery, finely chopped
2	cups tomato juice
½	cup white wine
3	tablespoons red wine vinegar
1	tablespoon lemon juice
2	tablespoons basil
1	teaspoon salt
½	teaspoon pepper
1	teaspoon Worcestershire sauce
	Dash of Tabasco sauce

Combine the tomato, onion, cucumber, green pepper and celery in a bowl and mix well. Add the tomato juice, white wine, red wine vinegar, lemon juice, basil, salt, pepper, Worcestershire sauce and Tabasco sauce and mix well. Chill, covered, for 24 hours. Garnish with sour cream and chopped fresh herbs.

YIELD: 6 SERVINGS

White Chicken Chili

1	cup melted butter
1	cup flour
2	tablespoons olive oil
3	large cloves of garlic, minced
1	large white onion, chopped
2	large green bell peppers, chopped
4	ribs celery, chopped
8	(8-ounce) boneless, skinless chicken breast halves, cut into bite-size pieces
1	teaspoon cumin
1	teaspoon white pepper
1	teaspoon hot sauce
½	cup sliced jalapeños
12	cups chicken broth, or 2 (48-ounce) cans chicken broth
4	cups cooked white kidney beans, or 2 (19-ounce) cans cannellini, rinsed, drained
1	cup sour cream
	Shredded Monterey Jack cheese

Melt the butter in a medium saucepan over low heat. Add the flour gradually, stirring constantly until smooth. Remove the roux from the heat. Heat the olive oil in a large stockpot over medium heat. Add the garlic. Sauté for 1 to 2 minutes or until golden brown. Add the onion, green peppers and celery. Sauté until tender-crisp. Add the chicken, cumin, white pepper and hot sauce. Cook until the chicken is cooked through. Add the jalapeños and chicken broth. Bring to a boil and reduce the heat. Add the roux. Cook until thickened, stirring constantly. Add the beans. Simmer until heated through or until serving time. Ladle into individual serving bowls. Dollop with sour cream and sprinkle with cheese.

YIELD: 12 SERVINGS

Corn and Red Pepper Chowder

1 tablespoon olive oil
1 large onion, chopped
4 medium red bell peppers, chopped
3 cloves of garlic, minced
10 cups fresh corn kernels
2 pounds red potatoes, chopped
10 cups vegetable or chicken stock
  Salt and freshly ground pepper to taste
2 teaspoons chopped fresh thyme, or
  1 teaspoon dried thyme
1 tablespoon olive oil
4 to 5 cups skim milk
¼ cup chopped fresh sage

Heat 1 tablespoon olive oil in a heavy stockpot over medium heat. Add the onion and ½ of the red peppers. Cook until the onion begins to soften, stirring constantly. Add ½ of the garlic. Cook for 5 minutes or until the onion and red peppers are tender. Add the remaining garlic, corn, potatoes, stock, salt, pepper and thyme. Bring to a boil and reduce the heat. Simmer, covered, for 35 minutes. Heat 1 tablespoon olive oil in a nonstick skillet over medium heat. Add the remaining red peppers. Sauté for 5 to 8 minutes or until tender. Remove from the heat. Pour ½ of the soup in a blender or food processor container and process until smooth. Return to the stockpot. Stir in 4 cups milk and sautéed red peppers. Season with salt and pepper. Cook for 10 minutes or until heated through; do not boil. Stir in enough of the remaining milk for the desired consistency. Stir in the sage. Serve immediately.

YIELD: 12 SERVINGS

Classic Oyster Stew

12 ounces shucked fresh stewing oysters
1 tablespoon butter or margarine
2 (12-ounce) cans evaporated milk
1 cup water
  Salt and pepper to taste

Sauté the oysters in the butter in a skillet over medium heat until the edges curl. Add the evaporated milk and water. Bring to a boil, stirring frequently. Season with salt and pepper to taste. Serve immediately.

YIELD: 4 SERVINGS

One ear of corn yields about ½ cup of corn kernels and has about 89 calories. Corn is very low in sodium and provides about 2.9 grams of fiber per ½ cup. Sweet corn also provides some vitamin C, and the yellow varieties also contain vitamin A.

Cheesy Ham and Potato Chowder

1½ cups water
4   cups potatoes, chopped
½   cup thinly sliced celery
¼   cup chopped onion
1   teaspoon salt
¼   teaspoon pepper
¼   cup butter or margarine
¼   cup flour
2   cups milk
2   cups shredded sharp Cheddar cheese
1   cup cubed cooked ham
4   slices bacon, crisp-fried, crumbled

Bring the water to a boil in a large stockpot. Add the potatoes, celery, onion, salt and pepper. Cover and reduce the heat. Simmer for 10 minutes or until the vegetables are tender. Melt the butter in a medium saucepan. Blend in the flour. Add the milk gradually, stirring constantly. Bring to a boil over medium heat. Boil for 1 minute. Add the cheese and stir until melted and smooth. Add to the vegetables gradually, stirring constantly. Stir in the ham. Sprinkle with the crumbled bacon.

YIELD: 6 SERVINGS

Broccoli Bisque

1   large bunch broccoli
¼   cup chopped onion
2   cups chicken broth
2   tablespoons butter
1   tablespoon flour
1   teaspoon salt
¼   teaspoon pepper
2   cups half-and-half

Rinse the broccoli and place in a steamer. Steam until tender. Chop the broccoli into small pieces and place in a saucepan. Add the onion and chicken broth. Bring to a boil and reduce heat. Simmer for 10 minutes. Purée in a blender until smooth. Melt the butter in a large saucepan. Add the flour, salt and pepper and stir until smooth. Stir in the half-and-half and broccoli purée. Cook over medium heat until bubbly, stirring constantly. Serve immediately or chill, covered, in the refrigerator.

YIELD: 6 SERVINGS

Tortellini Soup

1½ **pounds ground beef**
1 **cup chopped onion**
1 **teaspoon minced garlic**
5½ **cups broth**
½ **cup dry red wine**
2 **cups crushed tomatoes**
1 **cup thinly sliced carrots**
½ **teaspoon dried basil**
½ **teaspoon dried oregano**
1 **(8-ounce) can tomato sauce**
1½ **cups chopped zucchini**
1 **(8-ounce) package frozen meat tortellini or cheese tortellini**
3 **tablespoons chopped fresh parsley**

Brown the ground beef in a skillet, stirring until crumbly. Drain, reserving 2 tablespoons drippings. Sauté the onion and garlic in the reserved drippings in a large saucepan until tender. Add the broth, wine, tomatoes, carrots, basil, oregano, tomato sauce and ground beef and mix well. Bring to a boil. Stir in the zucchini, tortellini and parsley. Reduce the heat. Simmer for 30 minutes.

YIELD: 4 TO 6 SERVINGS

Ham and Vegetable Soup

4 **cups tomato juice or vegetable juice cocktail**
1 **meaty ham bone**
4 **potatoes, chopped**
2 **cups frozen white Shoe Peg corn**
2 **carrots, sliced**
2 **ribs celery, sliced**
1 **medium onion, chopped**
2 **cups water**
1 **teaspoon pepper**
2 **(16-ounce) cans butter beans, drained**
   Tabasco sauce to taste

Combine the tomato juice, ham bone, potatoes, corn, carrots, celery, onion, water and pepper in a large stockpot. Simmer, covered, for 1 hour. Remove the bone to a platter. Remove the ham from the bone and discard the bone. Return the ham to the soup. Stir in the butter beans. Simmer for 15 minutes. Stir in Tabasco sauce.

YIELD: 8 SERVINGS

A quick and efficient way to slice celery is by cutting the entire stalk as you would a loaf of bread, instead of rib by rib.

Mexican Potato Soup

¼ **cup butter**
1 **large onion, chopped**
6 **cloves of garlic, chopped**
1 **(4-ounce) can green chiles, drained**
8 **cups chicken stock**
2 **large potatoes, peeled, chopped**
2 **medium tomatoes, chopped**
  Salt and pepper to taste
8 **ounces Monterey Jack cheese or**
  mozzarella cheese, shredded
¼ **cup chopped fresh cilantro**
2 **limes, cut into quarters**
  Tortilla chips

Melt the butter in a stockpot. Add the onion, garlic and green chiles. Sauté over medium-high heat until the onion is tender. Add the chicken stock and potatoes. Bring to a boil and reduce the heat. Simmer for 15 to 20 minutes. Add the tomatoes. Simmer for 5 minutes. Season with salt and pepper. Ladle into individual soup bowls. Sprinkle with the cheese and cilantro. Squeeze the lime wedges over each serving. Serve with tortilla chips.

YIELD: 6 SERVINGS

Spicy Tortilla Soup

½ **cup chopped onion**
1 **clove of garlic, minced**
1 **tablespoon vegetable oil**
3 **medium zucchini, sliced**
4 **cups chicken broth**
1 **(16-ounce) can stewed tomatoes**
1 **(12-ounce) can whole kernel corn**
1 **jalapeño, finely chopped**
1 **teaspoon cumin**
½ **teaspoon cayenne**
½ **teaspoon black pepper**
½ **cup shredded Monterey Jack cheese or**
  Cheddar cheese
  Tortilla chips

Sauté the onion and garlic in the vegetable oil in a stockpot. Add the zucchini, broth, undrained tomatoes, undrained corn, jalapeño, cumin, cayenne and black pepper. Bring to a boil. Cover and reduce heat. Simmer for 15 to 20 minutes. Ladle into individual serving bowls. Sprinkle with the cheese. Serve with tortilla chips.

YIELD: 4 SERVINGS

Lemons and limes are often interchangeable. Substitute the juice of one for another when looking for ways to brighten recipes. Juice many lemons or limes at one time. Freeze in ice cube trays and store in plastic bags for future use.

BLT Croissants

12 slices bacon
6 large croissants
6 ounces cream cheese, softened
3 ounces goat cheese, softened
⅓ cup oil-pack chopped sun-dried tomatoes
1 teaspoon dried basil
1½ cups torn Bibb lettuce

Cook the bacon in a skillet until crisp-fried. Remove the bacon to a plate lined with paper towels to drain. Cut the croissants into halves horizontally. Beat the cream cheese and goat cheese in a small bowl until smooth. Stir in the tomatoes and basil. Spread on each croissant half. Place on a baking sheet. Bake at 325 degrees for 5 minutes or until the cheese mixture begins to melt. Remove from the oven. Place 2 bacon slices on the bottom half of each croissant. Layer evenly with the lettuce and top with the croissant tops. Serve immediately.

Note: May chill the cheese mixture, covered, for 8 hours.

YIELD: 6 SERVINGS

Chicken Ham Pitas with Béarnaise Sauce

4 boneless, skinless chicken breast halves, cut into 2-inch strips
8 ounces cooked smoked ham, cut into 2-inch squares
Chopped fresh tarragon to taste
1 tablespoon light olive oil
½ cup (½-inch) scallion pieces
1 pint sliced fresh mushrooms
¾ cup Béarnaise Sauce
6 pita bread pockets

Sauté the chicken, ham and tarragon in the olive oil in a skillet until the chicken is cooked through. Drain and pat dry. Chill, wrapped in plastic wrap. Combine with the scallions and mushrooms. Add the Béarnaise Sauce and toss to mix well. Stuff the pita pockets.

Béarnaise Sauce

3 tablespoons white wine vinegar
1 teaspoon finely chopped green onions
1 teaspoon chopped fresh tarragon
¼ teaspoon chopped fresh chervil
⅛ teaspoon white pepper
4 egg yolks, beaten
1 tablespoon water
½ cup butter, cut into 3 equal portions and softened

Bring the vinegar, green onions, tarragon, chervil and pepper to a boil in a saucepan over high heat. Boil until reduced by half. Combine the egg yolks, water, vinegar mixture and 1 portion of the butter in a double boiler. Cook over boiling water until thickened, stirring constantly. Add remaining butter 1 portion at a time, stirring constantly. Cook until thickened, stirring constantly. Remove from heat.

YIELD: 6 SERVINGS

Chicken Parmigiana Sandwiches

½ cup tomato sauce
2 tablespoons tomato paste
¼ cup minced onion
2 cloves of garlic, minced
½ teaspoon oregano
Pinch of red pepper flakes
½ cup chicken broth
1 tablespoon dry sherry
4 (3-ounce) chicken cutlets
½ teaspoon oregano
¼ teaspoon freshly ground black pepper
2 tablespoons grated Parmesan cheese
2¼ ounces mozzarella cheese,
cut into 4 slices
4 (2-ounce) hard rolls, split, toasted

Combine the tomato sauce, tomato paste, onion, garlic, ½ teaspoon oregano and red pepper flakes in a small saucepan. Bring to a boil over medium heat and reduce the heat to low. Simmer for 2 minutes. Bring the chicken broth and sherry to a boil in a large nonstick skillet over medium-high heat. Add the chicken, ½ teaspoon oregano and black pepper. Cover and reduce the heat to low. Simmer until the chicken is cooked through, turning once every 5 minutes. Place the chicken on a foil-lined broiler pan. Spread each cutlet with ¼ of the sauce and sprinkle each with ¼ of the Parmesan cheese. Top each with a slice of mozzarella cheese. Broil 4 inches from the heat source for 10 to 20 seconds or until the cheese is melted. Place each chicken cutlet on the bottom half of each roll and replace the top. Serve immediately.

YIELD: 4 SERVINGS

Crab Meat and Cream Cheese Sandwiches

8 ounces cream cheese, softened
¼ cup butter, softened
1 pound steamed lump crab meat, flaked
1 teaspoon Worcestershire sauce
½ teaspoon grated onion
Salt to taste
6 (½-inch-thick) tomato slices
Shredded sharp Cheddar cheese
6 round sandwich buns, split

Beat the cream cheese and butter in a mixer bowl until smooth. Add the crab meat, Worcestershire sauce, onion and salt and mix well. Shape into 6 patties and place on a platter lined with waxed paper. Chill, covered, until ready to assemble the sandwiches. Layer the tomato, crab meat patties and cheese on the bottoms of the sandwich buns. Replace the tops. Bake at 350 degrees for 15 to 20 minutes or until heated through and the cheese melts.

YIELD: 6 SERVINGS

Roasted Vegetable Sandwiches

1   medium yellow squash, thinly sliced
1   medium zucchini, thinly sliced
1   medium red bell pepper, thinly sliced
1   small Japanese eggplant, thinly sliced
½   medium red onion, thinly sliced
½   tablespoon chopped Italian parsley
    Pinch of dried thyme
    Salt and pepper to taste
1   tablespoon extra-virgin olive oil
2   (9-inch) rounds focaccia loaves or pita bread
    Goat Cheese Pesto

Combine the vegetables in a bowl. Add the parsley, thyme, salt, pepper and olive oil and toss to mix well. Layer the vegetable mixture on a baking sheet. Bake at 500 degrees for 15 minutes or until the vegetables are tender. Remove from the oven and cool. Cut each loaf into halves horizontally. Spread each cut side with the Goat Cheese Pesto. Divide the vegetables between 2 of the bread halves. Cover with the remaining halves. Cut each round into quarters.

Goat Cheese Pesto

3   tablespoons pine nuts
1   cup loosely packed fresh basil leaves
1   tablespoon olive oil
6   pieces marinated sun-dried tomato
7   medium cloves of garlic, peeled
2   tablespoons grated Parmesan cheese
2   tablespoons balsamic vinegar
    Salt and pepper to taste
3   ounces fresh goat cheese

Cook the pine nuts in a nonstick skillet until brown and toasted, shaking the skillet often. Process with the basil, olive oil, tomato, garlic, Parmesan cheese, vinegar, salt and pepper in a food processor container until puréed. Add the goat cheese and process well.

YIELD: 8 SERVINGS

Spinach Sandwiches

8   ounces fresh mushrooms, finely chopped
1   bunch green onions, thinly sliced
2   (10-ounce) packages frozen chopped spinach, thawed, drained
    Alfalfa sprouts to taste
    Sunflower seed kernels to taste
    Dijon mustard to taste
12 to 16 slices bread
12 to 16 slices Cheddar cheese or mozzarella cheese
12 to 16 slices bacon, cooked
½   cup butter, softened

Sauté the mushrooms and green onions in a nonstick skillet until tender. Combine with the spinach, alfalfa sprouts and sunflower seed kernels in a bowl and mix well. Spread Dijon mustard on ½ of the bread slices. Layer the cheese, spinach mixture and bacon over the Dijon mustard. Top with the remaining bread. Spread both sides of each sandwich with butter. Place on a nonstick griddle. Bake until heated through and golden brown, turning once.

YIELD: 6 TO 8 SERVINGS

Historically, citrus, along with other fruits and vegetables, was shipped in common wooden boxes. Labels, displayed prominently on each crate, advertised the family name and identified each product. A. Duda and Sons, Inc., founded in 1926 by Andrew Duda, Sr., is still locally-owned and operated by the Duda family, and is the world's largest producer of celery.

SUNNY
SIDES

Side
Dishes

• • •

Section sponsored by

A. Duda and Sons, Inc.

Celery Bread Dressing

A. DUDA AND SONS, INC.

- 1 **package celery hearts**
- 1 **large onion**
- 1 **cup margarine**
- 2 **large loaves sliced white bread**
- ½ **teaspoon celery powder**
- 13 **eggs**

Cut the celery and onion into small pieces. Melt the margarine in a medium skillet. Add the celery and onion. Cook over medium to high heat until the margarine bubbles. Reduce the heat. Simmer until the onion is transparent. Set aside. Cut the bread into quarters and place in a large bowl. Sprinkle with celery powder. Add the eggs and mix well using clean hands. Add the celery and onions and mix well. Place in a greased loaf pan. Bake at 350 degrees for 45 minutes or until golden brown.

YIELD: 10 TO 12 SERVINGS

Golden Pear and Almond Gratin

HEATHER MCPHERSON, *THE ORLANDO SENTINEL*

- ½ **cup honey**
- ¼ **cup dry white wine**
- 1 **tablespoon lemon juice**
- 1 **tablespoon orange juice**
- ½ **cup chopped toasted almonds**
- 1 **tablespoon grated lemon peel**
- 1 **tablespoon grated orange peel**
- ½ **teaspoon cinnamon**
- 2 **pounds pears (about 5 medium pears)**
- ¼ **cup sliced toasted almonds**

Bring the honey, wine, lemon juice and orange juice to a boil in a saucepan, whisking constantly. Reduce the heat. Simmer for 15 minutes or until the liquid is reduced by half. Set aside. Mix the chopped almonds, lemon peel, orange peel and cinnamon in a small bowl. Peel the pears and cut into halves lengthwise. Cut the pear halves into ½-inch-thick slices. Layer ½ of the pear slices in a greased 10-inch baking dish. Sprinkle with the chopped almond mixture. Top with the remaining pear slices and sliced almonds. Pour the honey mixture over the top. Bake at 400 degrees for 25 minutes or until the top is golden brown. Serve warm or chilled.

YIELD: 6 TO 8 SERVINGS

Asparagus with Orange Mayonnaise

1 pound asparagus, trimmed
2 tablespoons water
2 tablespoons plain yogurt
1 tablespoon mayonnaise
½ teaspoon finely shredded orange peel
1 tablespoon orange juice
   Dash of ground red pepper

Arrange the asparagus in a shallow round baking dish with the tips toward the center. Add the water. Cover with clear plastic wrap, leaving a vent. Microwave on High for 7 to 9 minutes or until the asparagus is tender, rearranging once; drain. Combine the yogurt, mayonnaise, orange peel, orange juice and red pepper in a small bowl and mix well. Spoon over the hot asparagus. Garnish with orange slices.

YIELD: 6 SERVINGS

There are three forms of honey available on the market today. Liquid honey, the most common form sold in the United States, is a thick golden syrup that can be drizzled or spooned. It is extracted from the beeswax comb, strained, and sometimes heated and filtered to delay natural crystallization. Creme, whipped, or spun honey is a finely crystallized honey. Processors control the crystallization so the honey becomes satin smooth and spreadable at room temperature. Comb honey, sold in squares or rounds, is the most natural and the rarest form available. It comes just as the bees store the honey in the hive, encapsulated in dozens of honeycomb-shaped cells of edible beeswax.

Cuban Black Beans

1   small onion, chopped
½   green bell pepper, sliced
2   tablespoons olive oil
      Cumin to taste
      Salt and pepper to taste
3   cloves of garlic, crushed
      White wine to taste
2   (16-ounce) cans black beans, rinsed, drained
1   (2-ounce) jar pimento
½   teaspoon sugar
1   bay leaf
      White vinegar to taste

Sauté the onion and green pepper in olive oil in a skillet. Sprinkle with cumin, salt and pepper. Add garlic and wine. Sauté until the onion is almost translucent. Stir in the black beans, pimento, sugar and bay leaf. Simmer, covered, for 45 to 60 minutes or until of the desired consistency. Stir in the vinegar. Discard the bay leaf. Serve over hot cooked rice.

YIELD: 4 SERVINGS

Miniature Broccoli Timbales

2   cups chopped fresh broccoli, steamed
1   cup cooked rice
2   egg whites
3   tablespoons chopped onion
¼   cup whipping cream
2   tablespoons melted butter
½   teaspoon salt
¼   teaspoon freshly ground pepper
½   teaspoon chopped garlic
1   tablespoon grated Romano cheese

Combine the broccoli, rice, egg whites, onion, whipping cream, butter, salt, pepper, garlic and cheese in a large bowl and mix well. Spoon into greased miniature muffin cups. Set in a larger baking pan filled with hot water. Bake at 350 degrees for 35 minutes or until set. Remove the muffin pan from the larger pan. Let stand until cool. Loosen the edges with a knife and invert onto a serving plate.

YIELD: 16 TO 18 SERVINGS

Nutty Brussels Sprouts

1½ **pounds fresh brussels sprouts**
½   **cup water**
¼   **cup unsalted butter or margarine**
⅓   **cup firmly packed brown sugar**
3   **tablespoons soy sauce**
¼   **teaspoon salt**
¼   **cup finely chopped toasted pecans**
¼   **cup chopped toasted almonds**

Rinse the brussels sprouts and remove discolored leaves. Cut off the stem end. Cut a shallow "X" in the bottom of each brussels sprout. Bring ½ cup water to a boil in a large saucepan. Add the brussels sprouts. Cover and reduce the heat. Simmer for 8 to 10 minutes or until tender-crisp; drain. Melt the butter in a medium skillet. Stir in the brown sugar, soy sauce and salt. Bring to a boil, stirring constantly. Add the pecans and almonds; reduce the heat. Simmer for 5 minutes, stirring occasionally. Stir in the brussels sprouts. Cook over medium heat for 5 minutes. Stir well before serving.

YIELD: 6 SERVINGS

Carrot Soufflé

1   **pound carrots, peeled, sliced**
½   **cup butter or margarine, softened**
3   **eggs**
1   **cup sugar**
3   **tablespoons flour**
1   **teaspoon baking powder**
1½ **teaspoons vanilla extract**

Cook the carrots in boiling water to cover in a saucepan until tender; drain. Place the carrots and butter in a blender container and process until smooth. Add the eggs, sugar, flour, baking powder and vanilla. Process until smooth. Spoon into a greased 1-quart soufflé dish. Bake at 350 degrees for 45 minutes or until set.

YIELD: 6 SERVINGS

Corn on the cob is the favorite way to eat fresh corn. Cook corn on the cob in water to cover for 3 to 4 minutes or until tender-crisp. Do not add salt to the water because it will toughen the kernels. Corn on the cob can also be wrapped in plastic wrap or waxed paper and microwaved for 1½ minutes. Grilled corn on the cob is also delicious. Remove the silk from the corn and wrap the ears back in the husk. Soak in water to cover for 10 minutes to prevent the corn from drying out. Place on a grill rack. Grill for 15 to 20 minutes or until tender-crisp. Serve hot corn on the cob with melted herb butter, guacamole, salsa, cheese sauce, sour cream, or seasoned mayonnaise.

Orange-Glazed Carrots

½ teaspoon salt
2 pounds carrots, peeled, cut into 2-inch pieces
1 tablespoon sugar
2 teaspoons cornstarch
¾ cup orange juice

Bring 1 inch of water to a boil in a large saucepan. Add ¼ teaspoon of the salt and the carrots. Cook, covered, for 10 minutes or until the carrots are tender; drain. Combine the sugar, cornstarch, remaining ¼ teaspoon salt and orange juice in a saucepan. Cook over medium heat until thickened, stirring constantly. Add the cooked carrots. Cook for 3 minutes or until heated through.

YIELD: 6 SERVINGS

Parmesan Corn on the Cob

4 ears of fresh corn
¼ cup melted butter or margarine
¼ cup grated Parmesan cheese
½ teaspoon Italian seasoning

Remove the husks and silk from the corn. Wrap each ear in heavy-duty plastic wrap. Microwave on High for 10 to 13 minutes or until tender, turning twice. Combine the butter, Parmesan cheese and Italian seasoning in a bowl and mix well. Unwrap the corn. Brush with the butter mixture.

Note: May wrap the corn in foil and bake at 500 degrees for 20 minutes.

YIELD: 4 SERVINGS

Green Beans Neapolitan Style

2 pounds green beans or pole beans
¼ cup extra-virgin olive oil
1 pound plum tomatoes, cut into quarters
4 cloves of garlic, cut into quarters
   Salt to taste
2 small red peppers, dried, crumbled, or
   ¼ teaspoon red pepper flakes
   Fresh chopped basil to taste

Rinse the green beans and trim the ends. Snap each green bean into halves. Pour the olive oil in a large saucepan. Add the green beans, tomatoes and garlic. Cook, covered, over medium-high heat for 5 to 10 minutes. Stir in the salt and red pepper. Cook, covered, for 5 minutes. Stir in the basil. Cook for 5 minutes. Serve hot or at room temperature.

YIELD: 4 SERVINGS

Green Beans and Mushrooms with Garlic Sauce

2   tablespoons olive oil
1   pound fresh green beans, trimmed
6   ounces fresh mushrooms
¼   cup soy sauce
1   tablespoon minced garlic, or to taste
1   tablespoon honey
2   teaspoons minced peeled fresh ginger, or to taste

Heat the olive oil in a wok or large heavy skillet over high heat. Add the green beans and mushrooms. Sauté for 5 minutes or until the green beans are tender-crisp. Add the soy sauce, garlic, honey and ginger. Boil for 2 minutes or until the sauce is thickened and coats the vegetables. Serve immediately.

Note: Garlic sauce is also good over steamed broccoli.

YIELD: 6 TO 8 SERVINGS

Drunken Mushrooms

½   cup chopped green onions
1   tablespoon minced fresh parsley
½   cup butter or margarine
½   cup chicken broth
¼   cup dry white wine
1   teaspoon salt
¼   teaspoon coarsely ground pepper
1   pound medium mushrooms

Sauté the green onions and parsley in melted butter in a skillet until tender. Add the chicken broth, wine, salt and pepper. Wipe the mushrooms clean with a damp towel. Cut off the tips of the mushroom stems. Place the mushrooms in a 1-quart baking dish. Add the broth mixture. Bake, covered, at 350 degrees for 20 minutes.

YIELD: 4 TO 6 SERVINGS

Grilled Portobello Mushrooms

8 ounces portobello mushrooms
3 tablespoons extra-virgin olive oil
2 large cloves of garlic, finely chopped
1 tablespoon chopped flat-leaf parsley
⅛ teaspoon dried marjoram
Salt and freshly ground pepper to taste
Juice of ½ lemon (optional)

Wipe the mushrooms clean with a damp towel. Remove the stems from the caps and thinly slice the stems. Combine the olive oil, garlic, parsley, marjoram, salt, pepper and lemon juice in a small bowl and mix well. Brush the mushroom caps and stems with the olive oil mixture. Place rounded side down on a grill rack. Grill for 2 minutes. Turn the caps and stems over and brush with the olive oil mixture. Grill for 2 to 3 minutes or until tender and light brown. Serve hot or at room temperature.

Note: May use porcini or shiitake mushrooms, discarding the stems if using shiitake mushrooms.

YIELD: 4 SERVINGS

Grilled Onion Slices

9 tablespoons Dijon mustard
2 tablespoons wine vinegar
3 tablespoons chopped fresh parsley
3 large red onions, cut into ½-inch-thick slices
Salt and freshly ground pepper to taste
Butter-flavored cooking spray

Combine the Dijon mustard, wine vinegar and parsley in a small bowl and mix well. Arrange the onion slices on a grill rack. Sprinkle with salt and pepper to taste. Grill for 10 minutes or until golden brown, turning 2 or 3 times and brushing with the mustard mixture and spraying with the butter-flavored cooking spray.

YIELD: 6 SERVINGS

For Bleu Cheese Mushrooms, remove the stems from 12 to 14 extra-large mushrooms and reserve the caps. Chop the stems and sauté in ¼ cup butter until tender. Stir in ¼ cup crumbled bleu cheese and 2 tablespoons fine bread crumbs. Season with salt and pepper to taste. Fill the mushroom caps with the bleu cheese mixture. Place on an ungreased baking sheet and sprinkle with 3 tablespoons fine bread crumbs. Bake at 350 degrees for 12 minutes and serve hot.

Gratin Dauphinois

- **4**   cloves of garlic, finely chopped
- **2⅔** cups whipping cream
- **2**   pounds baking potatoes, peeled, thinly sliced
- **3**   shallots, finely chopped
       Salt and freshly ground white pepper to taste
       Freshly ground nutmeg to taste
- **2**   teaspoons dried thyme
- **2**   eggs, beaten
- **1¾** cups mixture of grated Parmesan cheese and
       Gruyère cheese
- **5**   tablespoons unsalted butter

Butter an 8x12-inch baking dish. Sprinkle with the garlic. Bring the cream to a boil in a medium saucepan. Remove from the heat. Cover to keep warm. Pat the potatoes dry with paper towels and place in a large bowl. Add the shallots, salt, white pepper, nutmeg and thyme and toss to mix well. Add the eggs and ½ cup of the cheese mixture and mix well. Arrange the potato mixture in the prepared baking dish. Pour the warm cream over the top. Sprinkle with the remaining cheese mixture. Dot with the butter. Cover the baking dish with buttered foil. Place the dish on a baking sheet. Bake at 350 degrees for 45 minutes. Remove the foil. Bake for 30 to 45 minutes longer or until the potatoes are tender. Let stand for 10 minutes before serving.

YIELD: 6 TO 8 SERVINGS

Roasted Rosemary Potatoes

- **2½** tablespoons melted unsalted butter
- **2**   russet potatoes, cut into ¼-inch slices
- **1**   teaspoon kosher salt, or to taste
- **½**   teaspoon dried rosemary
       Pepper to taste

Pour ½ of the melted butter in an 8-inch baking pan. Layer the potatoes in rows, overlapping slightly. Sprinkle with kosher salt, rosemary and pepper. Pour the remaining butter over the top. Bake at 425 degrees for 45 to 60 minutes or until golden brown and crisp, turning each row once. Sprinkle with kosher salt.

YIELD: 2 SERVINGS

Potatoes con Queso

5   **tablespoons butter or margarine**
3   **tablespoons flour**
2   **cups milk**
2   **cups 4-cheese Mexican blend shredded cheese**
1   **(2-ounce) jar chopped pimento**
1   **(4-ounce) can chopped green chiles, drained**
2   **tablespoons chopped pickled jalapeño**
2   **pounds baking potatoes, peeled, thinly sliced**

Melt the butter in a medium saucepan over low heat. Stir in the flour until smooth. Cook for 1 minute, stirring constantly. Add the milk gradually. Cook over medium heat until thickened, stirring constantly. Stir in 1½ cups of the cheese. Remove from the heat. Stir until the cheese is melted. Add the pimento, green chiles and jalapeño and mix well. Layer the potatoes and cheese sauce ½ at a time in a 7x11-inch baking dish sprayed with nonstick cooking spray. Bake, covered, at 350 degrees for 20 minutes. Bake, uncovered, for 40 minutes longer. Sprinkle with the remaining ½ cup cheese. Bake for 5 minutes.

YIELD: 6 SERVINGS

Acorn Squash Rings with Orange Marmalade

2   **(12-ounce) acorn squash**
1   **tablespoon soy sauce**
1   **tablespoon orange marmalade**
½   **teaspoon ginger**

Cut the squash horizontally into ½-inch slices. Remove the seeds and pith. Mix the soy sauce, orange marmalade and ginger in a small bowl. Arrange the squash rings on a baking sheet sprayed with nonstick cooking spray. Brush with the marmalade mixture. Bake at 350 degrees for 40 minutes or until the squash is tender.

YIELD: 10 SERVINGS

Did you know you can place thick strips of lemon peel in a warm oven to dispel unwanted odors or rub hands with a cut lemon to remove odors?

Garden-Stuffed Yellow Squash

6	medium yellow squash
1	cup chopped onions
1	cup chopped tomatoes
½	cup chopped green bell pepper
½	cup shredded Cheddar cheese
6	slices bacon, cooked, crumbled
	Salt and pepper to taste
¼	cup butter

Place the squash in water to cover in a large saucepan. Bring to a boil and reduce the heat. Simmer, covered, for 8 to 10 minutes or until the squash is tender but firm. Drain and cool slightly. Trim the stems. Cut the squash into halves lengthwise. Remove the pulp to a bowl, reserving the shells. Chop the pulp. Add the onions, tomatoes, green pepper, cheese, bacon, salt and pepper and mix well. Place the squash shells in a 9x13-inch baking dish. Spoon the vegetable mixture into the shells. Dot with butter. The squash can be assembled to this point and refrigerated until baking time. Bake at 400 degrees for 20 to 25 minutes or until heated through.

YIELD: 12 SERVINGS

Squash Baked with Herbed Vegetables and Gouda

2	tablespoons olive oil
1½	cups fresh vegetables such as broccoli florets, cauliflowerets, sliced zucchini, sliced summer squash, snow peas and chopped scallions
15	carrot slices
16	mushrooms, sliced
1½	teaspoons herbes de Provence
	Salt and pepper to taste
1	cup white wine
1	tablespoon lime juice
2	acorn squash, cut into halves, seeded, steamed
8	teaspoons brown sugar
8	ounces gouda cheese, grated

Heat the olive oil in a large deep skillet. Add the vegetables and mushrooms. Sauté for 4 to 6 minutes or until tender-crisp. Stir in the herbes de Provence, salt, pepper, wine and lime juice. Simmer for 4 minutes. Place the acorn squash halves on a baking sheet. Coat the inside of each acorn squash half with 2 teaspoons brown sugar. Fill with the hot vegetable mixture. Top each with ½ cup cheese. Bake at 350 degrees for 15 minutes or until heated through. Serve immediately.

YIELD: 4 SERVINGS

Fresh Vegetables with Basil and Parmesan Cheese

2	small yellow squash, sliced
2	medium zucchini, sliced
1	small onion, sliced
1	tomato, sliced
2	tablespoons freshly grated Parmesan cheese
½	tablespoon salt
½	tablespoon basil
½	tablespoon thyme

Combine the squash, zucchini, onion and tomato in a bowl. Add the Parmesan cheese, salt, basil and thyme and toss gently Spoon into a greased 8x8-inch baking dish. Bake at 325 degrees for 30 minutes.

YIELD: 6 TO 8 SERVINGS

Squash Pie

10	to 12 small yellow squash, sliced
1	Vidalia or white onion, chopped
1	cup sour cream
1	cup shredded Monterey Jack cheese
1	cup shredded sharp Cheddar cheese
1	tomato, sliced
4	to 6 slices bacon, crisp-fried, crumbled
	Bread crumbs
	Butter

Bring the squash and onion in water to cover to a boil in a large saucepan. Boil for 5 minutes or until tender; drain. Add the sour cream, Monterey Jack cheese and Cheddar cheese and mix well. Spoon into a greased baking dish. Layer tomato slices over the top. Sprinkle with bacon and bread crumbs. Dot with butter. Bake at 350 degrees for 30 minutes.

YIELD: 6 TO 10 SERVINGS

Orange Pecan-Stuffed Squash

4	acorn squash
¼	cup water
2	tablespoons light brown sugar
½	teaspoon finely grated orange peel
½	teaspoon salt
2½	tablespoons butter, softened
2	to 3 teaspoons orange juice
⅓	cup chopped pecans

Cut the squash into halves and remove the seeds. Arrange cut side down in a shallow baking pan. Add the water to the pan. Bake at 350 degrees for 30 minutes or until tender. Remove from the oven. Cool cut side down for 15 minutes. Remove the pulp from the cooled squash and place in a medium bowl, reserving the shells. Add 1½ tablespoons of the brown sugar, orange peel, salt, butter and orange juice to the squash pulp and beat until fluffy. Spoon into the reserved squash shells. Place in a greased 6x10-inch baking dish. Sprinkle with the remaining ½ tablespoon brown sugar. Sprinkle with the pecans. Bake for 10 minutes.

YIELD: 8 SERVINGS

Orange Sweet Potatoes

5 to 6 medium sweet potatoes
   Salt and pepper to taste
5 tablespoons butter
¾ cup packed brown sugar
½ teaspoon nutmeg
½ teaspoon cinnamon
2 oranges, sliced

Scrub the potatoes. Place on a foil-lined baking sheet. Bake at 350 degrees for 45 minutes or until cooked through but still firm. Cool slightly. Peel and slice into ½-inch-thick slices. Spray a shallow 2-quart baking dish with nonstick cooking spray. Layer the sweet potatoes, salt, pepper, butter, brown sugar, nutmeg and cinnamon ½ at a time in the prepared dish. Top with the orange slices. Bake at 375 degrees for 30 minutes or until hot and bubbly.

YIELD: 6 TO 8 SERVINGS

Make an orange cup by marking a sawtooth edge around the center of the orange. Cut in toward the center with a sharp knife following the markings. Scoop out the pulp. Fill the shells with fruit salad, whipped sweet potatoes, or stewed cranberries.

Tomato and Mushroom Pastry

3 medium tomatoes
1 (9-inch) pie shell, baked
   Salt and pepper to taste
⅛ teaspoon herbs of choice
1 small Vidalia onion, finely chopped
1 tablespoon finely chopped bell pepper (optional)
1 (4-ounce) can sliced mushrooms, drained
3 ounces Monterey Jack jalapeño cheese, grated
½ cup shredded mozzarella cheese
¾ cup mayonnaise
¼ cup freshly grated Parmesan cheese
   Paprika to taste

Peel the tomatoes. Cut into thin slices and place on paper towels to drain. Pat dry with paper towels. Arrange ½ of the tomatoes in the pie shell. Season with salt, pepper and herbs. Top with ½ of the onion, ½ of the bell pepper and ½ of the mushrooms. Cover with ½ of the Monterey Jack cheese. Layer the remaining tomatoes, Monterey Jack cheese, onion and mushrooms over the layers. Sprinkle with the mozzarella cheese. Spread the mayonnaise over the top. Sprinkle with Parmesan cheese and paprika. Place on a baking sheet. Bake at 350 degrees for 45 minutes. Cool slightly. Chill, covered, in the refrigerator for 8 to 10 hours. Cut into slices. Bake at 350 degrees for 20 minutes. Serve with asparagus and melon.

YIELD: 4 TO 6 SERVINGS

Italian Baked Zucchini

2   large or 3 small zucchini, sliced
½   cup Italian bread crumbs
½   cup chopped fresh parsley
¼   cup grated Parmesan cheese
2   cloves of garlic, minced
    Salt to taste
1   tablespoon vegetable oil

Layer the zucchini, bread crumbs, parsley, Parmesan cheese, garlic and salt to taste in a baking dish. Drizzle with vegetable oil. Bake, covered, at 350 degrees for 45 minutes. Bake, uncovered, for 10 minutes longer.

YIELD: 8 SERVINGS

Ratatouille

4   large yellow squash, cut into ½-inch pieces
2   small zucchini, cut into ½-inch pieces
1   large onion, thinly sliced
2   medium green bell peppers, thinly sliced
2   cloves of garlic, peeled, chopped
2   tablespoons olive oil
2   (15-ounce) cans Italian stewed tomatoes
¼   cup grated Parmesan cheese

Sauté the squash, zucchini, onion, green peppers and garlic in the olive oil in a large skillet over medium-high heat until the vegetables are light brown. Remove from the heat. Stir in the tomatoes. Spoon into a medium baking dish. Sprinkle with the Parmesan cheese. Bake at 350 degrees for 30 minutes.

YIELD: 6 SERVINGS

Apple Almond Rice

2   cups apple juice
1   tablespoon butter
1   teaspoon salt
1   cup long grain and wild rice
2   red apples, chopped
½   cup slivered almonds, toasted
1   tablespoon grated orange peel
    Salt and freshly ground pepper to taste

Bring the apple juice, butter and 1 teaspoon salt to a boil in a small saucepan. Stir in the rice. Return to a boil. Cover and reduce the heat. Simmer for 25 to 30 minutes or until the rice is tender and the liquid is absorbed. Fold in the apples, almonds and orange peel. Season with salt and pepper to taste.

YIELD: 6 SERVINGS

Lemon Rice

2½ cups canned chicken broth
½ teaspoon salt, or to taste
1 clove of garlic, minced
1 cup long grain rice
1 tablespoon finely grated lemon zest
3 tablespoons chopped fresh dill
2 tablespoons unsalted butter
   Freshly ground pepper to taste

Bring the broth, salt and garlic to a boil in a heavy saucepan. Stir in the rice. Simmer, covered, for 20 minutes or until the liquid is absorbed. Remove from the heat. Stir in the lemon zest. Let stand, covered, for 5 minutes. Stir in the dill and butter. Sprinkle with pepper. Serve immediately.

Note: For a more lemony flavor, add the lemon zest and let stand for 2 hours or longer. Add ½ cup additional chicken broth and boil until evaporated. Proceed as above.

YIELD: 4 TO 6 SERVINGS

Herbed Lemon Almonds Pilaf

1 onion, chopped
2 cloves of garlic, minced
2 tablespoons olive oil
1 teaspoon turmeric
   Juice of ½ lemon
2 tablespoons soy sauce
½ cup chopped fresh basil
1 teaspoon thyme
½ cup chopped fresh parsley
3 cups cooked rice
¼ cup hot water
   Salt and pepper to taste
⅓ cup chopped toasted almonds

Sauté the onion and garlic in the olive oil in a saucepan until tender. Stir in the turmeric, lemon juice and soy sauce. Reduce the heat. Add the basil, thyme and parsley. Stir in the rice. Drizzle with hot water and cover. Steam over low heat for 5 minutes. Season with salt and pepper. Sprinkle with almonds.

YIELD: 4 SERVINGS

Reggae Rice

½ cup butter
1½ cups long grain white rice
3 cups chicken broth
1 cup chopped carrots
¾ cup chopped fresh parsley
½ cup sliced green onions
½ cup chopped red pepper
½ cup chopped celery

Melt the butter in a skillet. Stir in the rice. Sauté for 3 to 5 minutes or until light brown. Pour the chicken broth into a 2-quart baking dish. Add the rice. Bake, covered, at 350 degrees for 45 minutes. Stir in the carrots, parsley, green onions, red pepper and celery. Bake for 10 minutes or until the vegetables are tender-crisp.

YIELD: 8 TO 10 SERVINGS

Texas Rice

½ cup chopped onion
2 tablespoons margarine
1 (4-serving) package rice, cooked
1 cup sour cream
½ cup cottage cheese
Salt and pepper to taste
1 (4-ounce) can chopped green chiles, drained
2 cups shredded sharp Cheddar cheese

Sauté the onion in margarine in a small skillet for 5 minutes but do not brown. Mix the rice, sour cream, cottage cheese, sautéed onion and salt and pepper in a bowl. Layer ½ of the rice mixture, green chiles, 1 cup of the Cheddar cheese and remaining rice mixture in a greased deep round 1½-quart baking dish. Sprinkle with the remaining cheese. Bake at 350 degrees for 30 minutes.

YIELD: 6 SERVINGS

Celery can be used and served in many different ways. Try braising celery by baking in bouillon with onion, parsley, bacon bits and bread crumbs. For an oriental touch, sauté celery with mushrooms and chestnuts and serve with rice. Make an omelet filling by mixing chopped celery, chopped parsley and chopped tomatoes together. Serve cooked celery with a cream sauce and toasted slivered almonds. To add extra crunch and flavor to sandwich fillings, add some chopped fresh celery. Serve celery curls as a garnish.

Wild Rice Dressing

1   cup raisins
½   cup dark rum
6   cups water
1   teaspoon salt
1½   cups wild rice
1½   cups white rice
2   cups whipping cream
15   to 20 sprigs of fresh thyme
     Freshly ground pepper to taste

Combine raisins and rum in a small saucepan. Cook over low heat for 3 hours. Bring 2 cups of the water to a boil in a saucepan. Add ½ teaspoon of the salt and wild rice. Cook, covered, for 45 minutes. Bring 2 cups of the remaining water to a boil in a separate saucepan. Add the remaining salt and white rice. Cook, covered, for 30 minutes. Bring the whipping cream and thyme to a boil in a heavy saucepan, stirring frequently. Reduce the heat. Cook, covered, for 18 minutes. Combine the raisin mixture, wild rice and white rice in a large bowl and mix well. Strain the cream mixture over the rice mixture, discarding the thyme. Add the pepper and mix well. Spoon into a large greased baking dish. Bake, loosely covered, at 350 degrees for 30 minutes.

YIELD: 6 SERVINGS

Kona Stuffing

1   large loaf white or whole wheat bread
1   small onion, coarsely chopped
2   ribs celery, coarsely chopped
4   ounces pork link sausage, coarsely chopped
½   cup butter
1   tablespoon sage
1   tablespoon poultry seasoning
2   tablespoons chopped garlic
½   cup macadamia nuts, toasted, coarsely chopped
2   quarts turkey or chicken stock

Trim the crusts from the bread. Cut the bread into ½-inch cubes. Spread on a baking sheet. Bake at 350 degrees for 5 minutes or until crisp. Sauté the onion, celery and sausage in the butter in a large saucepan until the sausage is cooked through. Add the sage, poultry seasoning, garlic and nuts. Cook for 10 minutes. Add the turkey stock. Bring to a boil and remove from the heat. Stir in the toasted bread cubes. Line a large baking pan with oiled parchment paper. Line with foil. Spoon the stuffing into the prepared pan. Bake at 350 degrees for 25 to 30 minutes or until set.

YIELD: 8 TO 10 SERVINGS

FAIRVILLA

ORANGES · GRAPEFRUIT · TANGERINES

ORLANDO, FLORIDA · **CITRUS FRUIT PRODUCTS** INC.   DR. PHILLIPS, FLORIDA

Dr. Philip Phillips was Central Florida's citrus king and, at one time, the world's largest citrus grower, overseeing 5,000 acres of groves. He was responsible for developing the pasteurization process that produced better-tasting canned juices. He also received an endorsement from the American Medical Association stating that Florida grapefruit was a "winter essential" for fighting colds. This label shows the Dr. Phillips House in downtown Orlando, which is now a bed and breakfast inn.

SUN
DRIED

Pasta

• • •

Section sponsored by

Holiday Inn International Drive and Holiday Inn Select

Tortellini Alla Pana

CHEF ED WHITTAKER, HOLIDAY INN
INTERNATIONAL DRIVE

- ¾ **cup clarified butter**
- 2 **tablespoons chopped shallots**
- 2 **cloves of garlic, chopped**
- 3 **ounces sun-dried tomatoes, julienned**
- 2 **tablespoons julienned fresh basil**
- ½ **teaspoon salt and pepper mix**
- 3 **cups whipping cream**
- 12 **ounces grated Parmesan cheese**
- 2 **pounds tortellini, cooked**

Heat the clarified butter in a sauté pan. Add the shallots and garlic. Sauté until the shallots are translucent. Add the sun-dried tomatoes, basil and salt and pepper mix. Sauté for 1 minute. Add the cream. Bring to a boil. Cook until the mixture is reduced by ¼. Stir in the Parmesan cheese. Remove from the heat. Pour over hot cooked tortellini in a large bowl and toss to mix well.

YIELDS: 4 TO 6 SERVINGS

Summer Brie Pasta

- 5 **to 6 large tomatoes**
- 1 **ounce fresh basil**
- 4 **to 5 cloves of garlic**
- 1 **(8-ounce) round Brie cheese**
- ½ **cup olive oil**
- ½ **teaspoon salt, or to taste**
- 16 **ounces linguini**

Plunge the tomatoes into boiling water in a saucepan and remove. Peel the tomatoes and remove the core over a large glass bowl to catch the juice. Cut the tomatoes into chunks and place in the bowl. Remove the stems from the basil and discard. Chop the basil into medium pieces. Add to the tomatoes. Peel the garlic. Cut the garlic into large pieces. Add to the tomato mixture. Remove the rind from the Brie. Cut the Brie into pieces. Add to the tomato mixture and mix well. Stir in the olive oil and salt. Let stand, tightly covered with plastic wrap, for 2 to 3 hours. Cook the linguini in boiling water in a large saucepan until al dente and drain. Place on serving plates. Top with the tomato mixture.

Note: May sprinkle with toasted pine nuts or serve with grilled chicken breast.

YIELD: 4 TO 6 SERVINGS

Black Bean and Orzo Salad

3½ cups cooked orzo
1 cup chopped red bell peppers
¼ cup chopped purple onion
½ cup chopped fresh parsley
¼ cup chopped fresh basil
1 (15-ounce) can black beans, drained
¼ cup red wine vinegar
3 tablespoons water
2 tablespoons balsamic vinegar
1 tablespoon olive oil
½ teaspoon sugar
1 teaspoon pepper
¾ teaspoon salt
2 cloves of garlic, minced

Combine the orzo, red peppers, onion, parsley, basil and black beans in a large bowl and toss to mix well. Combine the red wine vinegar, water, balsamic vinegar, olive oil, sugar, pepper, salt and garlic in a bowl and mix well. Pour over the orzo mixture and toss to mix well. Chill, covered, until serving time.

YIELD: 6 SERVINGS

Presto Pesto Pasta Salad

16 ounces penne
2 envelopes dry pesto sauce mix
1 cup water
3 tablespoons olive oil or vegetable oil
2 cloves of garlic, minced
　 Juice of ½ lemon, or to taste
2 tablespoons grated Parmesan cheese, or to taste
2 (14-ounce) jars artichoke hearts
1 (16-ounce) package frozen broccoli, cauliflower and carrots, thawed
1 (3-ounce) can pitted black olives
1 (2-ounce) jar pine nuts

Cook the penne using package directions. Combine the pesto sauce mix and water in a small saucepan. Stir in the olive oil. Cook over medium heat for 5 minutes. Add the garlic, lemon juice and Parmesan cheese. Reduce the heat. Simmer for 10 minutes or until thickened, stirring constantly. Drain the pasta and place in a large serving bowl. Add the pesto sauce and toss to mix well. Add the artichoke hearts, vegetables and olives and toss to mix well. Add the pine nuts and toss to mix well. Sprinkle with additional Parmesan cheese. Serve immediately.

YIELD: 8 SERVINGS

Spaghetti Salad

1 cup Italian salad dressing
1 cup mayonnaise
1 teaspoon to 1 tablespoon catsup
3 cloves of garlic, minced
1 teaspoon Dijon mustard
  Seasoned salt to taste
  Pepper to taste
16 ounces vermicelli, cooked, drained
½ green bell pepper, coarsely chopped
1½ tomatoes, coarsely chopped
1 cucumber, coarsely chopped
2 ribs celery, coarsely chopped
1 bunch scallions, coarsely chopped

Let the salad dressing stand in the glass measure until the oil rises to the top. Pour off and discard the oil, reserving the remaining salad dressing. Combine the reserved salad dressing, mayonnaise, catsup, garlic, mustard, seasoned salt and pepper in a large bowl and mix well. Add the pasta and toss to mix well. Add the green pepper, tomatoes, cucumber, celery and scallions and toss to mix well. Chill, covered, for 8 to 10 hours before serving.

Note: May store in the refrigerator for 1 week.

YIELD: 6 TO 8 SERVINGS

Pasta Kabobs

1 (9-ounce) package refrigerated cheese or pesto tortellini
12 ounces Gouda cheese, cut into 1-inch cubes
1 (12-ounce) jar marinated artichoke hearts, drained
1 (12-ounce) jar roasted red bell peppers, drained
8 ounces fresh mushrooms
1 (5-ounce) jar pimento-stuffed olives, drained
1 (3-ounce) package sliced pepperoni
1 (8-ounce) bottle Greek salad dressing

Cook the tortellini using the package directions. Drain and rinse with cold water. Drain well. Combine the tortellini, cheese, artichoke hearts, red peppers, mushrooms, olives, pepperoni and salad dressing in a heavy-duty sealable plastic bag. Seal the bag. Marinate in the refrigerator for 8 hours, turning occasionally. Drain the pasta mixture, discarding the marinade. Thread the pasta, cheese, artichoke hearts, red peppers, mushrooms, olives and pepperoni alternately onto skewers. Serve immediately.

YIELD: 12 SERVINGS

Lemon Linguini

16	ounces linguini
½	cup butter
2	cups sour cream
	Juice of 1 lemon
1	teaspoon grated lemon peel
	Freshly ground pepper to taste
¼	cup minced fresh parsley
	Grated Parmesan cheese to taste

Cook the pasta using package directions. Melt the butter in a small saucepan and remove from the heat. Stir in the sour cream, lemon juice and lemon peel. Drain the pasta. Add the sauce and toss to mix well. Spoon into a large baking dish. Bake at 400 degrees for 20 to 25 minutes. Sprinkle with pepper, parsley and Parmesan cheese.

YIELD: 8 SERVINGS

Easy Fettuccini Alfredo

16	ounces fettuccini
1	cup whipping cream
½	cup butter
2	cloves of garlic, minced
	Salt and pepper to taste
4	ounces fresh Parmesan cheese, grated
	Parsley flakes to taste

Cook the pasta using the package directions. Combine the cream, butter, garlic, salt and pepper in a glass 9x13-inch dish. Microwave on Medium-High until the butter melts. Stir in the Parmesan cheese. Drain the pasta and add to the sauce. Toss until the pasta is well coated. Sprinkle with the parsley flakes. Serve immediately.

YIELD: 5 OR 6 SERVINGS

Tortellini Primavera

2	tablespoons margarine
1	cup sliced mushrooms
½	cup chopped onion
1	clove of garlic, minced
1	(10-ounce) package spinach
8	ounces cream cheese
1	medium tomato, chopped
¼	cup milk
¼	cup grated Parmesan cheese
1	teaspoon Italian seasoning
¼	teaspoon salt
¼	teaspoon pepper
8	ounces frozen cheese tortellini

Melt the margarine in a large skillet. Add the mushrooms, onion and garlic. Sauté until the onion is transparent. Add the spinach, cream cheese, tomato, milk, Parmesan cheese, Italian seasoning, salt and pepper and mix well. Bring the mixture to a simmer, stirring occasionally. Stir in the tortellini. Cook until heated through.

YIELD: 4 SERVINGS

Lentil and Tomato Pasta Sauce

½ cup dried lentils
1 bay leaf
1½ cups water
1 cup chopped onion
1½ teaspoons freshly minced garlic
1½ teaspoons dried basil
1½ teaspoons dried oregano
¼ cup dry red wine
2½ cups tomato purée
8 ounces lean ground beef or ground turkey breast
Salt and pepper to taste

Rinse the lentils. Combine the lentils, bay leaf and water in a 2-quart saucepan. Cook over medium heat for 30 minutes. Sauté the onion, garlic, basil and oregano in the red wine in a 4-quart saucepan until the onion is softened. Add the tomato purée. Cook for 20 minutes or until thickened, stirring constantly. Brown the ground beef in a medium nonstick skillet, stirring until crumbly; drain on paper towels. Stir into the sauce. Drain the lentils, discarding the bay leaf. Add the lentils, salt and pepper to the sauce and mix well. Serve over hot cooked pasta.

YIELD: 8 CUPS

Spicy Spaghetti Sauce

1 pound ground turkey
1 (27-ounce) jar spaghetti sauce
1 tablespoon Heinz 57 steak sauce
1 tablespoon A.1. steak sauce
1 tablespoon Worcestershire sauce
1 tablespoon prepared mustard
1 tablespoon grated Romano cheese

Brown the ground turkey in a skillet, stirring until crumbly and drain. Add the spaghetti sauce, Heinz 57 sauce, A.1. steak sauce, Worcestershire sauce, mustard and cheese. Cook over medium heat for 30 minutes, stirring occasionally. Serve over pasta.

Note: Sauce may be frozen.

YIELD: 3 ½ TO 4 CUPS

Four-Cheese Lasagna

1   pound ground beef
½   cup chopped onion
1   (8-ounce) can tomato sauce
1   (6-ounce) can tomato paste
¼   cup water
1   tablespoon dried parsley flakes
2   teaspoons Italian seasoning
1   teaspoon instant beef bouillon
¼   teaspoon garlic powder
8   ounces cream cheese, softened
1   cup cottage cheese
¼   cup sour cream
2   eggs, beaten
8   ounces lasagna noodles, cooked, drained
1   (4-ounce) package sliced pepperoni
4   cups (16 ounces) shredded mozzarella cheese
½   cup grated Parmesan cheese
    Green pepper rings

There are three different kinds of grapefruit: royal, marsh, and ruby. Royal is a small grapefruit that is sweet in flavor and less tart than some grapefruit. Marsh is a tart seedless grapefruit that is good for sectioning. The sections from the marsh grapefruit also freeze well. Ruby is a pink grapefruit with few seeds. These grapefruit are all good for eating fresh and sectioning and can be used for making marmalades, preserves, and crystallized peel.

Brown the ground beef with the onion in a heavy skillet, stirring until the ground beef is brown and crumbly; drain. Stir in the tomato sauce, tomato paste, water, parsley flakes, Italian seasoning, instant bouillon and garlic powder. Cook over low heat for 10 minutes. Mix the cream cheese, cottage cheese, sour cream and eggs in a small bowl until smooth. Spoon a small amount of the sauce into a lightly greased 8x12-inch baking dish. Layer the lasagna noodles, cheese mixture, pepperoni, remaining sauce and mozzarella cheese ½ at a time in the prepared dish. Sprinkle with Parmesan cheese. Bake, covered, at 350 degrees for 30 minutes. Arrange the green pepper rings on top of the lasagna. Let stand for 10 minutes before serving.

YIELD: 6 SERVINGS

Lasagna Fiscaletti

1   pound lean ground beef
¾   cup chopped onion
2   tablespoon light olive oil
1   (16-ounce) can tomatoes, chopped
1   (12-ounce) can tomato paste
2   cups water
1   tablespoon chopped fresh parsley
2   teaspoons salt
1   teaspoon basil
1½ teaspoons sugar
1   teaspoon garlic powder
½   teaspoon pepper
½   teaspoon oregano
8   ounces lasagna noodles, cooked, drained
16 ounces ricotta cheese
6   ounces mozzarella cheese, sliced
6   ounces provolone, thinly sliced
1   cup freshly grated Romano cheese or
    Parmesan cheese, or ½ cup each

Brown the ground beef and onion in the olive oil in a large saucepan, stirring until the ground beef is crumbly; drain. Add the tomatoes, tomato paste, water, parsley, salt, basil, sugar, garlic powder, pepper and oregano. Simmer for 30 minutes, stirring occasionally. Spread 1 cup of the sauce in a nonstick 9x13-inch baking dish. Alternate layers of the lasagna, remaining sauce, ricotta cheese, mozzarella cheese, provolone cheese and Romano cheese in the prepared dish until all of the ingredients are used and ending with the Romano cheese. Bake at 350 degrees for 45 minutes or until bubbly. Let stand for 15 minutes before serving.

YIELD: 8 SERVINGS

Capellini D'Angelo

1   clove of garlic, minced
¼   cup extra-virgin olive oil
3   cups chopped canned peeled whole tomatoes
3   tablespoons chopped fresh basil
    Salt and pepper to taste
16 ounces capellini or angel hair pasta, cooked, drained
¼   cup freshly grated Parmesan cheese

Sauté the garlic in the olive oil in a sauté pan. Add the undrained tomatoes. Simmer for 20 minutes. Add the basil, salt and pepper. Simmer for 5 minutes. Place on individual serving plates. Spoon the sauce over the pasta. Sprinkle with Parmesan cheese.

YIELD: 2 SERVINGS

Drop a lemon wedge into simmering tomato sauce for pasta for an interesting taste treat.

Fusilli All'Amatriciana

3   tablespoons olive oil
6   bacon slices, finely chopped
1   large onion, chopped
⅓   cup dry white wine
1   (28-ounce) can Italian plum tomatoes, chopped
2   teaspoons dried basil
     Cayenne to taste
     Black pepper to taste
8   ounces fusilli or penne, cooked, drained
     Grated Parmesan cheese

Heat the olive oil in a large heavy skillet over medium-high heat. Add the bacon and onion. Cook for 8 minutes or until the bacon is almost crisp and the onion is golden brown, stirring occasionally. Add the wine. Cook for 2 minutes, stirring constantly. Add the undrained tomatoes and basil. Bring to a boil and reduce the heat. Simmer for 30 minutes or until thickened, stirring occasionally. Season with cayenne and black pepper. Place pasta in a large bowl. Add the sauce and toss to mix well. Serve with Parmesan cheese.

YIELD: 2 TO 4 SERVINGS

Pasta with Ham and Tomato

3   cloves of garlic, finely chopped
1   medium onion, chopped
¼   cup olive oil
1¼   pounds ham, trimmed, cut into ½-inch pieces
1   (28-ounce) can crushed tomatoes with purée
2½   tablespoons chopped fresh sage, or
     1 teaspoon dried sage
2   teaspoons sugar
1   teaspoon pepper
¾   teaspoon salt
     Hot cooked pasta, drained

Sauté the garlic and onion in the olive oil in a skillet over medium heat for 3 minutes or until the onion is translucent. Add the ham. Cook for 2 minutes. Add the tomatoes, sage, sugar, pepper and salt. Simmer for 15 to 20 minutes or until the sauce thickens, stirring frequently. Serve over hot cooked pasta.

YIELD: 4 TO 6 SERVINGS

Cajun Chicken Pasta

1½ tablespoons butter or margarine
2   teaspoons chopped garlic
1   cup sliced green bell pepper (1 medium)
8   ounces chicken breast, cut into bite-sized pieces
1   tablespoon Cajun poultry seasoning
1   (14-ounce) can stewed tomatoes
1   (8-ounce) can tomato sauce
3   slices bacon, cooked, crumbled
6   to 8 ounces pasta, cooked, drained

Melt the butter in a skillet over medium heat. Add the garlic, green pepper and chicken. Cook until the green pepper is tender-crisp and the chicken is brown. Sprinkle with poultry seasoning. Stir in the tomatoes and tomato sauce. Cook over low heat for 20 to 25 minutes or until the chicken is cooked through and the sauce is of the desired consistency, stirring frequently. Stir in the bacon. Serve immediately over hot cooked pasta.

Note: May stir in 1 teaspoon Tabasco sauce.

YIELD: 3 TO 4 SERVINGS

FAIRVILLA
ORANGES · GRAPEFRUIT · TANGERINES
ORLANDO, FLORIDA · CITRUS FRUIT PRODUCTS INC. · DR. PHILLIPS, FLORIDA

To make Minty Orange Pesto, process 1 cup packed fresh basil leaves, 1 cup packed fresh mint leaves, 2 cloves of garlic, ½ cup walnuts and 2 tablespoons frozen orange juice concentrate in a blender until almost smooth. Add ¼ cup or more olive oil gradually, processing constantly. Season with salt and pepper to taste.

Chicken and Tortellini Salad with Basil Dressing

2   boneless, skinless chicken breast halves
     Minced garlic to taste
2   tablespoons olive oil
     Salt and pepper to taste
12 ounces cheese tortellini, cooked
1   (14-ounce) can artichoke hearts, drained, coarsely chopped
½   small red onion, thinly sliced
⅓   cup red wine vinegar
¼   cup chopped fresh basil leaves
2   tablespoons sugar
¼   teaspoon minced garlic, or 1 clove of garlic, minced
½   cup extra-virgin olive oil

Cut the chicken into ½-inch pieces. Sauté the chicken and garlic to taste in 2 tablespoons olive oil in a skillet until the chicken is cooked through. Season with salt and pepper to taste. Combine the chicken, tortellini, artichoke hearts and onion in a large bowl and toss to mix well. Combine the wine vinegar, basil, sugar and ¼ teaspoon minced garlic in a food processor container. Process until puréed. Add the ½ cup olive oil gradually, processing constantly until smooth. Season with salt and pepper to taste. Pour over the chicken mixture and mix well. Serve immediately on lettuce-lined salad plates or chill, covered, for 8 to 10 hours to enhance the flavor before serving.

Note: Substitute balsamic vinegar for the wine vinegar and omit the basil for a different taste.

YIELD: 4 SERVINGS

Chicken and Shells with Pesto

- **1 bunch fresh broccoli**
- **1½ to 2 cups chopped cooked chicken breasts**
- **12 ounces pasta shells, cooked, drained**
- **3 green onions, chopped**
- **1 large tomato, chopped**
- **Pesto**

Cook the broccoli in a small amount of water until tender crisp; drain. Chop the broccoli into bite-size pieces. Combine the chicken and pasta in a large bowl. Add the broccoli, green onions and tomato and toss to mix well. Add the Pesto and toss to mix well. Let stand for 5 to 10 minutes before serving.

Pesto

- **1 chicken bouillon cube**
- **½ cup boiling water**
- **½ cup virgin olive oil**
- **½ cup fresh chopped basil, or 1 teaspoon dried basil**
- **12 ripe olives, cut into pieces**
- **2 to 3 cloves of garlic, minced**
- **½ cup ground pecans**
- **3 to 4 tablespoons grated Parmesan cheese**
- **Salt and pepper to taste**
- **Everglades seasoning or seasoned salt to taste**

Dissolve the bouillon cube in the boiling water in a bowl. Stir in the olive oil. Add the basil, olives, garlic, pecans and Parmesan cheese and mix well. Season with salt, pepper and Everglades seasoning.

YIELD: 4 SERVINGS

Chicken with Shiitake Tomato Sauce

- **4 ounces fresh shiitake mushrooms**
- **2 teaspoons olive oil**
- **4 boneless, skinless chicken breast halves**
- **1 (14-ounce) can whole tomatoes, chopped**
- **1 tablespoon chopped fresh parsley**
- **1 teaspoon dried whole basil leaves**
- **¼ teaspoon salt**
- **1 clove of garlic, minced**
- **1 tablespoon lemon juice**
- **Orange peel to taste**
- **2 cups hot cooked spinach fettuccini**

Wipe the mushrooms clean with a damp paper towel. Remove the caps, discarding the stems. Heat the olive oil in a large nonstick skillet over medium heat. Add the chicken. Cook for 3 minutes on each side or until light brown. Add the mushroom caps, tomatoes, parsley, basil leaves, salt, garlic, lemon juice and orange peel. Cook, covered, over medium heat for 10 minutes or until the chicken is cooked through. Remove the chicken from the skillet to a warm shallow serving platter and keep warm. Bring the sauce to a boil over medium-high heat. Cook for 5 minutes or until the sauce is reduced to 1¾ cups. Discard the orange peel. Spoon the sauce over the chicken. Serve over the fettuccini.

YIELD: 4 SERVINGS

Thai Nutty Chicken Pasta

1   **(14-ounce) can coconut milk**
1   **jar satay sauce**
1   **pound bite-size boneless, skinless chicken pieces**
1   **cup bean sprouts**
16 **ounces pasta, cooked, drained**
¼   **cup unsalted chopped peanuts**
½   **cup chopped scallions**

Bring the coconut milk to a boil in a saucepan. Stir in the satay sauce. Add the chicken. Cook until the chicken is cooked through. Stir in the bean sprouts. Place the pasta in a large bowl. Add the sauce and toss to mix well. Sprinkle with peanuts and scallions.

Note: May substitute medium shrimp for the chicken and cook until the shrimp turn pink.

YIELD: 4 SERVINGS

Penne Venezia

2   **teaspoons chopped garlic**
2   **teaspoons olive oil**
8   **boneless, skinless chicken breast halves**
½   **cup lemon juice**
½   **teaspoon garlic salt**
8   **ounces sliced mushrooms**
1   **tablespoon dried parsley flakes**
1   **teaspoon dried oregano**
1   **teaspoon dried basil**
2   **ounces capers, drained**
1   **large tomato, coarsely chopped**
1   **(3-ounce) package sun-dried tomatoes, hydrated, drained**
16 **ounces penne, cooked, drained**
1   **tablespoon olive oil**
9   **ounces evaporated milk**
¼   **cup grated Parmesan cheese**

Sauté the garlic in 2 teaspoons olive oil in a skillet for 2 to 3 minutes or until brown. Add the chicken, lemon juice and garlic salt. Cook over high heat for 5 minutes. Reduce the heat to medium. Cook for 10 minutes or until the chicken is cooked through. Remove the chicken to a plate using a slotted spoon. Shred the chicken. Add mushrooms, parsley, oregano and basil to the skillet. Bring to a boil. Boil for 5 to 8 minutes or until of the desired consistency. Reduce the heat to warm. Cook until the mixture stops boiling. Add the capers, shredded chicken, chopped tomato and sun-dried tomatoes. Cover and let stand over warm heat. Add 1 tablespoon olive oil to the pasta in a large bowl and toss to mix well. Add the chicken mixture and evaporated milk and toss to mix well. Stir in the Parmesan cheese. Let stand for 5 minutes before serving.

YIELD: 8 SERVINGS

Tri-Colored Pasta Tuna Toss

- 6 ounces tri-colored pasta
- 2 (6-ounce) cans tuna, drained
- ½ cup chopped yellow bell pepper
- ½ cup quartered cherry tomatoes
- ¼ cup chopped celery
- ¾ cup salsa
- ½ cup mayonnaise
- ½ teaspoon red pepper flakes

Cook the pasta using package directions and drain. Rinse the pasta with cold water and drain. Combine the pasta, tuna, yellow pepper, tomatoes and celery in a medium bowl and toss to mix well. Mix the salsa, mayonnaise and red pepper flakes in a small bowl. Add to the pasta mixture and toss to mix well. Chill, covered, until serving time. Serve with melba crackers.

YIELD: 4 TO 6 SERVINGS

Pig-Out Clam Pasta

MIKE THOMAS, *THE ORLANDO SENTINEL*

- 10 cloves (or more) of garlic, minced
- 2 tablespoons olive oil
- 1 small can chopped clams
- 2 tablespoons dry sherry
- 1 teaspoon (heaping) paprika
- ½ teaspoon cayenne
  Oregano to taste, or other favorite Italian spices
- 8 ounces pasta, cooked, drained

Sauté the garlic in the olive oil in an 8-inch skillet until the garlic just begins to change color. Add the clams. Rinse the clam can with the dry sherry and pour into the skillet. Add the paprika, cayenne and oregano and mix well. Cook until the sauce is reduced to the desired consistency, stirring occasionally and adding additional wine if needed. Add the sauce to the pasta and toss to mix well. Serve immediately.

YIELD: 4 SERVINGS

FAIRVILLA

ORANGES · GRAPEFRUIT · TANGERINES
ORLANDO, FLORIDA • CITRUS FRUIT PRODUCTS INC. • DR. PHILLIPS, FLORIDA

Try these tips for cooking perfect pasta: always cook pasta uncovered at a fast boil in at least one quart of water for every four ounces of uncooked pasta; stir frequently to prevent sticking; undercook slightly pasta that is to be used in a dish requiring further cooking; drain to stop cooking but rinse only if the recipe says to do so; and do not overcook.

Blackened Shrimp Stroganoff

1   pound fresh shrimp, unpeeled
2   cups water
1   tablespoon olive oil or vegetable oil
2   tablespoons blackened seasoning
8   ounces fresh mushrooms, sliced
1   shallot, chopped
1   tablespoon butter or margarine
⅔   cup dry vermouth or white wine
½   cup sour cream
1   tablespoon cornstarch
6   ounces roasted red bell peppers, drained,
    cut into thin strips
1   tablespoon drained capers (optional)
    Salt to taste
    Hot cooked fettuccini

Peel and devein the shrimp, reserving the shells. Bring the shells and 2 cups water to a boil in a saucepan and reduce the heat. Simmer for 10 minutes. Strain, reserving 1 cup broth; discard the shells. Combine the shrimp and olive oil in a small bowl. Add the blackened seasoning and stir until the shrimp are coated. Sauté the mushrooms and shallot in melted butter in a 10-inch skillet until tender. Remove to a bowl. Add the shrimp mixture to the skillet. Cook over medium-high heat for 2 minutes or until the shrimp turn pink. Remove to a bowl. Add vermouth to the skillet. Boil for 2 to 3 minutes or until reduced to ¼ cup. Mix the sour cream and cornstarch in a bowl. Add the reserved shrimp broth and mix well. Add to the vermouth in the skillet and mix well. Cook until thickened, stirring constantly. Cook for 1 minute longer. Add the shrimp, red peppers, mushroom mixture and capers. Cook until heated through. Season with salt. Serve over fettuccini.

YIELD: 4 SERVINGS

FAIRVILLA

ORANGES · GRAPEFRUIT · TANGERINES
ORLANDO, FLORIDA · CITRUS FRUIT PRODUCTS Inc. DR. PHILLIPS, FLORIDA

To make Sun-Dried Tomato and Olive Pesto, drain ⅔ cup oil-packed sun-dried tomatoes into a 1-cup glass measure. Add enough olive oil to measure ¼ cup. Process the drained sun-dried tomatoes, ¾ cup packed basil leaves, ⅔ cup drained canned pitted black olives, ½ cup pine nuts and 2 cloves of garlic in a blender until finely chopped. Add the olive oil mixture gradually, processing constantly until well blended and adding additional olive oil if needed for desired consistency. Season with salt and pepper to taste. Pesto may be covered and stored in the refrigerator for up to 2 days or frozen for up to 1 week. Bring to room temperature before using.

Oriental Orzo and Shrimp

1   pound fresh mushrooms, sliced
1   tablespoon minced fresh ginger
2   teaspoons minced garlic
3   tablespoons vegetable oil
1⅓ cups orzo
2   (14-ounce) cans chicken broth
¼   cup hoisin sauce
¼   teaspoon ground red pepper
12   ounces cooked shrimp, deveined
½   cup 1-inch pieces green onions

Sauté the mushrooms, ginger and garlic in hot vegetable oil in a large saucepan for 5 minutes or until the mushrooms are tender. Stir in the pasta, chicken broth, hoisin sauce and red pepper. Bring to a boil and reduce the heat. Simmer, covered, for 10 minutes or until the orzo is firm-tender and some liquid still remains, stirring occasionally. Stir in the shrimp and green onions. Cook for 1 to 2 minutes or until the shrimp are heated through.

YIELD: 4 SERVINGS

Seafood Vermicelli

1¼ pounds cooked shrimp
1¼ pounds cooked crab meat
½   cup fresh lemon juice
1   cup mayonnaise
¼   cup Italian salad dressing
1½ teaspoons celery seed
1   red onion, chopped
1   green bell pepper, chopped
     Chopped fresh herbs such as parsley, oregano and chives to taste
14   ounces vermicelli, cooked, drained
     Salt and pepper to taste

Marinate the cooked seafood in lemon juice in a glass bowl for 8 to 10 hours. Combine with the mayonnaise, salad dressing, celery seed, onion, green pepper and herbs in a large bowl and mix well. Add the hot pasta and toss to mix well. Season with salt and pepper.

Note: May combine the cooked seafood in any proportion to equal 2½ pounds.

YIELD: 6 SERVINGS

Another popular theme was Florida's native flora.
This label shows the vines that lined the property of the
Avalon Orange Groves in west Orange County. At one time,
this company was the largest citrus grower in Florida.

SUN SEASONED

· *Meats* ·

· · ·

Section sponsored by

Omni Rosen Hotel

Everglades Rack of Lamb with Minted Onion

OMNI ROSEN HOTEL

- 1 teaspoon lime juice
- 1 cup barbecue sauce
- 1 cup olive oil
- 6 tablespoons teriyaki sauce
- 1 bunch basil, chopped
- 1 bay leaf
- 1 tablespoon chopped garlic
- 1 teaspoon cracked pepper
- 1 Frenched rack of lamb (domestic)
  Minted Onion

Combine the lime juice, barbecue sauce, olive oil, teriyaki sauce, basil, bay leaf, garlic and pepper in a glass dish and mix well. Add the lamb. Marinate, covered, in the refrigerator for 48 hours. Drain the lamb, discarding the bay leaf and marinade. Flat sear the lamb in a skillet until brown on all sides. Place in a large baking pan. Bake at 350 degrees for 20 minutes for medium-rare or until the lamb is of the desired degree of doneness. Serve with Minted Onion.

Minted Onion

- 1 large onion, chopped
- 1 teaspoon butter
- 1 cup beef demi-glace or brown gravy
- 2 tablespoons mint jelly
  Salt and pepper to taste

Sauté the onion in butter in a skillet until light brown. Add demi-glace and mint jelly. Cook for 5 minutes, stirring frequently. Add salt and pepper to taste.

YIELD: 2 SERVINGS

Beef Tenderloin du Chef

- 1 (3- to 4-pound) beef tenderloin
- 2 cups chopped mushrooms
- ½ cup minced fresh parsley
- ¼ cup minced scallions
- ¼ cup butter
- 2 tablespoons brandy
- 3 slices bacon, cooked, crumbled

Place the beef in a roasting pan. Bake at 450 degrees for 30 to 40 minutes or to the desired degree of doneness. Sauté the mushrooms, parsley and scallions in the butter in a skillet until light brown. Stir in the brandy and bacon. Cut the beef at an angle into slices and place on a serving platter. Pour the sauce over the tenderloin.

YIELD: 8 TO 10 SERVINGS

Tangy Beef Over Noodles

2	tablespoons brown sugar
⅓	cup soy sauce
1½	cups unsweetened orange juice
⅓	cup dry sherry
2	cloves of garlic, sliced
1	tablespoon Worcestershire sauce
2	bay leaves
1½	pounds beef for stew
8	ounces bacon
½	cup flour
1	teaspoon salt
½	teaspoon pepper
½	teaspoon garlic powder
2	(14-ounce) cans beef broth
1	(28-ounce) can tomatoes
1	cup dry red wine
1	cup orange juice
5	potatoes, peeled, cubed
5	carrots, chopped
4	ribs celery, chopped
3	or 4 pearl onions, peeled
2	teaspoons garlic powder
1	teaspoon chili powder
16	ounces noodles, cooked, drained

Dissolve the brown sugar in the soy sauce in a large bowl. Add the orange juice, sherry, garlic, Worcestershire sauce and bay leaves and mix well. Add the beef, stirring until coated. Marinate, covered, in the refrigerator for 2 hours to overnight. Cook the bacon in a large stockpot until crisp. Remove the bacon and crumble; set aside, reserving the drippings. Combine the flour, salt, pepper and garlic powder in a large sealable plastic bag and mix well. Drain the beef, discarding the bay leaves and marinade. Add the beef to the flour mixture and shake until all of the pieces are coated. Brown the beef in the reserved bacon drippings. Remove the beef from the stockpot and set aside. Deglaze the stockpot with a small amount of the beef broth. Pour in the remaining beef broth and the tomatoes. Simmer over medium heat for 10 minutes. Add the wine, orange juice and beef. Simmer for 30 minutes, stirring occasionally. Stir in the potatoes, carrots, celery and onions. Cook for 1½ hours or until the vegetables are tender, stirring occasionally. Stir in the bacon, garlic powder and chili powder. Simmer for 10 minutes or until the broth is of the desired consistency. Serve over noodles.

YIELD: 8 SERVINGS

Keep the following tips in mind when marinating food. Always pierce the meat or poultry with a fork before placing in the marinade to allow for flavor penetration. Plan on ⅓ to ½ cup marinade per pound of food. Use a covered glass dish or a heavy-duty sealable plastic food storage bag for marinating. Always marinate foods in the refrigerator, never at room temperature. Marinating times vary because foods and marinades differ in how they react. Over-marinating can cause foods to have a flavor that is too strong or can make the food mushy. Basting foods during grilling increases the flavor, but always reserve a portion of the marinade to use for basting before it comes in contact with uncooked food.

Ropa Vieja

1 (2-pound) flank steak
1 bay leaf
1 small onion
1 tomato
1 rib celery, cut into halves
1 tablespoon salt
¼ cup olive oil
1 small onion, finely chopped
½ green bell pepper, finely chopped
2 cloves of garlic, minced
1 bay leaf
½ teaspoon oregano
¼ teaspoon cumin
1 (10-ounce) can tomato sauce
¼ teaspoon sugar
1 tablespoon red wine vinegar
1 teaspoon salt
¼ cup dry red wine

Combine the steak, 1 bay leaf, 1 onion, tomato, celery and 1 tablespoon salt in a large stockpot. Cover with cold water. Bring to a boil, skimming often. Reduce heat. Cook for 1 hour or until the steak is tender. Remove from the heat. Let stand until cool. Remove the steak to a 2½-quart saucepan and shred. Strain the stock, reserving ½ cup. Sauté the chopped onion and green pepper in the olive oil in a large skillet until transparent. Add the garlic, bay leaf, oregano and cumin. Cook for 5 minutes. Add a mixture of the tomato sauce, reserved stock, sugar, vinegar, salt and wine and mix well. Bring to a boil and reduce the heat. Simmer for 30 minutes, stirring frequently. Remove the bay leaf. Pour the sauce over the shredded steak and mix well. Simmer, covered, for 20 to 30 minutes or until the desired consistency, stirring occasionally. Serve over white rice.

YIELD: 6 TO 8 SERVINGS

Beef Burgundy

8 slices bacon
1 cup flour
4 pounds London broil, cut into cubes
1 (10-ounce) can cream of mushroom soup
1 envelope dry onion soup mix
2 cups burgundy
1 cup beef bouillon
1 bay leaf
¼ teaspoon ground pepper
½ teaspoon garlic powder
½ teaspoon salt
1 carrot, thinly sliced
1 rib celery, thinly sliced
1 pound fresh mushrooms, sliced
¼ cup butter or margarine
24 small white onions
1 (8-ounce) can sliced water chestnuts

Cook the bacon in a skillet until crisp. Remove the bacon. Combine the flour and beef in a sealable plastic food storage bag. Seal the bag and shake until the beef is coated. Brown the beef in the bacon drippings in the skillet. Remove the beef and place in a Dutch oven. Combine the mushroom soup and onion soup mix in a bowl. Add the wine and bouillon gradually, mixing constantly until smooth. Add the bay leaf, pepper, garlic powder and salt and mix well. Stir in the carrot and celery. Pour over the beef. Bake at 325 degrees for 2 to 2½ hours, adding additional wine if the sauce becomes too thick. Sauté the sliced mushrooms in the butter in a skillet. Remove the mushrooms with a slotted spoon. Sauté the onions in the skillet until tender. Add the sautéed mushrooms, sautéed onions and water chestnuts to the beef mixture and mix well. Bake, covered, for 30 minutes. Remove the bay leaf. Serve over rice or noodles. Garnish with parsley.

YIELD: 10 SERVINGS

Herbed Burgundy Beef Kabobs

2	pounds beef tenderloin, cut into 1-inch cubes
¾	cup burgundy or other dry red wine
½	cup vegetable oil
⅓	cup soy sauce
3	tablespoons Worcestershire sauce
4	large cloves of garlic, minced
2	teaspoons dried rosemary
2	teaspoons coarsely ground pepper
1	teaspoon dried thyme
12	boiling onions
2	large red bell peppers, cut into 1½-inch pieces
2	large yellow bell peppers, cut into 1½-inch pieces
2	medium zucchini, cut into 1-inch pieces
12	large mushrooms
	Hot cooked rice

Place the beef in a large shallow container. Combine the wine, oil, soy sauce, Worcestershire sauce, garlic, rosemary, pepper and thyme in a bowl and mix well. Pour over the beef. Marinate, covered, in the refrigerator for 30 minutes. Parboil the onions in a small amount of boiling water in a saucepan for 3 minutes; drain. Parboil the pepper pieces in a small amount of boiling water in a saucepan for 1 minute; drain. Drain the beef, reserving the marinade. Pour the reserved marinade in a small saucepan. Bring to a boil and remove from the heat. Thread the beef, onions, pepper pieces, zucchini and mushrooms alternately on twelve 12-inch metal skewers. Place the kabobs on a grill rack sprayed with nonstick cooking spray. Grill over medium hot coals for 6 to 8 minutes on each side or to the desired degree of doneness, basting often with the boiled reserved marinade. Serve the kabobs over rice.

YIELD: 6 SERVINGS

FLAME VINE
BRAND

PACKED BY
AVALON ORANGE GROVES CO.
ORLANDO · FLORIDA

For Teriyaki Marinade, combine 1 cup soy sauce, 1 cup water, ¾ cup sugar, ¼ cup Worcestershire sauce, 3 tablespoons vinegar, 3 tablespoons vegetable oil, ½ cup fresh chopped chives and 2 teaspoons garlic powder in a bowl and mix well. Use to marinate flank steak in the refrigerator for 8 hours before grilling, or to marinate chicken in the refrigerator for 2 hours before grilling.

Mushroom and Marsala Beef Tenderloin

1 **(5- to 6-pound) beef tenderloin, trimmed**
¾ **cup marsala**
¼ **cup minced onion**
¼ **cup olive oil**
2 **tablespoons red wine vinegar**
½ **teaspoon salt**
½ **teaspoon pepper**
1 **pound fresh mushrooms, sliced**
⅓ **cup sliced green onions**
2 **cloves of garlic, crushed**
3 **tablespoons melted butter or margarine**
½ **cup marsala**
1½ **cups soft whole wheat bread crumbs**
 Garlic salt to taste
 Freshly ground pepper to taste
8 **slices bacon**
 Tomato roses (optional)
 Fresh parsley sprigs (optional)

Place tenderloin in a large shallow dish. Combine ¾ cup wine, onion, olive oil, vinegar, salt and pepper in a small bowl and mix well. Pour marinade over tenderloin. Marinate, covered, in the refrigerator for 8 hours, turning occasionally. Sauté the mushrooms, green onions and garlic in butter in a large skillet over medium heat until tender. Add ½ cup wine. Simmer until the liquid evaporates. Remove from the heat. Add the bread crumbs and toss gently. Drain the tenderloin, discarding the marinade. Cut the tenderloin lengthwise to but not through the center, leaving one long side connected. Spoon the stuffing mixture into the opening of the tenderloin. Fold the top side over the stuffing and tie securely with heavy string at 2-inch intervals. Sprinkle with garlic salt and pepper. Place seam side down on a rack in a roasting pan. Insert meat thermometer into the thickest portion of the tenderloin. Bake, uncovered, at 425 degrees for 30 minutes. Cut strings and remove from tenderloin. Arrange bacon slices in a crisscross pattern over the tenderloin and secure at ends with wooden picks. Bake for 15 to 20 minutes or until the bacon is crisp and the thermometer registers 140 degrees for rare, 150 degrees for medium-rare or 160 degrees for medium. Remove wooden picks. Garnish with tomato roses and parsley.

YIELD: 10 TO 12 SERVINGS

FLAME VINE
BRAND

PACKED BY
AVALON ORANGE GROVES CO.
ORLANDO · FLORIDA

To make Citrus Cartwheels, select firm lemons, limes, or oranges with thick rinds. Cut evenly spaced grooves from tip to tip using a citrus stripper. Cut the fruit crosswise into thin slices. Float several citrus cartwheels in a punch bowl filled with fruit punch or in a pitcher of lemonade. Garnish individual beverages by making a cut from the outside edge to the center of the cartwheel and placing it on the rim of the glass.

Beef Tenderloin Steaks with Peppercorn Cream

1   tablespoon olive oil
2   (6-ounce) beef tenderloin steaks
    Salt and pepper to taste
¼   cup brandy
1   large clove of garlic, minced
1   teaspoon crushed multicolored peppercorns
½   teaspoon dried oregano
⅛   teaspoon salt
⅔   cup whipping cream
1½ tablespoons sour cream
    Hot cooked rice
    Sprigs of fresh oregano

Heat the olive oil in a medium skillet until hot. Sprinkle the steaks with salt and pepper. Sear the steaks on both sides in the skillet. Place the steaks on a rack in a broiler pan. Broil 5½ inches from the heat source for 5 to 7 minutes on each side or until a meat thermometer registers 140 degrees for rare, 150 degrees for medium-rare or 160 degrees for medium. Remove from the oven and keep warm. Add brandy to the drippings in the skillet. Bring to a boil, stirring to deglaze the skillet. Add minced garlic, peppercorns, oregano and salt. Cook for 1 minute. Add the whipping cream. Bring to a boil. Cook for 6 to 7 minutes or until the sauce is reduce by half. Remove from the heat. Whisk in the sour cream. Place the beef on a serving plate. Spoon the sauce over the beef. Serve with rice. Garnish with sprigs of oregano.

YIELD: 2 SERVINGS

Tournedos Roquefort

4   (4-ounce) beef tenderloin steaks
2   teaspoons finely chopped fresh thyme, or
    1 teaspoon dried thyme
¼   teaspoon salt
¼   teaspoon pepper
1   tablespoon butter
1   tablespoon olive oil
1   cup dry white wine
½   cup beef consommé
½   cup half-and-half
8   small asparagus spears
1½ ounces crumbled Roquefort cheese

Rub the steaks with thyme, salt and pepper. Melt the butter in a large skillet over medium heat. Stir in the olive oil. Add the steaks. Cook for 1 to 3 minutes on each side or to the desired degree of doneness. Remove the steaks to a warm platter and keep warm. Stir the wine and consommé into the drippings in the skillet. Cook over high heat until reduced to ½ cup, stirring frequently. Stir in the half-and-half. Cook until reduced to ½ cup or to the desired consistency, stirring constantly. Keep warm. Snap off tough ends of the asparagus. Remove the scales with a vegetable peeler. Cut the spears into halves. Place in a steamer basket. Place over boiling water in a saucepan. Steam, covered, for 8 minutes or until tender-crisp. Arrange steaks on a rack in a broiler pan. Arrange the asparagus over the steaks and sprinkle with cheese. Place in the oven and leave the door partially open. Broil 6 inches from the heat source for 2 minutes or until the cheese melts. Serve immediately with the sauce.

YIELD: 4 SERVINGS

Steak Diane

2	(6-ounce) filets mignons
⅛	teaspoon salt
⅛	teaspoon freshly ground pepper
2	tablespoons butter
1	teaspoon Dijon mustard
2	tablespoons shallots, minced
1	tablespoon butter
1	tablespoon lemon juice
1½	teaspoons Worcestershire sauce
1	tablespoon fresh chives, minced
1	teaspoon brandy
1	tablespoon fresh parsley, minced

Season both sides of the steaks with salt and pepper. Melt 2 tablespoons butter in a heavy skillet. Stir in the mustard and shallots. Sauté over medium heat for 1 minute. Add the steaks. Cook for 3 minutes on each side or to the desired degree of doneness. Remove the steaks to a serving plate and keep warm. Add 1 tablespoon butter, lemon juice, Worcestershire sauce and chives to the pan drippings in the skillet. Cook for 2 minutes. Stir in the brandy. Pour over the steaks. Sprinkle with parsley.

YIELD: 2 SERVINGS

Steak au Poivre

1	tablespoon cracked peppercorns
2	(1¼-inch-thick) tenderloin steaks
2	tablespoons butter
1	tablespoon minced shallots
2	tablespoons cognac
2	tablespoons red wine
¼	cup beef broth
2	tablespoons whipping cream

Press the peppercorns into the steaks. Heat the butter in a heavy skillet. Add the steaks. Sear on both sides over medium-high heat. Reduce the heat to medium. Cook until the steaks are of the desired degree of doneness, turning frequently. Remove the steaks to a platter and keep warm. Add the shallots to the skillet. Sauté for 1 minute. Add the cognac and wine. Boil for 2 minutes, stirring constantly. Add the beef broth. Boil for 2 minutes, stirring to deglaze the skillet. Stir in the whipping cream. Cook until heated through; do not boil. Pour the sauce over the steaks. Serve immediately.

YIELD: 2 SERVINGS

Herbed Flank Steak

1   **pound flank steak**
    Meat tenderizer to taste
½   **teaspoon salt**
½   **teaspoon pepper**
2   **teaspoons minced garlic**
2   **tablespoons dried rosemary**
1   **teaspoon dried thyme**
1   **teaspoon dried tarragon**
    Juice of ½ lemon
2   **teaspoons Worcestershire sauce**

Place the steak in a 9x13-inch baking pan. Sprinkle both sides with meat tenderizer, salt and pepper and rub in with the tines of a fork. Let stand for a few minutes. Spread 1 teaspoon garlic on each side of the steak; press into the steak with the tines of a fork. Sprinkle both sides of the steak with rosemary, thyme and tarragon and press in with the tines of a fork. Let stand for 5 minutes. Sprinkle both sides with lemon juice and Worcestershire sauce. Chill, covered, for 1 hour. Place the steak on a rack in a broiler pan. Bake at 450 degrees for 5 minutes per side. Cut into thin slices. Serve immediately.

Note: To make gravy, cover the steak with foil and bake at 350 degrees for 20 minutes. This steak is also good grilled.

YIELD: 4 SERVINGS

Korean Barbecue

1¼ **pounds sirloin or flank steak, partially frozen**
¼   **cup soy sauce**
2   **tablespoons honey**
1   **tablespoon brown sugar**
3   **tablespoons dark sesame oil**
3   **tablespoons sesame seeds, toasted**
2   **cloves of garlic, minced**
1   **inch fresh gingerroot, minced**
2   **scallions, finely chopped**
    Pinch of red pepper flakes
10 **twists of freshly ground black pepper**

Cut the beef cross grain into very thin slices. Place in a shallow glass dish. Combine the soy sauce, honey, brown sugar, sesame oil, sesame seeds, garlic, gingerroot, scallions, red pepper and black pepper in a bowl and mix well. Pour over the beef. Marinate, covered, in the refrigerator for 15 minutes. Drain the beef, reserving the marinade. Heat a wok or skillet over high heat. Add the beef with a small amount of the reserved marinade. Stir-fry for 2 minutes or until done to taste. Serve with hot cooked rice.

Note: The marinade is also good with chicken and pork.

YIELD: 2 TO 3 SERVINGS

FLAME VINE

PACKED BY
AVALON ORANGE GROVES CO.
ORLANDO · FLORIDA

To make Green Onion Butter, mix ¼ cup butter, softened, ¼ cup sliced green onions, ½ teaspoon dry mustard and ½ cup finely shredded Cheddar cheese in a bowl. Use to spread over grilled steaks.

Veal Saltimbocca

3   veal scallops
    Flour
3   tablespoons olive oil
3   slices Monterey Jack cheese
3   thin prosciutto slices
⅓   cup white wine
½   cup beef broth
3   tablespoons grated Parmesan cheese
    Chopped fresh parsley to taste
    Pepper to taste

Place the veal between 2 pieces of waxed paper. Pound until very thin. Dredge the veal in flour on a flat surface, pressing to coat both sides. Sauté the veal in the olive oil in a skillet until brown on both sides; drain. Layer the cheese and prosciutto on the veal. Add the wine and broth to the skillet. Sprinkle with Parmesan cheese and parsley. Cook until the cheese melts and the sauce thickens. Add pepper to taste.

Note: Add ¼ cup spaghetti sauce for a different taste.

YIELD: 1 SERVING

Honey-Glazed Barbecued Spareribs

HEATHER MCPHERSON, *THE ORLANDO SENTINEL*

4   pounds lean pork spareribs
    Salt and pepper to taste
½   cup honey
¼   cup lemon juice
2   teaspoons grated lemon peel
2   teaspoons grated ginger
1   clove of garlic, minced
1   teaspoon crushed rosemary
½   teaspoon crushed red chile peppers
½   teaspoon sage

Place spareribs in a large stockpot or very deep skillet. Add water to cover. Bring to a boil over medium heat and reduce the heat. Simmer for 4 minutes; drain. Season the spareribs with salt and pepper. Place on a rack in a roasting pan and cover loosely with foil. Bake at 450 degrees for 15 minutes. Combine the honey, lemon juice, lemon peel, ginger, garlic, rosemary, red chile peppers and sage in a bowl and mix well. Reduce the oven temperature to 350 degrees. Brush the spareribs with the honey mixture. Bake for 1 hour longer or until cooked through, basting with the honey mixture every 15 minutes.

Note: To grill the spareribs, prepare as above, placing the spareribs on a grill rack. Grill over hot coals for 30 minutes per side or until cooked through, brushing with the honey mixture 2 times during the last 15 minutes of grilling.

YIELD: 4 TO 6 SERVINGS

Peppercorn-Crusted Pork Loin

1	(4-pound) lean boneless pork loin roast, trimmed
½	teaspoon salt
¼	cup Dijon mustard
1	tablespoon buttermilk
2	cups soft whole wheat bread crumbs
1	tablespoon cracked black peppercorns
1	tablespoon whole assorted peppercorns, crushed
2	teaspoons chopped fresh thyme
	Sprigs of fresh thyme (optional)

Sprinkle the roast with salt. Combine the mustard and buttermilk in a small bowl and mix well. Spread over the roast. Combine the bread crumbs, black peppercorns, assorted peppercorns and chopped thyme in a small bowl and mix well. Press evenly over the roast. Place on a lightly greased rack in a roasting pan. Bake at 325 degrees for 2 hours or until a meat thermometer registers 160 degrees. Let stand for 10 minutes. Garnish with sprigs of thyme.

YIELD: 8 TO 10 SERVINGS

Orange Pork Tenderloin

⅔	cup orange juice
¼	cup soy sauce
3	cloves of garlic, chopped
1	to 2 pounds pork tenderloin or pork loin roast

Combine the orange juice, soy sauce and garlic in a large sealable plastic food storage bag and mix well. Add the pork and seal. Marinate in the refrigerator for 4 to 5 hours. Drain the pork. Place in a large baking pan. Bake at 375 degrees for 45 minutes or until cooked through.

Note: Meat may also be grilled.

YIELD: 6 TO 8 SERVINGS

To prepare Honey-Mustard Marinade, mix ½ cup honey, ¼ cup Dijon mustard, ¼ cup lemon juice, ¼ cup soy sauce and 2 cloves of garlic, crushed, in a bowl. Use to marinate pork tenderloin, covered, in the refrigerator for 8 hours before grilling.

Pork Tenderloin in Cranberry Orange Sauce

1 (16-ounce) can whole cranberry sauce
1 (12-ounce) jar orange marmalade
1 package pork chop seasoning with cooking bag
2 pork tenderloins

Combine the cranberry sauce, orange marmalade and ¾ of the pork chop seasoning in a saucepan and mix well. Cook over low heat for 30 minutes. Rub the tenderloins with the remaining pork chop seasoning. Place in the cooking bag and place in a shallow baking pan. Spread 3 tablespoons of the sauce over each tenderloin and close the bag. Bake at 350 degrees for 25 minutes. Remove tenderloins from the bag and place on a platter, discarding the cooking bag and drippings. Cut the tenderloins into slices. Serve with the remaining sauce.

YIELD: 6 SERVINGS

Prepare Garlic-Honey Marinade by combining ¼ cup lemon juice, ¼ cup honey, 2 tablespoons soy sauce, 1 tablespoon dry sherry and 4 cloves of garlic, minced, in a bowl and mix well. Pour over boneless pork and marinate, covered, in the refrigerator for 8 hours before grilling.

Pork Medallions with Orange Caramelized Onion Sauce

1 teaspoon cornstarch
¼ cup water
½ tablespoon butter
½ tablespoon vegetable oil
2 cups (⅛-inch) red onion slices
¼ teaspoon salt
⅛ teaspoon pepper
¼ cup spiced rum
1 tablespoon balsamic vinegar
¾ cup orange juice
12 (3-ounce) pork medallions
   Salt and pepper to taste
6 tablespoons olive oil
6 tablespoons spiced rum
2½ tablespoons butter
18 (¼-inch-thick) orange wheels
   Chopped fresh parsley

Dissolve the cornstarch in the water in a bowl. Melt ½ tablespoon butter in the vegetable oil in a sauté pan over medium heat. Add the onions, ¼ teaspoon salt and ⅛ teaspoon pepper. Sauté until the onions are golden brown. Add ¼ cup rum, stirring to deglaze the skillet. Stir in the vinegar and orange juice. Bring to a boil. Add the cornstarch mixture gradually, stirring constantly. Return to a boil and reduce the heat. Simmer for 2 minutes. Remove from the heat and keep warm. Pat the pork dry and season with salt and pepper. Heat the olive oil in a sauté pan. Add the pork. Cook until the pork is cooked through. Remove the pork to a warm platter. Add the remaining rum to the pan, stirring to deglaze the pan. Stir in the onion sauce. Add the remaining butter. Cook until the butter is melted. Spoon over the pork medallions. Garnish with orange wheels and parsley.

YIELD: 6 SERVINGS

Pork Chops Stuffed with Rice and Apricots

1	(7-ounce) package long grain and wild rice
2	teaspoons instant chicken bouillon
4	large (1-inch-thick) pork chops with pockets
2	to 3 tablespoons butter or margarine
½	cup chopped celery
½	cup chopped onion
1	(10-ounce) can apricot halves, drained
⅓	cup salted sunflower seed kernels
2	tablespoons dry white wine
½	teaspoon bouquet garni
½	teaspoon salt

Prepare the rice using the package directions, adding the instant bouillon. Brown the pork chops on both sides in a nonstick skillet. Remove the pork chops to a platter to keep warm. Add butter to the skillet. Heat until melted. Add the celery and onion. Sauté until tender. Remove from the heat. Reserve 4 apricot halves for garnish. Chop the remaining apricots. Stir the apricots, celery and onion into the rice. Add sunflower seeds, wine, bouquet garni and salt and mix well. Fill the pork chops with the rice mixture. Arrange in a 12x12-inch or 9x13-inch glass baking dish. Spoon the remaining rice around the pork chops. Bake, covered, at 350 degrees for 30 minutes. Bake, uncovered, for 30 minutes longer or until cooked through. Garnish with the reserved apricot halves.

YIELD: 4 SERVINGS

Sherried Pork Chops

6	thick pork chops
2	tablespoons vegetable oil
3	apples, cored, sliced
½	cup packed light brown sugar
½	teaspoon cinnamon
2	tablespoons butter or margarine
	Salt and pepper to taste
½	cup sherry

Brown the pork chops in the vegetable oil in a heavy skillet. Arrange the apples in a greased 9x13-inch baking dish. Sprinkle with a mixture of brown sugar and cinnamon. Dot with butter. Arrange the pork chops on the apples. Sprinkle with salt and pepper. Pour the sherry over the top. Bake, covered, at 350 degrees for 1 to 1½ hours or until the pork chops are cooked through.

YIELD: 6 SERVINGS

Honey-Gingered Pork Loin

2   (12-ounce) pork tenderloins
¼   cup honey
¼   cup soy sauce
¼   cup oyster sauce
2   tablespoons brown sugar
1   tablespoon minced fresh gingerroot
1   tablespoon minced garlic
1   tablespoon catsup
½   teaspoon onion powder
½   teaspoon ground red pepper
¼   teaspoon ground cinnamon
     Fresh sprigs of parsley (optional)

Place tenderloins in a 7x11-inch baking dish. Combine the honey, soy sauce, oyster sauce, brown sugar, gingerroot, garlic, catsup, onion powder, red pepper and cinnamon in a bowl and mix well. Pour over the tenderloins. Marinate, covered, in the refrigerator for 8 hours, turning occasionally. Drain the tenderloins, reserving the marinade. Bring the reserved marinade to a boil in a saucepan. Boil for 3 minutes. Remove from the heat. Place the tenderloins on a grill rack. Grill over medium-hot coals for 25 to 35 minutes, turning frequently and basting with the reserved marinade until a meat thermometer inserted into the thickest portion of the tenderloin registers 160 degrees. Cut tenderloins into thin slices and arrange on a serving platter. Garnish with fresh parsley sprigs.

YIELD: 6 SERVINGS

Orange-Glazed Ham Steak

¼   cup orange marmalade
1   teaspoon Dijon mustard
1   pound (½-inch-thick) cooked center-cut ham slice

Mix the marmalade and mustard in a bowl. Place the ham on a grill rack. Grill over medium-hot coals 4 to 6 inches from the heat source for 5 to 10 minutes or until heated through, brushing with the glaze and turning once.

YIELD: 4 SERVINGS

Parsleyed Rack of Lamb

2   tablespoons olive oil
1   teaspoon curry
     Salt and freshly ground pepper to taste
2   (1- to 1½-pound) racks of lamb, trimmed
2   cups fresh bread crumbs
1   tablespoon finely chopped shallots
1   teaspoon chopped garlic
1   teaspoon fresh thyme
1   tablespoon melted butter
3   tablespoons finely chopped parsley

Combine the olive oil, curry and salt and pepper in a small bowl and mix well. Brush over the lamb. Place in a shallow baking dish with the lamb racks side by side. Bake at 450 degrees 4 inches from the heat source for 3 minutes. Turn the lamb over. Bake for 2 minutes longer. Combine the bread crumbs, shallots, garlic, thyme, butter, 2 tablespoons parsley and salt and pepper to taste in a bowl. Sprinkle over the lamb. Bake for 5 to 6 minutes or until of the desired degree of doneness. Sprinkle with the remaining 1 tablespoon parsley.

YIELD: 6 SERVINGS

Roasted Leg of Lamb with Orzo

1	(4- to 5-pound) boneless leg of lamb, rolled and tied
2	tablespoons vegetable oil
5	to 6 cloves of garlic, peeled, minced
1	teaspoon salt
1	teaspoon pepper
1	teaspoon oregano
1	teaspoon garlic powder
¼	cup melted butter or margarine
1	teaspoon salt
1	teaspoon oregano
1	teaspoon garlic powder
	Baked Orzo

Unroll the leg of lamb and brush with vegetable oil. Sprinkle with the garlic, 1 teaspoon salt, 1 teaspoon pepper, 1 teaspoon oregano and 1 teaspoon garlic powder. Roll up the lamb and tie with heavy string. Melt the butter and remaining seasonings in a small saucepan. Arrange the lamb in a shallow roasting pan. Brush with the seasoned butter. Bake at 350 degrees for 2 hours, basting frequently with the seasoned butter. Serve with Baked Orzo.

Baked Orzo

2	quarts water
1	teaspoon salt
1	pound orzo
4	cups water
1	(16-ounce) can tomatoes, mashed
¼	cup vegetable oil
¼	cup butter or margarine, softened
1	teaspoon instant chicken bouillon
1	tablespoon tomato paste
1	teaspoon garlic powder
1	teaspoon oregano
1	teaspoon paprika
1	teaspoon pepper

Bring 2 quarts water and salt to a boil in a large saucepan. Add the orzo. Cook for 15 minutes. Drain and rinse with cold water. Combine the orzo, 4 cups water, undrained tomatoes, vegetable oil, butter, instant bouillon, tomato paste and seasonings in a large bowl and mix well. Spoon into a greased 2-quart casserole. Bake at 350 degrees for 30 minutes or until the liquid has been absorbed.

YIELD: 10 TO 12 SERVINGS

FLAME VINE
BRAND

PACKED BY
AVALON ORANGE GROVES CO.
ORLANDO · FLORIDA

To make Grapefruit Mint Jelly, bring 2¼ cups unsweetened grapefruit juice, ¾ cup water and 1 package fruit pectin to a boil in a large saucepan over high heat. Stir in 3½ cups sugar. Return to a boil. Boil for 30 seconds, stirring constantly. Remove from the heat and skim. Stir in 6 to 8 drops of oil of spearmint and enough green food coloring to tint as desired. Pour into hot sterilized jars, leaving ¼ inch headspace; seal with 2-piece lids.

WISSAHICKON BRAND

PINEAPPLE

ORANGES

FAMOUS MARION COUNTY CITRUS

PRODUCE OF U. S. A.

PACKED BY O. D. HUFF Jr., GROVES, Inc., McIntosh, Fla.

In the 1930s, sugar broker Victor Perley teamed up with Joseph Musante to develop orange groves in Citra, Florida. Their Wissahickon label was named after a park in Philadelphia. The Pineapple orange is a sweet, early-season orange. O. D. Huff, Jr. was the name of the packer for this fruit. In many instances the packers and grove owners were separate entities, which is reflected in this label.

SUN BAKED

· *Poultry* ·

. . .

Section sponsored by

Missy and John Guentz

Chicken in Honeyed Tomatoes

HEATHER MCPHERSON, *THE ORLANDO SENTINEL*

- 6 boneless, skinless chicken breast halves
  Salt and pepper to taste
- 3 tablespoons olive oil
- 1 small onion, chopped
- 1 clove of garlic, minced
- 1 (28-ounce) can plum tomatoes, drained, chopped
- ½ cup dry white wine
- 6 tablespoons honey
- ½ teaspoon crushed dried thyme leaves
- ½ teaspoon crushed dried tarragon leaves
- 1 cup pitted black olive halves
- 3 tablespoons chopped fresh parsley

Pound the chicken between 2 pieces of waxed paper until flattened. Sprinkle both sides with salt and pepper. Heat the olive oil in a large skillet over medium heat. Add half the chicken. Cook for 3 minutes per side or until brown and cooked through. Remove and keep warm. Repeat with the remaining chicken. Add the onion and garlic to the skillet. Cook for 3 minutes or until tender. Stir in the tomatoes, wine, honey, thyme and tarragon. Simmer for 15 minutes or until thickened, stirring constantly. Return the chicken to the skillet and add olives. Cook, covered, for 3 minutes. Season with salt and pepper to taste. Divide the chicken and sauce evenly between serving plates. Sprinkle with the parsley.

YIELD: 6 SERVINGS

HONEY NUTRITION FACTS

- Most types of honey are about 17 percent moisture. About 98 percent of the remaining solids are carbohydrates.
- One tablespoon of honey contains about 64 calories. Because of its high fructose content, honey has a higher sweetening power than sugar.
- Raw honey contains traces of thiamine, riboflavin, vitamin C, calcium, iron, and manganese. However, most of the honey that consumers buy is not raw. Much of it is strained, pasteurized, thinned, and blended to meet health standards and consumer preferences.
- Honey is a "simple sugar" meaning it's already broken down into glucose and fructose that the human body assimilates without further digestion. Sugar requires digestion to convert it into glucose that the body can use.

Low Country Chicken with Cinnamon-Curried Rice

½ cup raisins
2 medium apples, peeled, cored, finely chopped
½ cup sliced almonds
1 (8-ounce) can water chestnuts, finely chopped
½ cup butter or margarine, melted
1 teaspoon cinnamon, or to taste
2 teaspoons curry powder, or to taste
½ to ¾ cup packed brown sugar
8 boneless, skinless chicken breasts
　 Cinnamon-Curried Rice

Combine the raisins, apples, almonds, water chestnuts, butter, cinnamon, curry powder and brown sugar in a bowl and mix well. Place 1 tablespoon of the apple mixture on each chicken breast. Bring up corners and secure with a wooden pick. Arrange seam side down in a 9x13-inch baking dish. Spoon remaining apple mixture on top of each chicken breast. Bake, tightly covered with foil, at 350 degrees for 35 to 40 minutes, basting at least 2 times with the pan juices. Bake, uncovered, for 5 minutes longer or until slightly brown. Spoon Cinnamon-Curried Rice on a serving platter. Arrange the chicken on top.

Cinnamon-Curried Rice

2½ cups uncooked white rice
3 cups chicken broth
1½ teaspoons curry powder, or to taste
1 teaspoon cinnamon

Combine the rice, chicken broth, curry powder and cinnamon in a saucepan and mix well. Simmer, covered, for 45 minutes or until the liquid has been absorbed.

YIELD: 8 SERVINGS

Chicken Pastry with Mushroom Sauce

4 cups finely chopped cooked chicken
¾ cup finely chopped celery
1 green onion, chopped
¾ cup mayonnaise
2 tablespoons chopped fresh parsley
1 to 2 teaspoons salt
1 sheet puff pastry
　 Melted butter
　 Mushroom Sauce

Combine the chicken, celery, green onion, mayonnaise, parsley and salt in a bowl and mix well. Roll the puff pastry slightly on a lightly floured surface. Spread the chicken mixture over the puff pastry. Roll as for a jelly roll. Place seam side down on a nonstick baking sheet. Brush with melted butter. Bake at 375 degrees for 25 minutes or until brown. Serve with Mushroom Sauce.

Mushroom Sauce

2 cups heavy cream
1 cup sliced fresh mushrooms
½ cup chicken broth
　 Salt and pepper to taste
¼ cup dry sherry

Bring the cream to a boil in a 10-inch skillet. Boil until the cream is reduced to ⅓. Add the mushrooms. Stir in the broth. Simmer for 10 minutes. Season with salt and pepper. Stir in the sherry just before serving.

YIELD: 4 SERVINGS

Baked Chicken Curry

½ cup flour
1 teaspoon salt
¼ teaspoon pepper
12 boneless chicken breast halves
1 tablespoon butter, melted
  Curry Sauce
¾ cup flaked coconut

Combine the flour, salt and pepper in a shallow dish. Add the chicken and coat well. Arrange skin side down in a large baking pan and drizzle with butter. Bake at 450 degrees for 20 minutes. Pour Curry Sauce over the chicken. Sprinkle with coconut. Reduce the oven temperature to 350 degrees. Bake for 40 minutes longer or until the chicken is cooked through.

Curry Sauce

½ cup chopped yellow onion
1 tablespoon curry powder
2 tablespoons applesauce
8 ounces bacon, cut into small pieces
1 tablespoon tomato sauce
1 cup beef consommé
1 teaspoon sugar
¼ cup lemon juice
  Pinch of garlic powder

Combine the onion, curry powder, applesauce, bacon, tomato sauce, consommé, sugar, lemon juice and garlic powder in a saucepan and mix well. Cook over medium heat for 10 to 15 minutes or until the bacon is cooked through, stirring occasionally.

YIELD: 12 SERVINGS

Spicy Chicken Fajitas

1½ teaspoons ground cumin
1½ teaspoons dried oregano
¾ teaspoon salt
¾ teaspoon ground coriander
¾ teaspoon ground cayenne
8 to 10 boneless, skinless chicken breast halves, cut into strips
  Olive oil
2 green bell peppers, sliced
2 medium onions, sliced
  Soft tortillas
  Shredded Cheddar cheese
  Salsa
  Sour cream

Combine the cumin, oregano, salt, coriander and cayenne in a sealable plastic food storage bag and mix well. Add the chicken. Seal the bag and shake well until the chicken is coated. Chill for 30 minutes. Sauté the chicken in olive oil in a skillet until brown. Remove the chicken and keep warm. Add the peppers and onions to the skillet. Sauté until the onions begin to caramelize. Return the chicken to the skillet. Cook until heated through. Stack the tortillas on a microwave-safe plate, placing a damp paper towel between each tortilla. Microwave for 1 minute. Place a portion of the chicken mixture in each tortilla. Sprinkle with cheese. Add salsa and sour cream. Roll up to enclose the filling. Serve immediately.

YIELD: 4 OR 5 SERVINGS

Orange Fried Chicken with Jalapeño Honey Sauce

5   cups buttermilk
1   tablespoon minced garlic
1   medium jalapeño, minced
5   pounds chicken breast halves
1½ cups flour
1   tablespoon grated orange peel
1   teaspoon salt
½   teaspoon dried basil
¼   teaspoon cayenne
     Vegetable oil for frying
1   tablespoon minced garlic
     Jalapeño slices
     Jalapeño Honey Sauce

Combine the buttermilk, 1 tablespoon of the garlic and jalapeño in a large bowl. Add the chicken. Chill, covered, in the refrigerator for 2 hours. Combine the flour, 1 tablespoon orange peel, salt, basil and cayenne in a shallow dish and mix well. Drain the chicken, discarding the marinade. Coat chicken in the flour mixture, shaking off the excess. Place on waxed paper. Let stand at room temperature for 20 minutes. Heat ¼ to ½ inch oil in a heavy 12-inch skillet over medium heat until the oil sizzles when sprinkled with water. Stir in 1 tablespoon garlic. Add the chicken in batches. Cook for 6 minutes per side or until golden brown. Drain on paper towels. Arrange on a serving platter. Garnish with jalapeño slices. Serve with Jalapeño Honey Sauce.

Note: Substitute orange juice for the buttermilk in the marinade for a stronger orange flavor.

Jalapeño Honey Sauce

½   cup butter or margarine
1   medium jalapeño, minced
1   teaspoon grated orange peel
½   cup honey

Melt the butter in a medium saucepan over low heat. Add jalapeño and orange peel. Cook for 1 minute. Stir in honey. Bring to a boil and reduce the heat. Simmer for 10 minutes. Cover and keep warm.

YIELD: 6 TO 8 SERVINGS

Basil Grilled Chicken

1   teaspoon coarsely ground pepper
4   boneless, skinless chicken breast
     halves, skinned
⅓   cup melted butter or margarine
⅓   cup chopped fresh basil
½   cup butter or margarine, softened
2   tablespoons minced fresh basil
2   tablespoons grated Parmesan cheese
½   teaspoon minced garlic
¼   teaspoon each salt and pepper
     Sprigs of fresh basil (optional)

Press the pepper into the chicken. Combine ⅓ cup melted butter and ⅓ cup basil in a small dish and mix well. Reserve ½ of the butter mixture. Brush the chicken with the remaining butter mixture. Combine ½ cup butter, 2 tablespoons basil, Parmesan cheese, garlic, salt and pepper in a small mixer bowl. Beat at low speed until smooth. Spoon into a small serving bowl. Place the chicken on a grill rack. Grill over medium-hot coals for 8 to 10 minutes on each side, basting frequently with the reserved butter mixture. Serve with the basil butter. Garnish with sprigs of basil.

YIELD: 4 SERVINGS

Tipsy Chicken

2 tablespoons chopped fresh rosemary
½ cup lemon juice
2 tablespoons Dijon mustard
1 teaspoon (scant) salt
1 teaspoon (heaping) pepper
1 cup olive oil
20 boneless, skinless chicken breast halves
10 shallots
6 cloves of garlic, chopped
½ cup olive oil
5 tablespoons (heaping) chopped fresh rosemary
1½ pounds fresh shiitake mushrooms, sliced
2 ounces dry mixed wild mushrooms, hydrated, chopped
2 ounces sun-dried tomatoes, hydrated, chopped
5 tablespoons flour
6 cups rich beef stock
½ cup whipping cream
½ cup whiskey, or to taste
Salt and pepper to taste

Whisk the rosemary, lemon juice, Dijon mustard, 1 teaspoon salt and 1 teaspoon pepper in a small bowl. Add 1 cup olive oil gradually, whisking constantly. Arrange the chicken in a shallow dish. Pour the marinade over chicken. Marinate, covered, in the refrigerator for 1 hour or longer. Sauté the shallots and garlic in ¼ cup of the olive oil in a large skillet until golden brown. Stir in the remaining ¼ cup olive oil, rosemary, shiitake mushrooms, wild mushrooms and tomatoes. Sprinkle with the flour and add the beef stock gradually, stirring constantly. Stir in the cream, whiskey, salt and pepper. Bring to a boil and reduce the heat. Simmer for 8 minutes. Remove from the heat and add more whiskey, if desired. Drain the chicken, discarding the marinade. Place on a grill rack. Grill over hot coals until cooked through. Arrange on a serving platter and top with the sauce.

YIELD: 12 TO 20 SERVINGS

Chicken Laura

8 boneless, skinless chicken breast halves
6 cloves of garlic, minced
2 tablespoons dried oregano
Kosher salt to taste
Ground pepper to taste
¼ cup wine vinegar
¼ cup slightly drained capers
3 bay leaves
½ cup packed light brown sugar
½ cup white wine
2 tablespoons minced cilantro

Combine the chicken, garlic, oregano, salt, pepper, vinegar, capers and bay leaves in a sealable plastic food storage bag and seal. Marinate in the refrigerator for 6 to 8 hours. Drain the chicken, reserving the marinade and discarding the bay leaves. Place the chicken in a single layer in a glass baking dish. Spoon the reserved marinade over the chicken. Sprinkle with brown sugar. Pour the wine over the top. Bake at 350 degrees for 50 to 60 minutes or until the chicken is cooked through, basting frequently. Sprinkle with cilantro just before serving.

YIELD: 8 SERVINGS

Savory Grilled Chicken

¾   cup vegetable oil
⅓   cup soy sauce
3   tablespoons Worcestershire sauce
¼   cup red wine vinegar
    Juice of 1 lemon
1   tablespoon dry mustard
1   teaspoon salt
2   tablespoons minced fresh parsley
1   clove of garlic, crushed
2   whole frying chickens, cut into pieces

Combine the vegetable oil, soy sauce, Worcestershire sauce, vinegar, lemon juice, dry mustard, salt, parsley and garlic in a large sealable plastic food storage bag and mix well. Add the chicken pieces. Marinate, covered, in the refrigerator for 6 to 24 hours. Drain the chicken, reserving the marinade. Bring the reserved marinade to a boil in a small saucepan. Boil for 3 minutes. Remove from the heat. Place the chicken on a grill rack. Grill over medium-hot coals for 15 to 20 minutes or until cooked through, basting frequently with the reserved marinade.

YIELD: 6 SERVINGS

Lemon Basil Grilled Chicken

½   cup vegetable oil
¼   cup lemon juice
2   tablespoons white wine vinegar
1   teaspoon grated lemon peel
1   tablespoon dried basil, or 2 tablespoons fresh basil
2   cloves of garlic, minced
½   teaspoon salt
¼   teaspoon freshly ground pepper
4   boneless, skinless chicken breast halves

Combine the vegetable oil, lemon juice, vinegar, lemon peel, basil, garlic, salt and pepper in a shallow dish and mix well. Add the chicken, turning once to coat both sides. Marinate, covered, in the refrigerator for 30 to 45 minutes, turning once. Drain the chicken, discarding the marinade. Place the chicken on a grill rack. Grill 3 to 4 inches from the hot coals for 3 to 5 minutes on each side or until cooked through.

YIELD: 4 SERVINGS

Make Black Eagle's Barbecue Sauce by mixing ½ cup butter or margarine, 1 cup white vinegar, juice and rind of 1 lemon, 1 cup tomato juice or vegetable juice cocktail, 1 teaspoon dry mustard, 2 tablespoons Worcestershire sauce, 1 teaspoon crushed red pepper, or to taste, ⅛ teaspoon black pepper and 1 tablespoon Tabasco sauce in a saucepan. Bring to a boil and reduce the heat. Simmer for 30 minutes, stirring occasionally. Use with pork or poultry.

Mediterranean Grilled Chicken with Dried Tomato Pesto

½ cup lemon juice
¼ cup olive oil
4 cloves of garlic, minced
½ teaspoon salt
6 boneless, skinless chicken breast halves
4 ounces sun-dried tomatoes
⅓ cup olive oil
¼ cup grated Parmesan cheese
¼ cup chopped toasted pine nuts or walnuts
¼ cup minced fresh basil
½ cup water
2 cloves of garlic, minced

Combine the lemon juice, ¼ cup olive oil, 4 cloves of garlic and salt in a shallow dish and mix well. Add the chicken, turning to coat. Marinate, covered, in the refrigerator for 8 to 10 hours, turning occasionally. Bring the tomatoes with water to cover to a boil in a small saucepan. Cook for 5 minutes; drain. Process the tomatoes, ⅓ cup olive oil, Parmesan cheese, pine nuts, basil, ½ cup water and 2 cloves of garlic in a blender until smooth. Drain the chicken, discarding the marinade. Place the chicken on a grill rack. Grill for 9 to 10 minutes on each side or until cooked through. Spoon the pesto over the chicken to serve.

YIELD: 6 SERVINGS

Grilled Orange Chicken Drumsticks Tandoori

¾ cup fresh orange juice
½ cup plain yogurt
1 large clove of garlic, minced
¼ teaspoon cayenne
¼ cup vegetable oil
12 chicken drumsticks
½ cup sweet orange marmalade
2 tablespoons fresh orange juice
2 tablespoons minced fresh rosemary leaves
Pinch of salt

Combine ¾ cup orange juice, yogurt, garlic and cayenne in a bowl and mix well. Whisk in the vegetable oil. Arrange the chicken in a shallow dish. Pour the marinade over the chicken. Marinate, covered, in the refrigerator for 1 to 3 hours. Combine the marmalade, 2 tablespoons orange juice, rosemary and salt in a saucepan. Cook over medium-low heat until the marmalade is melted, stirring occasionally. Cover and keep warm. Drain the chicken, reserving the marinade. Bring the reserved marinade to a boil in a small saucepan. Boil for 3 minutes. Remove from the heat. Place the chicken on a grill rack. Grill over hot coals until cooked through, turning and basting frequently with the cooked reserved marinade. Brush the chicken with the orange glaze. Grill for 3 minutes longer.

YIELD: 12 SERVINGS

Sesame Chicken Kabobs

6	boneless, skinless chicken breast halves
¼	cup plus 2 tablespoons teriyaki sauce
¼	cup soy sauce
2	tablespoons sesame seeds
3	tablespoons vegetable oil
2	tablespoons dark sesame oil
2	medium red bell peppers, cut into 1-inch pieces
2	medium yellow bell peppers, cut into 1-inch pieces
4	small purple onions, cut into wedges
	Sprigs of fresh basil (optional)

Cut the chicken into 1-inch pieces. Arrange in a shallow dish. Combine the teriyaki sauce, soy sauce, sesame seeds, vegetable oil and sesame oil in a small bowl and mix well. Pour over the chicken. Marinate, covered, in the refrigerator for 3 hours. Soak six 12-inch wooden skewers in water for 30 minutes or longer. Drain the chicken, reserving the marinade. Bring the reserved marinade to a boil in a small saucepan. Boil for 3 minutes. Remove from the heat. Thread the chicken, peppers and onions alternately onto the skewers. Place on a grill rack. Grill over medium-hot coals for 3 to 5 minutes on each side or until the chicken is cooked through, basting frequently with cooked reserved marinade. Garnish with sprigs of basil.

YIELD: 6 SERVINGS

To prepare fresh orange juice for freezing, squeeze the juice into a pitcher, being careful not to get the oil from the rind. Pour into freezer containers, leaving 1 inch headspace and seal. Label and date the containers. Freeze until firm. Store in the freezer for 3 to 4 months.

Note: The Valencia orange produces the best juice for freezing. To prepare fresh grapefruit juice for freezing, prepare as above adding ½ cup sugar and ¾ teaspoon crystalline ascorbic acid for each 4 quarts of juice.

Teriyaki Kabobs

1 cup soy sauce
½ cup packed brown sugar
1 cup pineapple juice
½ cup vinegar
4 cloves of garlic, minced, or 2 teaspoons garlic powder
3 pounds chicken cubes
2 fresh pineapples, cubed

Mix the soy sauce, brown sugar, pineapple juice, vinegar and garlic in a large bowl and mix well. Add the chicken, stirring to coat. Marinate, covered, in the refrigerator for 6 to 7 hours. Drain the chicken, reserving the marinade. Bring the reserved marinade to a boil in a small saucepan. Boil for 3 minutes. Remove from the heat. Thread the chicken and fresh pineapple alternately onto skewers. Place on a grill rack. Grill over hot coals until the chicken is cooked through, turning and basting frequently with the cooked reserved marinade.

YIELD: 6 SERVINGS

To prepare Puerto Rican Seasoning, crush 1 small clove of garlic, peeled, 1 whole black peppercorn and ¼ teaspoon dried oregano in a mortar with a pestle. Add 1 teaspoon salt, 1 teaspoon olive oil and ½ teaspoon vinegar and mix well. Use to rub inside and outside of turkey. Chill, covered, for several hours before roasting.

Garlic Herb Chicken

1 (17-ounce) package frozen puff pastry, thawed
1 (4-ounce) container garlic and spice cheese spread
6 boneless, skinless chicken breast halves
1 egg, beaten
1 tablespoon water

Unfold the pastry sheets. Roll each into a 12x14-inch rectangle. Cut 1 sheet into four 6x7-inch rectangles. Cut the remaining sheet into two 6x7-inch rectangles and one 6x12-inch rectangle. Set the large rectangle aside. Spread the 6 small rectangles with cheese, leaving 1 inch around the edges. Place a chicken breast in the center of each. Fold pastry around the chicken, sealing all seams. Place each bundle seam side down on a lightly greased baking sheet. Cut the remaining large rectangle into twenty-four ¼-inch strips. Braid 2 strips together and place crosswise on a bundle; braid 2 additional strips and place lengthwise on the bundle. Trim excess and tuck edges under. Repeat with the remaining strips and chicken bundles. Chill, covered, in the refrigerator for up to 2 hours, if desired. Brush bundles with a mixture of egg and water. Place on the lower oven rack. Bake at 400 degrees for 25 minutes or until the bundles are golden brown and the chicken is cooked through.

YIELD: 6 SERVINGS

Cheese-Stuffed Chicken in Phyllo

8	boneless, skinless chicken breast halves
	Salt and pepper to taste
4	cups chopped fresh spinach
1	cup chopped onion
2	tablespoons olive oil or vegetable oil
4	ounces cream cheese, cubed, softened
1	cup shredded mozzarella cheese
½	cup crumbled feta cheese
½	cup shredded Cheddar cheese
1	egg yolk, beaten
1	tablespoon flour
½	teaspoon ground nutmeg
½	teaspoon ground cumin
16	sheets phyllo dough (14x18-inch rectangles)
⅔	cup melted margarine or butter

Pound each chicken breast half between 2 sheets of heavy plastic wrap with the flat side of a meat mallet until ⅛ inch thick. Season with salt and pepper. Sauté the spinach and onion in olive oil in a large skillet until the onion is tender. Remove from the heat. Stir in the cream cheese until blended. Add the mozzarella cheese, feta cheese, Cheddar cheese, egg yolk, flour, nutmeg and cumin and mix well. Place about ¼ cup of the spinach mixture on each chicken breast half. Roll up as for a jelly roll. Place 1 sheet of phyllo on a work surface, keeping the remaining sheets covered with a damp towel to prevent drying out. Brush with some of the margarine. Place another phyllo sheet on top of the first and brush with some of the margarine. Place 1 chicken roll seam side down near a short side of the phyllo and roll chicken and phyllo over once to cover the chicken. Fold in the long sides and continue rolling from the short side. Place in a shallow baking pan. Repeat with the remaining chicken, phyllo sheets and some of the margarine. Brush with the remaining margarine. Bake, uncovered, at 350 degrees for 30 to 35 minutes or until the chicken is cooked through.

YIELD: 8 SERVINGS

Rosemary Walnut Chicken

1	tablespoon olive oil
½	cup coarsely chopped walnuts
½	teaspoon rosemary
½	clove of garlic, minced
¼	teaspoon salt
¼	cup flour
½	teaspoon salt
¼	teaspoon pepper
6	boneless, skinless chicken breast halves
3	tablespoons olive oil
2	cloves of garlic, minced
1	tablespoon rosemary
1	tablespoon thyme
2	cups dry white wine
2	cups chicken stock
¼	cup balsamic vinegar
½	cup crumbled feta cheese
¼	cup thinly sliced green onions

Heat 1 tablespoon olive oil in a small skillet. Add the walnuts, ½ teaspoon rosemary, ½ clove of garlic and ¼ teaspoon salt. Sauté for 3 to 4 minutes or until the walnuts are toasted. Mix the flour, ½ teaspoon salt and pepper in a shallow dish. Dredge the chicken in the flour mixture. Heat 3 tablespoons olive oil in a large skillet over medium-high heat. Add the chicken. Cook for 3 minutes on each side or until light brown. Remove the chicken to a warm platter and keep warm. Reduce the heat to medium. Add 2 cloves of garlic, 1 tablespoon rosemary and thyme. Cook for 2 minutes. Stir in the wine, chicken stock and vinegar. Simmer for 10 to 12 minutes or until thickened, stirring occasionally. Return the chicken to the skillet. Simmer for 10 to 12 minutes or until the chicken is cooked through. Sprinkle the feta cheese over the chicken. Place the chicken on individual serving plates. Spoon the sauce over the chicken. Sprinkle with green onions and toasted walnuts. Serve immediately.

YIELD: 6 SERVINGS

Chicken Marsala

2 boneless, skinless chicken breasts
2 tablespoons butter
6 mushrooms, sliced
½ cup marsala or dry white wine
⅛ teaspoon salt
 Dash of salt and pepper
1 teaspoon lemon juice
2 teaspoons fresh chopped parsley

Roll or pound each piece of chicken between 2 sheets of waxed paper until ¼ inch thick using a rolling pin or meat mallet. Melt the butter in a medium skillet. Add the chicken. Cook over low heat for 3 to 4 minutes on each side or until brown and cooked through. Remove the chicken to a serving platter. Add the mushrooms, wine, salt, pepper and lemon juice to the skillet. Cook until the mushrooms are tender, stirring occasionally. Pour over the chicken. Sprinkle with parsley.

YIELD: 2 SERVINGS

To prepare East-West Marinade, combine 6 tablespoons soy sauce, 2 tablespoons vinegar, ½ teaspoon sugar (optional), 2 cloves of garlic, 6 tablespoons catsup, ½ cup vegetable oil and ½ teaspoon pepper in a saucepan and mix well. Bring to a boil and reduce the heat. Simmer until of the desired consistency. Use to marinate meat or chicken for 30 minutes to overnight.

Parmesan Chicken Fingers

⅓ cup buttermilk, or ⅓ cup milk plus 2 teaspoons vinegar
1 large clove of garlic, chopped
¾ teaspoon Tabasco sauce
1 pound boneless, skinless chicken breasts, cut into ¼-inch strips
¾ cup saltine cracker crumbs
1 teaspoon paprika
½ teaspoon salt
2 tablespoons grated Parmesan cheese

Combine the buttermilk, garlic and Tabasco sauce in a large bowl and mix well. Add the chicken, stirring until evenly coated. Refrigerate, covered, for 30 minutes. Line a baking sheet with foil and spray with nonstick cooking spray. Combine the cracker crumbs, paprika, salt and 1 tablespoon of the Parmesan cheese in a shallow dish. Drain the chicken. Place the chicken in the cracker crumb mixture, turning to coat both sides. Arrange on the prepared baking sheet. Sprinkle with remaining 1 tablespoon Parmesan cheese. Bake at 450 degrees for 8 to 10 minutes or until cooked through.

Note: Chicken can be frozen up to 1 month ahead. Freeze the coated chicken on a baking sheet. Place in a sealable freezer bag and seal. To bake, place frozen chicken on a foil-lined baking sheet and bake at 450 degrees for 12 minutes or until cooked through. These are great dipped in your favorite salad dressing.

YIELD: 4 SERVINGS

Pecan-Crusted Chicken Breasts

¼ **cup butter**
3 **tablespoons Dijon mustard**
4 **boneless, skinless chicken breast halves**
1 **cup finely chopped pecans**
¼ **cup butter**
   Toasted pecan halves
   Mustard Sauce

Melt ¼ cup butter in a saucepan. Whisk in the mustard. Dip the chicken in the mustard mixture. Place in the chopped pecans, turning to coat well. Sauté the chicken in ¼ cup of butter in a skillet until light brown on both sides. Place in a greased baking dish. Bake at 350 degrees for 15 to 20 minutes or until cooked through. Drizzle with Mustard Sauce. Garnish with pecan halves.

Mustard Sauce

1   **tablespoon butter**
⅔   **cup sour cream**
1   **tablespoon Dijon mustard**
    Salt and pepper to taste

Melt the butter in a saucepan. Whisk in the sour cream, mustard, salt and pepper. Cook until heated through; do not boil.

YIELD: 4 SERVINGS

Country Chicken Piccata

¼ **cup milk**
1 **egg, lightly beaten**
⅓ **cup flour**
⅓ **cup crushed cornflakes**
¼ **teaspoon salt**
   Pinch of pepper
4 **boneless, skinless chicken breast halves**
6 **tablespoons butter**
1 **teaspoon minced fresh garlic**
2 **tablespoons lemon juice**
1 **cup (1-inch) green onion slices**
1 **cup fresh mushrooms halves**
   Fresh lemon slices
   Sprigs of fresh parsley

Combine the milk and egg in a shallow dish and mix well. Combine the flour, cornflakes, salt and pepper in a shallow dish and mix well. Pound the chicken between 2 sheets of waxed paper until ¼ inch thick using a meat mallet. Dip the chicken into the milk mixture and then into the flour mixture, turning to coat. Melt 4 tablespoons of the butter in a large skillet. Add the garlic and chicken. Cook over medium heat for 5 to 6 minutes or until golden brown and cooked through, turning occasionally. Place on a serving platter and keep warm. Add the remaining 2 tablespoons butter to the skillet. Heat until the butter melts. Stir in the lemon juice. Add the green onions and mushrooms. Cook until heated through, stirring occasionally. Spoon over the chicken. Garnish with lemon slices and sprigs of parsley. Serve with fresh herbed linguini.

YIELD: 4 SERVINGS

Crunchy Fried Chicken Strips with Creole Mustard Sauce

1   cup flour
1   teaspoon onion powder
1   teaspoon garlic powder
½   teaspoon pepper
4   cups Cap'n Crunch cereal
3   cups cornflakes
1   egg
1   cup milk
2   pounds boneless, skinless chicken breasts, cut into 1-ounce tenders
    Vegetable oil for frying
    Creole Mustard Sauce

Mix the flour, onion powder, garlic powder and pepper in a shallow bowl. Crush the Cap'n Crunch cereal and cornflakes in a shallow bowl. Beat the egg and milk in a bowl. Dredge the chicken in the seasoned flour until well coated and shake off the excess flour mixture. Dip into the egg mixture, coating well. Dredge in the cereal mixture until well coated. Heat vegetable oil to 325 degrees in a large skillet. Add the coated chicken carefully to the hot vegetable oil. Fry for 3 to 5 minutes or until cooked through and golden brown. Remove to paper towels to drain. Serve with Creole Mustard Sauce.

Creole Mustard Sauce

1   cup mayonnaise
¼   cup Creole mustard or Dijon mustard
1   tablespoon prepared mustard
1   tablespoon prepared horseradish
½   teaspoon cider vinegar
    Dash of Worcestershire sauce
1   teaspoon red wine vinegar
1   teaspoon water
½   teaspoon cayenne
½   teaspoon salt
1   tablespoon (¼-inch) sliced green onions
1   tablespoon oil-packed crushed garlic
1   teaspoon finely chopped green bell pepper
1   teaspoon finely chopped celery
1   teaspoon finely chopped onion

Combine the mayonnaise, Creole mustard, prepared mustard, horseradish, cider vinegar, Worcestershire sauce, red wine vinegar, water, cayenne and salt in a bowl and mix well. Stir in the green onions, garlic, green pepper, celery and onion.

YIELD: 8 SERVINGS

For Lime Marinade for Grilled Chicken, combine ½ cup fresh lime juice, ¼ cup vegetable oil, 2 tablespoons dark brown sugar, 2 tablespoons minced onion, 2 garlic cloves and salt and freshly ground pepper to taste in a bowl and mix well. Use to marinate chicken in the refrigerator for 6 to 8 hours before grilling.

Honey Curry Chicken

¼ **cup melted margarine**
¼ **cup honey**
¼ **cup prepared or spicy brown mustard**
¼ **teaspoon salt**
1 **teaspoon curry powder**
6 **boneless, skinless chicken breast halves**

Combine the margarine, honey, mustard, salt and curry powder in a bowl and mix well. Dip the chicken into the mustard mixture. Place in a greased baking dish. Bring the remaining sauce to a boil in a saucepan. Cook for 3 minutes, stirring constantly. Remove from the heat. Bake the chicken at 375 degrees for 1 hour or until the chicken is cooked through, basting with the cooked sauce.

YIELD: 4 TO 6 SERVINGS

Orange Cornish Game Hens

4 **Cornish game hens**
2 **oranges, cut into quarters**
1 **bunch of rosemary, stems removed**
 Salt and pepper to taste

Heat the grill until the coals are almost white, adding hickory chips for flavor. Rinse the hens and pat dry. Squeeze the juice of 4 orange quarters over the hens. Sprinkle with ½ of the rosemary, salt and pepper. Place the 4 squeezed orange quarters inside the hens. Season inside the hens with the remaining rosemary, salt and pepper. Place the hens breast side up on a grill rack. Grill, covered, for 15 minutes or until cooked through, squeezing remaining orange quarters over the hens and placing them inside the hens as they are used. Cut into halves and serve over wild rice.

YIELD: 8 SERVINGS

Rock Cornish Hens with Sherry Sauce

1 **(6-ounce) package wild rice**
½ **cup grated onion**
½ **cup chopped green bell pepper**
½ **cup margarine**
2 **teaspoons salt**
½ **teaspoon sage**
½ **teaspoon pepper**
¼ **teaspoon tarragon**
¼ **cup cream sherry**
6 **Cornish game hens, thawed**
 Sherry Sauce

Cook the wild rice using the package directions. Sauté the onion and green pepper in the margarine in a skillet until the onion is light brown. Stir in salt, sage, pepper, tarragon and sherry. Add the rice and mix well. Stuff the hens with the rice mixture. Arrange in a shallow baking pan. Bake, tightly covered, at 425 degrees for 1 hour. Bake, uncovered, for 30 minutes or until cooked through. Serve with Sherry Sauce.

Sherry Sauce

¼ **cup butter**
¼ **cup flour**
1 **teaspoon paprika**
¾ **cup cream sherry**
¾ **cup chicken broth**
1 **cup sour cream**

Melt the butter in a saucepan. Add the flour, stirring until smooth. Stir in the paprika. Add the sherry and broth gradually, whisking constantly. Cook until thickened, whisking constantly. Whisk in the sour cream.

YIELD: 6 SERVINGS

Caruso's
BLUE BIRD
BRAND

REG. U.S. PAT. OFF.

SOUTHERN FRUIT DISTRIBUTORS INC.
GROWERS, PACKERS AND CANNERS
ORLANDO, FLORIDA

*The Blue Bird Company was owned and operated by four generations
of the Caruso family in Orlando between 1926 and 1986.
This label is patented and is still in use today. The colors on crate labels
indicated the grades of fruit. Blue meant top grade, red meant middle grade,
and yellow or green indicated lower grade fruit.*

SUNFISH

Seafood

...

Section sponsored by

Downeast Orvis Winter Park

Grilled Cilantro Lime Shrimp

EXECUTIVE CHEF ALAN GOULD, HYATT REGENCY
GRAND CYPRESS

½	**cup orange marmalade**
¼	**cup fresh lime juice**
1	**teaspoon minced garlic**
3	**tablespoons chopped fresh cilantro**
3	**tablespoons olive oil**
1	**tablespoon teriyaki sauce**
¼	**teaspoon red pepper flakes**
20	**large shrimp, peeled, deveined**

Combine the orange marmalade, lime juice, garlic, cilantro, olive oil, teriyaki sauce and red pepper flakes in a bowl and mix well. Reserve ½ cup of the marmalade mixture. Add the shrimp to the remaining marmalade mixture. Marinate, covered, in the refrigerator for 1 hour. Drain, discarding the marinade. Place the shrimp on a grill rack. Grill until the shrimp turn pink. Place 2 tablespoons of the reserved marmalade mixture into each of 4 ramekins. Place each ramekin in the center of a serving plate. Arrange the grilled shrimp around the ramekin.

YIELD: 4 SERVINGS

Follow these juicing tips to gain the most juice from your lemons or limes.
- Room-temperature lemons or limes will yield more juice than those that are chilled.
- **Cooking the lemon or lime in a microwave for a few seconds before squeezing will enable you to extract more juice.**
- **Using the palm of your hand, roll the lemon or lime around on the countertop a few times before squeezing.**
- **Pierce the skin of the lemon or lime with a wooden pick if just a few drops of juice are needed. Store the fruit by reinserting the wooden pick, placing in a sealable plastic bag, and chilling.**

Charcoal-Grilled Shrimp in the Shell

2	pounds medium shrimp, unpeeled
1	cup vegetable oil
½	cup lemon juice
¼	cup soy sauce
½	teaspoon salt, or to taste
1	tablespoon chopped onion
2	tablespoons parsley flakes
¼	cup crushed tarragon
1	teaspoon dried basil

Using scissors, cut through the shell at the back of each raw shrimp and remove the black vein. Rinse the unpeeled shrimp thoroughly and drain on paper towels. Place in a large bowl. Combine the vegetable oil, lemon juice, soy sauce, salt, onion, parsley flakes, tarragon and basil in a bowl and mix well. Pour over the shrimp. Marinate, covered, in the refrigerator for 8 to 10 hours, turning the shrimp several times. Drain the shrimp, reserving the marinade. Bring the reserved marinade to a boil in a small saucepan. Boil for 3 minutes. Remove from the heat. Place the shrimp in a basket grill. Grill 4 inches from the heat source for 3 to 4 minutes per side or until the shells are slightly charred, basting frequently with the cooked reserved marinade.

Note: Place the grilled shrimp in a styrofoam chest lined with foil while the remaining shrimp are being grilled. Allow about 18 shrimp per serving.

YIELD: 2 OR 3 SERVINGS

Grilled Lemon Prawns

1	cup olive oil
1	tablespoon dried oregano
1	tablespoon dried thyme
2	teaspoons freshly grated lemon zest
2	teaspoons coarse salt
2	teaspoons freshly ground pepper
24	prawns or jumbo shrimp
3	tablespoons fresh lemon juice

Combine the olive oil, oregano, thyme, lemon zest, salt and pepper in a large bowl. Add the prawns and toss until well coated. Marinate, covered, in the refrigerator for 1 to 10 hours. Stir in the lemon juice. Let stand at room temperature for 30 minutes. Drain the prawns in a fine sieve. Place the prawns on a grill rack. Grill 4 inches from the hot coals for 3 minutes on each side or until the prawns turn pink. Serve with lemon wedges.

YIELD: 8 SERVINGS

Shrimp and Pepper Kabobs

1   **pound large fresh shrimp, unpeeled**
1   **cup lemon juice**
¾   **cup vegetable oil**
½   **cup soy sauce**
¼   **cup plus 2 tablespoons chopped fresh parsley**
⅓   **cup finely chopped onion**
1   **teaspoon pepper**
2   **cloves of garlic, minced**
2   **medium green bell peppers, cut into pieces**
2   **medium red bell peppers, cut into pieces**
    Hot cooked rice

Peel the shrimp and devein, leaving the tails intact. Arrange the shrimp in a large shallow dish. Mix the lemon juice, vegetable oil, soy sauce, parsley, onion, pepper and garlic in a medium bowl. Reserve ½ of the marinade. Pour the remaining marinade over the shrimp. Marinate, covered, in the refrigerator for 4 hours. Drain the shrimp, discarding the marinade. Thread the shrimp onto four 12-inch skewers alternately with the green and red peppers. Place on a grill rack. Grill over medium coals for 3 to 4 minutes on each side or until the shrimp turn pink, basting with the reserved marinade. Serve over hot cooked rice.

YIELD: 4 SERVINGS

Fired-Up Shrimp and Scallops

1   **pound large shrimp, peeled, deveined**
1   **pound scallops**
1   **large onion, cut into bite-size pieces**
2   **cups Catalina French salad dressing**
2   **tablespoons Worcestershire sauce**
2   **teaspoons garlic powder**
2   **teaspoons pepper**
2   **drops of Tabasco sauce**

Place the shrimp, scallops and onion in a large container or sealable plastic bag. Combine the salad dressing, Worcestershire sauce, garlic powder, pepper and Tabasco sauce in a bowl and mix well. Pour over the seafood, covering completely. Marinate, covered, in the refrigerator for 1 to 10 hours. Drain the seafood, reserving the marinade. Bring the reserved marinade to a boil in a saucepan. Boil for 2 to 3 minutes and remove from the heat. Thread the shrimp, scallops and onion onto skewers. Cover the grill rack with foil and punch several holes in the foil with a fork. Place the skewers on the prepared grill rack. Grill, covered, for 20 minutes or until the shrimp turn pink and the scallops are tender, basting with the cooked marinade.

YIELD: 2 SERVINGS

Black and Blue Shrimp

1 (15-ounce) can Italian tomatoes
1 medium onion, chopped
1 teaspoon basil
1 teaspoon oregano
  Tabasco sauce to taste
12 ounces fettuccini
1 tablespoon olive oil
2 medium zucchini, julienned
  Dried basil to taste
2 tablespoons olive oil
72 shrimp, peeled, deveined
  Creole Seasoning to taste
2 ounces blue cheese, crumbled

Combine the tomatoes, onion, 1 teaspoon basil, oregano and Tabasco sauce in a small saucepan and mix well. Cook until thickened to the desired consistency, stirring frequently. Cook the fettuccini using the package directions and adding 1 tablespoon olive oil. Sauté the zucchini with basil in 2 tablespoons olive oil in a skillet until tender. Remove the zucchini to a bowl using a slotted spoon, reserving the oil in the skillet. Sprinkle the shrimp with Creole Seasoning to taste. Add to the reserved oil in the skillet. Sauté until the shrimp turn pink. Drain the fettuccini and place in a large serving bowl. Pour the tomato sauce over the fettuccini. Arrange the shrimp and zucchini over the sauce. Sprinkle with the blue cheese.

Creole Seasoning

⅓ cup salt
⅓ cup paprika
¼ cup granulated garlic
¼ cup black pepper
2 tablespoons cayenne or red pepper
2 tablespoons dried thyme
2 tablespoons dried oregano
3 tablespoons onion powder

Combine the salt, paprika, garlic, black pepper, cayenne, thyme, oregano and onion powder in a bowl and mix well.

YIELD: 4 TO 6 SERVINGS

Use this fast and easy trick when zesting citrus peel. Cover the zest side of the grater with plastic wrap. Grate the fruit over the plastic wrap. Most of the zest will remain on the plastic wrap. Remove the plastic wrap and shake the zest onto a plate. Also, if you are using the fruit for the zest and juice, always grate the zest first and then squeeze the juice.

Shrimp Creole

1	tablespoon flour
1	tablespoon bacon drippings
2	onions, minced
2	cloves of garlic, crushed
1	green bell pepper, minced
2	tablespoons minced parsley
2	tablespoons olive oil
1	(28-ounce) can chopped tomatoes
1	teaspoon salt
¼	teaspoon red pepper
2	bay leaves
⅓	teaspoon celery seeds
¼	teaspoon dried thyme
2	teaspoons Worcestershire sauce
2	pounds shrimp, peeled, deveined

Brown the flour in the bacon drippings in a skillet over low heat, stirring constantly. Sauté the onions, garlic, green pepper and parsley in the olive oil in a skillet until the onions are slightly brown. Stir in the tomatoes, browned flour, salt, red pepper, bay leaves, celery seeds, thyme and Worcestershire sauce. Cook, covered, over low heat for 30 minutes, stirring frequently. Add the shrimp. Cook, covered, over low heat for 30 minutes, stirring frequently. Discard the bay leaves before serving.

YIELD: 4 TO 6 SERVINGS

Shrimp-Stuffed Eggplant

1	(1½-pound) eggplant
¼	cup chopped onion
1	tablespoon butter
1	pound cooked shrimp, peeled, devined
¼	cup fine dry bread crumbs
1	egg yolk
1	teaspoon salt
2	teaspoons chili powder
¼	teaspoon pepper
⅛	teaspoon garlic powder
¾	cup soft bread crumbs
2	tablespoons melted butter

Rinse the eggplant. Cut the eggplant into halves lengthwise. Place in water to cover in a saucepan. Parboil for 15 minutes and drain. Scoop the pulp from the eggplant into a bowl, leaving a ½-inch edge and forming a shell. Reserve the eggplant shells. Chop the eggplant pulp finely. Sauté the onion in 1 tablespoon butter in a skillet until transparent. Cut the shrimp into small pieces. Add the sautéed onion, shrimp, dry bread crumbs, egg yolk, salt, chili powder, pepper and garlic powder to the eggplant pulp and mix well. Spoon into the reserved eggplant shells. Place in a baking dish. Toss the soft bread crumbs with 2 tablespoons melted butter in a bowl. Sprinkle over the eggplant. Bake at 350 degrees for 35 to 40 minutes or until the crumbs are brown.

YIELD: 6 SERVINGS

Greek Shrimp Feta

2	cups chopped onions
2	cloves of garlic, minced
2	tablespoons butter
2	tablespoons olive oil
4	cups chopped, peeled, seeded fresh tomatoes
1	tablespoon fresh minced dill, or 1 teaspoon dried dillweed
1	tablespoon fresh minced basil, or 1 teaspoon dried basil
1	teaspoon dry mustard
1	teaspoon sugar
½	cup chopped fresh parsley
½	teaspoon pepper
2	pounds medium shrimp, peeled, deveined
½	cup white wine
8	ounces feta cheese, crumbled

Sauté the onions and garlic in the butter and olive oil in a large skillet until golden brown. Stir in the tomatoes, dill, basil, dry mustard, sugar, parsley and pepper. Simmer for 5 minutes. Add the shrimp and wine. Simmer for 3 minutes or until the shrimp turn pink, stirring constantly. Do not overcook. Turn off the heat. Sprinkle the cheese over the top. Cover and let stand for 5 minutes or until the cheese is slightly melted. Serve with crusty bread, green salad and hot cooked rice.

Note: The sauce may be prepared ahead of time. May substitute drained canned tomatoes for the fresh tomatoes.

YIELD: 6 SERVINGS

Sinful Shrimp in Wine and Mustard Cream

80	medium shrimp, peeled, deveined
¼	cup chopped garlic
¼	cup chopped shallots
1	cup butter
⅔	cup white wine
2	cups crème fraîche or sour cream
½	cup grainy mustard
1½	pounds fettuccini, cooked, drained
1	teaspoon herbes de Provence
	Salt and pepper to taste
40	snow peas, trimmed, blanched
40	(¼-inch-thick) slices red apples
8	sprigs of fresh dill (optional)
8	lemon slices (optional)

Sauté the shrimp, 1 tablespoon of the garlic and 1 tablespoon of the shallots in ½ cup of the butter in a skillet for 1 to 2 minutes. Stir in the wine, crème fraîche and mustard. Simmer for 5 minutes. Keep warm. Sauté the remaining garlic and remaining shallots in the remaining butter in a large skillet for 2 to 3 minutes. Add the pasta. Cook until heated through. Stir in the herbes de Provence and salt and pepper. Divide the pasta mixture among 8 serving plates. Alternate 8 to 10 warm shrimp, 5 snow peas and 5 apple slices clockwise over each serving. Drizzle with the remaining shrimp sauce. Garnish with the dill and lemon slices. Serve immediately.

YIELD: 8 SERVINGS

Tequila Lime Shrimp

¼ **cup fresh lime juice**
¼ **cup tequila**
½ **cup olive oil**
2 **cloves of garlic, chopped**
2 **shallots, chopped**
1 **teaspoon cumin**
1 **teaspoon salt**
½ **teaspoon pepper**
2½ **pounds large shrimp, peeled, deveined**

Whisk the lime juice, tequila and olive oil in a bowl. Stir in the garlic, shallots, cumin, salt and pepper. Pour over the shrimp in a bowl. Marinate, covered, in the refrigerator for 1 to 4 hours. Drain the shrimp, discarding the marinade. Place the shrimp in a baking dish. Bake at 400 degrees for 20 minutes or until the shrimp turn pink.

Note: For kabobs, soak bamboo skewers in water for 1 hour. Thread the shrimp onto the soaked skewers. Place on a grill rack. Grill until the shrimp turn pink.

YIELD: 4 TO 6 SERVINGS

Shrimp Scampi

½ **cup melted butter**
2 **tablespoons olive oil**
24 **large shrimp, peeled, deveined**
5 **cloves of garlic, crushed**
2 **tablespoons chopped fresh parsley**
2 **tablespoons dry white wine**
1 **tablespoon lemon juice**
  Salt and pepper to taste

Heat the butter and olive oil in a large skillet. Add the shrimp. Sauté for 5 minutes or until the shrimp turn pink. Drain, reserving the drippings. Arrange the shrimp in a serving dish. Combine the reserved drippings, garlic, parsley, wine, lemon juice and salt and pepper in a small saucepan. Cook over high heat for 1 minute. Pour over the shrimp. Serve immediately.

YIELD: 5 SERVINGS

Southern Barbecued Shrimp

5 **pounds shrimp, unpeeled**
2 **cups melted butter**
2 **to 4 tablespoons pepper**
1 **(16-ounce) bottle Italian salad dressing**
  Juice of 4 lemons

Rinse the shrimp thoroughly and pat dry. Place in a roasting pan. Combine the butter, pepper, salad dressing and lemon juice in a bowl and mix well. Pour over the shrimp. Bake, covered, at 350 degrees for 45 minutes. Serve with French bread.

YIELD: 4 TO 6 SERVINGS

Marinated Shrimp Scampi

1   cup olive oil
½   cup white wine
3   tablespoons chopped fresh basil
1   teaspoon salt
¼   teaspoon freshly ground pepper
     Juice of ½ lemon
     Zest of ½ lemon
3   cloves of garlic, minced, or to taste
30 jumbo shrimp, peeled, deveined
1   cup butter
¼   cup chopped parsley
1   tablespoon lemon juice
½   tablespoon lemon zest
½   teaspoon salt
2   cloves of garlic, minced
¼   teaspoon pepper
     Hot cooked pasta, drained

Combine the olive oil, wine, basil, 1 teaspoon salt, ¼ teaspoon pepper, juice of ½ lemon, zest of ½ lemon and 3 cloves of garlic in a large airtight container and mix well. Add the shrimp. Marinate, covered, in the refrigerator for 8 to 10 hours. Drain the shrimp, discarding the marinade. Place the shrimp on a broiler rack in a broiler pan or on a grill rack. Broil or grill until the shrimp turn pink. Melt the butter in a saucepan. Stir in the parsley, 1 tablespoon lemon juice, ½ tablespoon lemon zest, salt, 2 cloves of garlic and pepper. Place the pasta on a serving plate. Cover with the shrimp. Pour the butter sauce over the top. Serve immediately.

YIELD: 3 OR 4 SERVINGS

Make Basil White Wine Butter Sauce by sautéing 4 cloves of garlic, minced, in ½ cup butter in a skillet over low heat for 2 to 3 minutes. Whisk in ¼ cup dry white wine, the juice of ½ lemon and ¼ cup chopped fresh basil. Remove from the heat. Season with salt and pepper to taste. Use to marinate seafood, as a basting sauce for seafood and as a dipping sauce for seafood.

Crab Meat Cobbler

½ cup chopped onions
½ cup chopped green bell pepper
½ cup butter
½ cup flour
1 teaspoon dry mustard
½ teaspoon Accent
1½ cups milk
1 cup shredded Cheddar cheese
2 (6-ounce) cans crab meat, drained, flaked
1 (15-ounce) can tomatoes, drained
2 teaspoons Worcestershire sauce
½ teaspoon salt
1 cup flour
2 teaspoons baking powder
½ teaspoon salt
¼ cup shredded Cheddar cheese
2 tablespoons shortening
½ cup milk

Sauté the onions and green pepper in the butter in a skillet for 10 minutes or until tender. Stir in ½ cup flour, dry mustard, Accent, 1½ cups milk and 1 cup cheese. Cook until smooth and creamy, stirring constantly. Stir in the crab meat, tomatoes, Worcestershire sauce and ½ teaspoon salt. Spoon into a 9x13-inch baking dish. Sift 1 cup flour, baking powder and ½ teaspoon salt into a bowl. Add ¼ cup cheese. Cut in the shortening until crumbly. Add ½ cup milk and mix well until the mixture is moistened. Drop by rounded teaspoonfuls on top of the crab meat mixture. Bake at 425 degrees for 20 to 25 minutes or until golden brown.

YIELD: 4 SERVINGS

Crawfish or Shrimp Étouffé

2 cups margarine
1 cup flour
3 green bell peppers, finely chopped
2 bunches green onions, finely chopped
1 stalk celery, finely chopped
5 cloves of garlic, minced
1 (16-ounce) can tomatoes
3 tablespoons salt
3 tablespoons Worcestershire sauce
2 to 3 teaspoons cayenne
6 cups water
5 pounds crawfish tails or deveined peeled shrimp
4 cups rice, cooked

Melt the margarine in a large heavy stockpot. Add the flour. Cook until the flour is light brown, stirring constantly. Add the green peppers, green onions, celery, garlic and tomatoes and mix well. Add the salt, Worcestershire sauce and cayenne. Cook, covered, over low heat for 1 hour, stirring frequently. Stir in the water. Cook for 3 hours, adding additional water if needed for the desired consistency. Add the crawfish tails. Cook for 15 minutes. Spoon over the hot cooked rice.

YIELD: 12 SERVINGS

Lobster Mornay

5	tablespoons butter
3	tablespoons flour
½	teaspoon salt
1	cup milk
½	cup white wine
½	cup shredded sharp Cheddar cheese
3	dashes of Tabasco sauce
	Dash of garlic powder
	Pepper to taste
6	lobsters, cooked, peeled, cut into small pieces

Melt the butter in a small saucepan. Blend in the flour and salt. Add the milk, wine and cheese. Cook over low heat until thickened, stirring constantly. Add the Tabasco sauce, garlic powder and pepper and mix well. Line a shallow casserole with the lobster pieces. Pour the sauce over the lobster. Bake at 350 degrees for 25 to 30 minutes or until bubbly. Serve with wild rice.

YIELD: 6 TO 8 SERVINGS

Scallops with Garlic and Parsley

1½	pounds bay or sea scallops
3	tablespoons flour
	Salt to taste
	White pepper to taste
2	tablespoons olive oil
2	tablespoons butter
2	medium cloves of garlic, minced
⅓	cup chopped fresh parsley
	Lemon wedges

Rinse and drain the scallops thoroughly. Mix the flour, salt and white pepper in a bowl. Add the scallops and toss until well coated. Heat the olive oil and butter in a large skillet until the butter melts. Add the garlic. Sauté for 30 seconds. Add the scallops a single layer at a time. Cook for 4 minutes or until cooked through, turning once. Stir in the parsley. Serve with lemon wedges.

Note: Serve as an entrée with curried rice and broiled tomatoes. May substitute shrimp for the scallops.

YIELD: 4 SERVINGS

Grilled Garlic Scallops

⅓	cup fresh lemon juice
⅓	cup dry white wine or chicken broth
4	cloves of garlic, minced
2	bay leaves
1	teaspoon grated lemon peel
1	teaspoon pepper
1½	pounds sea scallops
4	cups large mushroom caps
3	medium red bell peppers, cut into 1-inch pieces
3	medium green bell peppers, cut into 1-inch pieces
2	large red onions, cut into 1-inch pieces

Combine the lemon juice, wine, garlic, bay leaves, lemon peel and pepper in a shallow glass dish and mix well. Reserve 3 tablespoons of the lemon juice mixture and set aside. Add the scallops to the dish and toss to coat well. Marinate, covered with plastic wrap, for 1 hour. Drain the scallops, discarding the marinade and bay leaves. Thread the scallops, mushrooms, red peppers, green peppers and onions alternately onto six 12-inch metal skewers. Place on a grill rack sprayed with nonstick cooking spray. Grill 6 inches from the hot coals for 7 to 8 minutes or until the scallops are cooked through, turning occasionally and basting frequently with the reserved lemon juice mixture. Serve immediately.

YIELD: 6 SERVINGS

Saucy Sole

½	cup grated Parmesan cheese
½	cup shredded mozzarella cheese
½	cup butter, softened
3	tablespoons mayonnaise
½	cup chopped scallions
½	cup sliced mushrooms
	Dash of Tabasco sauce
2	pounds fillet of sole
2	tablespoons lemon juice

Combine the Parmesan cheese, mozzarella cheese, butter, mayonnaise, scallions, mushrooms and Tabasco sauce in a bowl and mix well. Arrange the fish in a single layer on a well greased rack in a broiler pan. Brush with the lemon juice. Broil for 4 to 6 minutes or until the fish flakes easily with a fork. Remove from the oven. Spread the fish with the cheese mixture. Broil for 3 to 4 minutes or until light brown.

YIELD: 4 SERVINGS

Tropical Mahimahi with Pineapple Salsa

1   pound mahimahi, cut into fillets
½   cup orange juice
3   tablespoons lime juice
2   tablespoons honey
¼   teaspoon salt
1   clove of garlic, crushed
1   cup Pineapple Salsa

Place the fish in an ungreased baking dish. Mix the orange juice, lime juice, honey, salt and garlic in a bowl. Pour over the fish. Chill, covered, for 1 to 6 hours, turning once. Drain the fish, reserving the marinade. Bring the reserved marinade to a boil in a small saucepan. Boil for 3 minutes and remove from the heat. Place the fish on a grill rack. Grill for 12 to 15 minutes or until the fish flakes easily, turning and brushing with the heated reserved marinade. Serve with Pineapple Salsa.

Pineapple Salsa

½   cup finely chopped red bell pepper
¼   cup finely chopped red onion
1   small red chile, seeded, finely chopped
2   cups ½-inch pineapple pieces
2   tablespoons chopped cilantro or parsley
2   tablespoons lime juice

Sauté the red pepper, onion and chile in a skillet until tender. Stir in the pineapple, cilantro and lime juice. Chill, covered, for 2 hours.

YIELD: 4 TO 6 SERVINGS

Orange Roughy Italiano

½   cup sliced onion
2   cups thinly sliced zucchini
1   teaspoon dried oregano
3   tablespoons olive oil
1   tomato, chopped
1   pound orange roughy, cut into serving-size
      pieces
      Salt and pepper to taste
½   cup shredded provolone cheese

Sauté the onion, zucchini and oregano in the olive oil in a skillet over medium-high heat for 4 minutes. Layer the tomato and fish over the vegetables. Sprinkle with salt and pepper. Cover and reduce the heat. Simmer for 9 minutes or until the fish is opaque and flakes easily with a fork. Sprinkle with the cheese. Cook, covered, for 1½ minutes or until the cheese melts. Serve immediately.

YIELD: 4 SERVINGS

Grilled Salmon Steaks with Cilantro Pesto

¾ **cup tightly packed cilantro**
2 **serrano chiles, seeded, chopped**
2 **cloves of garlic, minced**
½ **cup coarsely chopped raw cashews**
1 **teaspoon grated lime zest**
1 **teaspoon grated orange zest**
2½ **teaspoons fresh lime juice**
½ **teaspoon sugar**
1 **teaspoon white pepper**
5 **tablespoons light olive oil**
1 **tablespoon rice vinegar**
1½ **teaspoons tamari soy sauce**
   Salt to taste
4 **(8-ounce) salmon fillets, 1 inch thick**

Process the cilantro, chiles, garlic, cashews, lime zest, orange zest, lime juice, sugar and white pepper in a food processor until finely minced. Add the olive oil in a fine stream, processing constantly. Scrape into a bowl. Stir in the vinegar, soy sauce and salt. Reserve a small amount of the pesto and set the remaining pesto aside. Rinse the salmon and pat dry. Brush with the reserved pesto. Place on a grill rack. Grill for 4 to 5 minutes on each side or until the salmon flakes easily and is lightly charred. Serve with the remaining pesto.

YIELD: 4 SERVINGS

Make Lemon Peel Roses by cutting the peel from a lemon in a spiral shape. Coil the peeling into a rose shape. Use to garnish **meat loaf, roast, poultry, etc.**

Mediterranean Salmon Bake

½ **cup mayonnaise**
⅓ **cup sliced pimento-stuffed green olives**
¼ **cup chopped fresh parsley**
1 **tablespoon drained capers**
½ **teaspoon Worcestershire sauce**
¼ **teaspoon white pepper**
1½ **pounds salmon fillets**

Combine the mayonnaise, green olives, parsley, capers, Worcestershire sauce and white pepper in a small bowl and mix well. Arrange the salmon skin side down in a large baking dish. Spread the olive mixture evenly over the salmon. Bake at 375 degrees for 20 to 25 minutes or until the salmon is opaque. Do not overcook. Serve immediately.

YIELD: 4 SERVINGS

Bourbon Orange Salmon Over Citrus Couscous

½   cup bourbon
¼   cup teriyaki sauce
2   cups orange juice
6   (6-ounce) skinless salmon fillets, ½ inch thick
1   tablespoon butter
¼   cup finely chopped almonds
¼   teaspoon curry powder
⅛   teaspoon cayenne
¼   teaspoon dried thyme
¼   teaspoon salt
2¼ cups orange juice
1½ cups couscous
    Salt and black pepper to taste
¼   cup vegetable oil
    Orange sections
    Trimmed fresh watercress

Combine the bourbon, teriyaki sauce and 2 cups orange juice in a shallow dish and mix well. Add the salmon. Marinate, covered, in the refrigerator for 3 hours. Drain the salmon, discarding the marinade. Melt the butter in a sauté pan over medium heat. Add the almonds, curry powder, cayenne and thyme. Sauté for 3 to 4 minutes or until the almonds are golden brown. Add ¼ teaspoon salt and 2¼ cups orange juice. Bring to a boil. Stir in the couscous. Cover the pan tightly and remove from the heat. Let stand for 5 minutes or until all of the liquid is absorbed. Stir with a fork to separate the grains. Pat the salmon dry. Season with salt and black pepper to taste. Sear the salmon in vegetable oil in a large skillet for 2 to 3 minutes per side. Garnish with orange sections and watercress. Serve the salmon with the couscous.

YIELD: 6 SERVINGS

Oranges can be used and served in many different ways. Serve fresh orange sections in salads or use the sections and the juice in pies. Fresh orange juice can be used in salad dressings, muffins, and cakes. Oranges can be cut into cartwheel shapes and used as garnishes. Orange half shells can be used to hold dressings, desserts, and relishes.

Pepper-Crusted Salmon with Orange Butter

½ cup cracked black peppercorns
4 salmon steaks
1 to 2 teaspoons olive oil
Orange Butter or ¼ cup bottled tomato citrus vinaigrette

Position a grill rack 2 inches from hot coals. Place a cast-iron griddle or large cast-iron skillet on the rack. Preheat over the hot coals for 10 to 15 minutes. Spread the pepper on a plate. Press the salmon into the pepper, turning to coat both sides. Add olive oil to the hot griddle. Add the salmon. Sear for 8 minutes, turning over halfway through grilling time. Serve with Orange Butter.

Orange Butter

½ cup butter, softened
2 to 3 tablespoons fresh orange juice

Mix the butter and orange juice in a bowl until smooth and creamy.

YIELD: 4 SERVINGS

Mediterranean Snapper

4 Italian plum tomatoes, seeded, chopped
2 tablespoons chopped kalamata olives
¼ cup drained capers
1 teaspoon minced garlic
2 tablespoons olive oil
1½ tablespoons fresh lemon juice
¼ cup dry white wine
¼ cup crumbled feta cheese
2 tablespoons minced shallots
2 tablespoons chopped fresh basil
Salt and pepper to taste
1 tablespoon olive oil
4 (6- to 8-ounce) snapper fillets
1½ tablespoons fresh lemon juice
¼ cup crumbled feta cheese

Combine the tomatoes, olives, capers, garlic, 2 tablespoons olive oil, 1½ tablespoons lemon juice, wine, ¼ cup feta cheese, shallots, basil and salt and pepper to taste in a bowl. Let stand at room temperature. Brush the bottom of a shallow baking dish with 1 tablespoon olive oil. Season both sides of the fish with salt and pepper to taste. Place in the prepared dish. Sprinkle 1½ tablespoons lemon juice over the fish. Spread the tomato mixture over the top. Sprinkle with ¼ cup feta cheese. Bake at 425 degrees for 15 minutes or until cooked through. Remove the fish to a serving plate. Spoon the pan juices over the top.

Note: May substitute grouper or halibut for the snapper.

YIELD: 4 SERVINGS

Grilled Swordfish with Capers, Lemon and Garlic

4　(4- to 6-ounce) swordfish steaks, ½ inch thick
1　tablespoon olive oil
　　Salt and pepper to taste
1　to 2 cloves of garlic, minced
2　tablespoons (heaping) capers
6　tablespoons fresh lemon juice
1　teaspoon olive oil

Brush the fish on both sides with 1 tablespoon olive oil. Sprinkle lightly with salt and pepper. Combine the garlic, capers, lemon juice and 1 teaspoon olive oil in a bowl and mix well. Season with pepper. Place the fish on a grill rack. Grill 3 to 4 inches from the hot coals for 2 to 2½ minutes on each side or until the fish flakes easily with a fork. Remove to a serving plate. Spoon the capers mixture over the fish. Serve with rice or pasta.

YIELD: 4 SERVINGS

Bayou Blackened Swordfish

1½　pounds swordfish
3　to 4 tablespoons melted butter or margarine
1　to 2 tablespoons Cajun seasoning, or to taste
¼　teaspoon ground red pepper, or to taste
　　Chopped fresh parsley

Preheat a heavy skillet over medium-high heat for 3 minutes or longer. Dip the fish in the butter. Sprinkle both sides evenly with the seasonings, pressing gently so the seasonings adhere to the fish. Cook for 10 minutes per inch thickness of the fish or until blackened and the fish flakes easily with a fork, turning once. Garnish with parsley.

YIELD: 4 SERVINGS

Prepare Fruity Salsa by combining 1 mango, chopped, 2 bananas, chopped, 1 green bell pepper, chopped, 1 red bell pepper, chopped, 2 tomatoes, chopped, ½ of a red onion, chopped, 3 tablespoons chopped fresh cilantro, 3 or 4 Key limes, peeled, chopped, balsamic vinegar to taste and a dash of salt and pepper in a bowl and mixing well.

Lemon-Grilled Swordfish

6	(1-inch-thick) swordfish steaks
½	cup lemon juice
2	tablespoons minced fresh parsley
2	tablespoons olive oil
½	teaspoon seasoned salt
½	teaspoon lemon pepper
	Hollandaise Sauce
	Chopped fresh chives
	Lemon wedges

Place the steaks in a shallow dish. Mix the lemon juice, parsley, olive oil, seasoned salt and lemon pepper in a bowl and mix well. Pour evenly over the steaks. Marinate, covered, in the refrigerator for 2 hours or longer, turning the steaks occasionally. Drain the steaks. Place on a grill rack. Grill over medium-hot coals for 7 to 8 minutes on each side or until the fish flakes easily with a fork. Spoon Hollandaise Sauce down the center of each steak. Sprinkle with chives. Serve with lemon wedges.

Hollandaise Sauce

3	egg yolks
⅛	teaspoon salt
	Dash of ground red pepper
2	tablespoons lemon juice
½	cup butter or margarine
¼	teaspoon lemon pepper

Beat the egg yolks, salt and red pepper in a double boiler. Add the lemon juice gradually, stirring constantly. Add about ⅓ of the butter. Cook over hot water until the butter melts, stirring constantly. Add half the remaining butter, stirring constantly. Cook until the butter melts, stirring constantly. Add the remaining butter and lemon pepper, stirring constantly. Cook until thickened, stirring constantly.

YIELD: 6 SERVINGS

To make lemon wheels, cut wedges of lemon peels lengthwise into thin strips. Cut the lemon crosswise into thin notched rounds to resemble wheels. Use as a garnish to float in punch. Or use to garnish a platter of fish or veal, placing a whole stuffed olive in the center of the wheel shape and sprinkling with parsley.

Grilled Swordfish with Tropical Salsa

¼ **cup fresh pineapple juice**
¼ **cup fresh lime juice**
2 **tablespoons olive oil**
1 **tablespoon minced fresh thyme, or**
    1 teaspoon dried thyme
½ **teaspoon minced garlic**
1 **teaspoon freshly grated lime zest**
4 **(6- to 8-ounce) swordfish steaks**
    Tropical Salsa

Combine the pineapple juice, lime juice, olive oil, thyme, garlic and lime zest in a small bowl and mix well. Place the fish in a shallow glass dish. Pour the marinade over the fish, turning to coat. Marinate, covered, in the refrigerator for 3 hours, turning once. Place on a grill rack. Grill over medium-hot coals for 10 minutes per inch of thickness or until the fish flakes easily with a fork, turning once. Arrange on individual serving plates. Spoon Tropical Salsa over each serving.

Tropical Salsa

1 **cup chopped fresh pineapple**
1 **red bell pepper, seeded, chopped**
3 **tablespoons minced green onions**
1 **small jalapeño, seeded, chopped**
½ **cup chopped peeled jicama**
1 **tablespoon minced fresh cilantro**
2 **tablespoons rice wine vinegar**
1 **tablespoon olive oil**
    Salt to taste

Combine the pineapple, red pepper, green onions, jalapeño, jicama, cilantro, wine vinegar, olive oil and salt in a glass bowl and mix well. Chill, covered, for 3 to 10 hours. Let stand at room temperature for 1 hour before serving.

YIELD: 4 SERVINGS

Honey Mustard Sesame Swordfish Kabobs

1 **medium zucchini**
1 **medium yellow squash**
1 **pound swordfish, cut into 1-inch pieces**
¼ **cup vegetable oil**
2 **tablespoons Dijon mustard**
2 **tablespoons honey**
2 **tablespoons lemon juice**
½ **teaspoon lemon zest**
½ **teaspoon salt**
¼ **teaspoon freshly ground pepper**
1 **medium red onion, cut into 1-inch pieces**
1 **tablespoon sesame seeds, toasted**

Cut the zucchini and squash into halves lengthwise. Cut each half into ½-inch pieces. Combine the zucchini, squash and swordfish in a large glass bowl. Mix the oil, Dijon mustard, honey, lemon juice, lemon zest, salt and pepper in a small bowl. Pour over the fish mixture and toss to coat. Marinate, covered, in the refrigerator for 1 hour, turning once. Drain, discarding the marinade. Thread the red onion, zucchini, swordfish and yellow squash alternately onto skewers until all the ingredients are used. Place on a grill rack. Grill 4 inches from the heat source for 6 minutes per side or until the fish is cooked through. Sprinkle with the sesame seeds.

YIELD: 4 SERVINGS

Southwestern Marinade

⅓ cup lime juice
⅓ cup olive oil
2 tablespoons tequila
2 tablespoons chopped fresh cilantro
1 clove of garlic, minced
1 jalapeño, seeded, chopped
¼ teaspoon salt
¼ teaspoon pepper

Combine the lime juice, olive oil, tequila, cilantro, garlic, jalapeño, salt and pepper in a bowl and mix well. Use to marinate shrimp and soft-shell crab in the refrigerator for 2 hours before grilling.

YIELD: ¾ CUP

There are four different kinds of limes. The Key lime is grown chiefly in the Florida Keys, but can be grown in Central Florida with care. It is hard to grow, but delicious. The juice of this lime makes the famous Key lime pie. The Limequat lime is a small yellow fruit with the flavor of kumquat and the tartness of lime. It is a good lime to use in making marmalades. The Persin lime is a large green lime of good flavor, grown best in southern Florida. The Rangpur lime is orange in color. Its tart juice may be used as lime or lemon juice.

Citrus Marinade

¼ cup fresh lime juice
¼ cup fresh lemon juice
1 cup fresh orange juice
½ cup olive oil
2 teaspoons minced garlic
2 teaspoons coarsely ground pepper
3 bay leaves, crushed
2 tablespoons chopped fresh cilantro
Salt to taste

Combine the lime juice, lemon juice, orange juice, olive oil, garlic, pepper, bay leaves, cilantro and salt in a glass bowl and mix well. Let stand at room temperature for 30 minutes. Use to marinate shellfish in the refrigerator for 10 to 15 minutes and to marinate fish in the refrigerator for 30 to 60 minutes.

YIELD: 2 CUPS

Rosemary Citrus Marinade

½   **cup orange juice**
¼   **cup lemon juice**
¼   **cup lime juice**
2   **tablespoons vegetable oil**
2   **teaspoons dried rosemary**
¼   **teaspoon salt**
⅛   **teaspoon white pepper**

Combine the orange juice, lemon juice, lime juice, vegetable oil, rosemary, salt and white pepper in a bowl and mix well. Use to marinate orange roughy fillets or other fresh fish in the refrigerator for 8 hours before grilling.

YIELD: 1 CUP

Melon Salsa

½   **honeydew melon, chopped**
½   **cantaloupe, chopped**
1   **jalapeño, chopped**
2   **tablespoons lime juice**
1   **tablespoon olive oil**

Combine the honeydew melon, cantaloupe, jalapeño, lime juice and olive oil in a blender container. Process for 5 to 10 seconds or until blended. Serve over fish.

YIELD: 1 TO 1 ½ CUPS

The Ponderosa lemon and Meyer lemon are two types of lemons. The Ponderosa lemon is oblong in shape and as large as a grapefruit. It grows on a small tree. The peel is excellent for marmalades, preserves, and crystallized peel. The Meyer lemon is a smooth-skinned fruit with good-flavored, tart juice. It is a good lemon to use in cooking, in beverages, for marmalade, and for crystallized peel.

In the mid-1950s, the Leesburg Fruit Company converted its business from packing fresh citrus to producing juice concentrate. The Holloway family was one of several that started a concentrate plant in Groveland. Orange juice concentrate was first commercially produced in Central Florida in 1946, and today the majority of oranges grown in Florida are used for juice.

SUN SWEETS

Desserts

· · ·

Section sponsored by
Kelly's Cakes

Fancy Flourless Fudge Torte

CHEF KELLY ACREE, KELLY'S CAKES

- **7** **ounces semisweet chocolate, chopped**
- **10** **tablespoons unsalted butter, cut into pieces**
- **4** **eggs**
- **½** **cup superfine sugar**
- **1** **tablespoon vanilla extract**
- **1** **cup plus 3 tablespoons ground pecans**
- **1** **teaspoon cinnamon**
  Honey Chocolate Glaze
- **20** **toasted pecan halves**

Grease an 8-inch round cake pan. Line the bottom with parchment paper. Grease the parchment paper. Cook the chocolate and butter over low heat until melted, stirring constantly. Remove from the heat. Beat the eggs, sugar and vanilla in a mixer bowl for 1 to 2 minutes or until frothy. Stir in the melted chocolate mixture, ground pecans and cinnamon. Pour into the prepared pan. Place in a larger pan. Add enough boiling water to the larger pan to come ¾ up the side of the smaller pan. Bake at 350 degrees for 25 to 30 minutes or until the edges are set but the center is soft. Remove the pan from the water bath to a wire rack. Let stand until cool. Place a wire rack on a baking sheet. Invert the cooled cake onto the rack and remove the parchment paper. Reserve some of the Honey Chocolate Glaze for coating the pecans. Pour enough of the glaze over the top and side of the cake to cover, using a spatula to smooth the sides. Dip the pecan halves halfway into the reserved Honey Chocolate Glaze. Arrange around the edge of the cake. Store, covered, for 24 hours before serving.

Honey Chocolate Glaze

- **4** **ounces bittersweet chocolate, chopped**
- **¼** **cup unsalted butter, cut into pieces**
- **2** **tablespoons honey**
  Pinch of cinnamon

Cook the chocolate and butter with the honey and cinnamon in a small saucepan until melted, stirring constantly. Remove from the heat.

YIELD: 16 TO 20 SERVINGS

To prepare Chocolate Fondue, break two (8-ounce) packages semisweet chocolate baking squares into pieces and place in a small saucepan. Add 1 cup whipping cream. Cook over warm heat until smooth and creamy, stirring constantly. Remove from the heat. Stir in ½ cup chopped pecans (optional) and 2 tablespoons Chambord. Serve with pound cake, marshmallows, cheesecake and fresh fruit.

Chocolate Nut Cake with Grilled Oranges

1 cup pecans
1 cup hazelnuts
1 cup almonds
1 cup walnuts
7 ounces bittersweet chocolate, chopped
¾ cup sugar
8 eggs, separated
1 teaspoon freshly grated lemon zest
1 tablespoon freshly grated orange zest
12 navel oranges, peeled, sectioned
½ cup honey

Grease lightly a 9-inch springform pan. Line the bottom with parchment paper. Process the pecans, hazelnuts, almonds and walnuts a small amount at a time in a food processor until finely ground. Process the chocolate and 6 tablespoons of the sugar in a food processor until finely ground. Beat the egg yolks in a mixer bowl until thick and pale yellow. Add the chocolate mixture, lemon zest and orange zest and beat until combined. Beat the egg whites in a mixer bowl. Add the remaining 6 tablespoons sugar gradually, beating until soft peaks form. Fold the nut mixture and meringue into the egg yolk mixture gently. Spoon into the prepared pan. Bake at 350 degrees for 55 minutes or until a cake tester inserted in the center comes out clean. Cool in the pan on a wire rack. Remove the side of the pan. Toss the orange sections and honey in a bowl. Let stand for 10 minutes. Heat a ridged grill pan over high heat until hot. Grill the oranges a small amount at a time in the preheated pan for 10 seconds on each side. Cut the cake into serving portions and place on individual serving plates. Spoon the oranges over the cake.

YIELD: 12 TO 16 SERVINGS

Blueberry Citrus Cake

1 (2-layer) package lemon cake mix
½ cup orange juice
½ cup water
⅓ cup vegetable oil
3 eggs
1½ cups fresh blueberries
1½ tablespoons finely shredded orange peel
1½ tablespoons finely shredded lemon peel
   Citrus Frosting
   Orange peel curls

Combine the cake mix, orange juice, water, vegetable oil and eggs in a large mixer bowl. Beat at low speed for 30 seconds. Beat at medium speed for 2 minutes. Fold in the blueberries, orange peel and lemon peel. Spoon into two greased and floured 8- or 9-inch round cake pans. Bake at 350 degrees for 35 to 40 minutes or until a wooden pick inserted near the center comes out clean. Cool in the pans on wire racks for 10 minutes. Invert the layers onto wire racks to cool completely. Spread Citrus Frosting between the layers and over the top and side of the cake. Sprinkle with orange peel curls. Store, covered, in the refrigerator.

Citrus Frosting

3 ounces cream cheese, softened
¼ cup butter, softened
3 cups sifted confectioners' sugar
2 tablespoons orange juice
1 cup whipping cream, whipped
2 tablespoons finely shredded orange peel
1 tablespoon finely shredded lemon peel

Beat the cream cheese and butter in a medium mixer bowl until light and fluffy. Add the confectioners' sugar and orange juice and beat until smooth. Add the whipped cream, orange peel and lemon peel. Beat at low speed until blended.

YIELD: 12 SERVINGS

Italian Cream Cake

2   **cups sugar**
½   **cup shortening**
½   **cup vegetable oil**
5   **egg yolks**
1   **teaspoon baking soda**
1   **cup buttermilk**
2   **cups flour**
½   **cup flaked coconut**
5   **egg whites, beaten**
½   **teaspoon vanilla extract**
½   **teaspoon butter flavoring**
     Cream Cheese Frosting

Cream the sugar, shortening and oil in a mixer bowl until light and fluffy. Add the egg yolks 1 at a time, beating well after each addition. Stir the baking soda into the buttermilk. Add alternately with the flour to the creamed mixture, beating constantly. Fold in the coconut. Fold in the beaten egg whites. Stir in the flavorings. Spoon into a greased 10-inch cake pan. Bake at 350 degrees for 1 hour or until a cake tester inserted in the center comes out clean. Invert onto a wire rack to cool. Spread the Cream Cheese Frosting between the layers and over the top and side of the cake.

Cream Cheese Frosting

8   **ounces cream cheese, softened**
½   **cup margarine, softened**
1   **(16-ounce) package confectioners' sugar, sifted**
1½ **cups chopped pecans**
½   **teaspoon vanilla extract**
½   **teaspoon butter flavoring**

Beat the cream cheese and margarine in a mixer bowl until smooth. Add the confectioners' sugar gradually, beating constantly. Stir in the pecans and flavorings.

YIELD: 14 TO 16 SERVINGS

Southern Pecan Cake

3¼ **cups sifted flour**
½   **teaspoon baking powder**
4   **cups coarsely chopped pecans**
1   **(16-ounce) package golden raisins**
1   **cup butter, softened**
1   **(16-ounce) package light brown sugar**
6   **eggs, beaten**
⅓   **cup pineapple juice or whiskey**

Grease a 9-inch tube pan. Line the bottom with nonrecycled brown paper or parchment paper. Grease the paper. Sift the flour and baking powder together. Toss the pecans and raisins with a small amount of the flour mixture. Cream the butter and brown sugar in a mixer bowl until light and fluffy. Add in eggs and beat well. Add the remaining flour mixture gradually, beating constantly. Stir in the pecan and raisin mixture. Add the pineapple juice gradually, beating well after each addition. Spoon into the prepared pan. Bake at 225 degrees for 3 hours or until a wooden pick inserted in the center comes out clean.

YIELD: 15 TO 20 SERVINGS

Choco-Kahlúa Pound Cake

THIS IS THE MOST POPULAR RECIPE FROM *SUNSATIONAL*.

1	**(2-layer) package pudding-recipe devil's food cake mix**
½	**cup sugar**
⅓	**cup vegetable oil**
3	**eggs**
¾	**cup water**
¼	**cup bourbon**
½	**cup Kahlúa**
¾	**cup double-strength black coffee**
2	**teaspoons baking cocoa**
	Chocolate Icing

Combine the cake mix, sugar, vegetable oil, eggs, water, bourbon, Kahlúa, black coffee and baking cocoa in a large mixer bowl and mix well. Beat for 4 minutes. Spoon into a greased bundt pan. Bake at 350 degrees for 50 minutes or until the cake tests done. Let stand for 10 minutes. Invert onto a cake plate. Pour the hot Chocolate Icing over the cake immediately.

Chocolate Icing

¼	**cup butter**
1	**cup sugar**
⅓	**cup evaporated milk**
1½	**cups chocolate chips**

Bring the butter, sugar and evaporated milk to a boil in a saucepan, stirring constantly. Boil for 2 minutes, stirring constantly. Remove from the heat. Add the chocolate chips, stirring constantly until melted.

YIELD: 16 SERVINGS

Coconut Pound Cake

3	**cups flour**
¼	**teaspoon baking soda**
¼	**teaspoon salt**
1	**cup butter, softened**
3	**cups sugar**
6	**eggs**
1	**cup sour cream**
1	**cup flaked coconut**
1	**teaspoon coconut extract**
1	**teaspoon vanilla extract**

Mix the flour, baking soda and salt together. Beat the butter in a mixer bowl until smooth and creamy. Add the sugar gradually, beating constantly until light and fluffy. Add the eggs 1 at a time, beating well after each addition. Add the sour cream alternately with the flour mixture, beating well after each addition and beginning and ending with the sour cream. Stir in the coconut and flavorings. Spoon into a greased and floured 10-inch tube pan. Bake at 350 degrees for 1¼ hours or until a wooden pick inserted in the center comes out clean. Cool in the pan for 10 to 15 minutes. Invert onto a wire rack to cool completely.

YIELD: 10 TO 12 SERVINGS

Cream Cheese Pound Cake

3   cups flour
     Dash of salt
1   cup margarine, softened
½   cup butter, softened
8   ounces cream cheese, softened
3   cups sugar
6   eggs
1½   teaspoons vanilla extract
½   cup packed light brown sugar
1   teaspoon cinnamon

Mix the flour and salt together. Beat the margarine, butter and cream cheese in a large mixer bowl until smooth and creamy. Add the sugar 1 cup at a time, beating well after each addition. Add 2 of the eggs and a small amount of the flour mixture and mix well. Add the remaining flour mixture and remaining eggs alternately, beating well after each addition and beginning and ending with the flour mixture. Stir in the vanilla. Spoon into a greased 10-inch tube pan. Sprinkle with a mixture of the brown sugar and cinnamon. Place in a cold oven. Bake at 300 degrees for 1½ hours.

Note: May top with sliced strawberries.

YIELD: 16 SERVINGS

Lemon Pound Cake

3   cups cake flour
1   cup unsalted butter, softened
3   cups sugar
6   eggs
1   cup whipping cream
2   teaspoons lemon extract
2   teaspoons vanilla extract

Sift the cake flour 3 times. Beat the butter and sugar in a mixer bowl until light and fluffy. Add the eggs 1 at a time, beating well after each addition. Add the cake flour and whipping cream alternately a small amount at a time, beating well after each addition. Stir in the flavorings. Spoon into a greased and floured 10-inch tube pan. Place in a cold oven. Bake at 325 or 350 degrees for 50 to 60 minutes or until the cake tests done.

YIELD: 16 SERVINGS

For Orange Pecan Sauce, combine 1 cup sugar, 1 cup orange juice, grated peel of 1 orange, 8 egg yolks, beaten, and a pinch of salt in a double boiler. Cook over medium-high heat until thickened, stirring constantly. Remove from the heat. Whip 1 cup whipping cream in a bowl until soft peaks form. Fold the whipped cream and 1 cup chopped pecans into the orange mixture. Chill, covered, in the refrigerator until ready to serve.

Orange Sunshine Cake

3   cups flour
1   tablespoon baking powder
½   teaspoon salt
1   cup plus 2 tablespoons unsalted butter or
      margarine, softened
2⅓   cups sugar
5   eggs
1   cup orange juice
2   teaspoons grated orange peel
      Orange Filling
      Sunshine Frosting
      Slivered orange peel

Grease three round 9-inch cake pans. Line the bottom of the pans with waxed paper. Mix the flour, baking powder and salt in a medium bowl. Beat 1 cup of the butter and 2 cups of the sugar at medium speed in a large mixer bowl until creamy. Add the eggs 1 at a time, beating well after each addition. Add the flour mixture alternately with ¾ cup of the orange juice, beating well after each addition. Beat in the orange peel. Pour into the prepared pans. Bake at 350 degrees for 25 to 30 minutes or until a cake tester inserted in the center comes out clean. Loosen the layers around the edges with a spatula. Invert onto wire racks. Remove the waxed paper. Invert the layers and prick all over with a wooden pick. Melt the remaining 2 tablespoons butter with the remaining ⅓ cup sugar and ¼ cup orange juice in a small saucepan. Cook until the sugar dissolves, stirring constantly. Spoon gradually over the warm layers, letting the syrup soak in. Let stand until cooled completely. Place 1 cake layer on a cake plate. Spread with ½ of the Orange Filling. Top with another cake layer. Spread with ½ of the Sunshine Frosting. Top with the remaining cake layer. Spread with the remaining Orange Filling. Spread the remaining Sunshine Frosting over the side of the cake. Garnish with slivered orange peel.

Orange Filling

1½   teaspoons unflavored gelatin
¼   cup orange juice
⅓   cup plus 2 tablespoons sugar
½   cup unsalted butter or margarine
2   eggs, separated

Soften the gelatin in the orange juice in a small saucepan. Add ⅓ cup of sugar. Cook over low heat until the sugar dissolves, stirring constantly. Add the butter. Cook until the butter melts, stirring constantly. Beat the egg yolks in a small bowl. Stir a small amount of the hot mixture into the egg yolks. Stir the egg yolks into the hot mixture. Cook over low heat until thickened, stirring constantly. Remove from the heat. Let stand until cool. Beat the egg whites with the remaining 2 tablespoons sugar in a mixer bowl until stiff peaks form. Fold into the cooled orange mixture. Chill for about 10 minutes or until thick and of spreading consistency.

Sunshine Frosting

2   egg whites
⅔   cup sugar
3½   tablespoons light corn syrup
2   tablespoons water
¼   teaspoon cream of tartar
½   teaspoon vanilla extract

Mix the egg whites, sugar, corn syrup, water and cream of tartar in a double boiler. Beat for 7 minutes over boiling water or until stiff and glossy. Remove from the heat. Beat in the vanilla.

YIELD: 10 TO 12 SERVINGS

Florida Orange Nut Cake

3   cups sifted flour
1½   teaspoons baking soda
1   teaspoon salt
¾   cup butter or margarine, softened
1   cup sugar
1   tablespoon grated orange peel
1   teaspoon vanilla extract
3   eggs
1   cup orange marmalade
1   cup chopped pecans
½   cup orange juice
½   cup evaporated milk
1   cup orange juice
1   cup sugar

Sift the flour, baking soda and salt together. Beat the butter, 1 cup sugar, orange peel and vanilla in a mixer bowl until light and fluffy. Add the eggs 1 at a time, beating well after each addition. Stir in the marmalade and pecans. Add the flour mixture alternately with a mixture of ½ cup orange juice and evaporated milk, beating well after each addition. Pour into a greased parchment-lined 9-inch tube pan. Bake at 350 degrees for 1 hour. Cool in the pan for 10 minutes. Heat 1 cup orange juice and 1 cup sugar in a small saucepan over medium heat until the sugar dissolves, stirring constantly. Invert the hot cake onto a cake plate. Spoon the orange syrup over the hot cake. Serve warm or cold.

YIELD: 12 SERVINGS

To make a Soaking Syrup for Cakes, bring 2 parts water and 1 part sugar to a boil in a saucepan over high heat. Cook until the mixture is reduced and golden brown. The syrup can be used immediately to coat cakes to keep them moist for a longer period of time.

Orange Fruit Cake

- **2 cups flour**
- **1 teaspoon baking soda**
- **½ cup chopped pecans**
- **1 cup chopped dates**
- **¼ cup flour**
- **½ cup butter, softened**
- **1 cup sugar**
- **2 eggs**
- **2 tablespoons minced orange peel**
- **⅔ cup buttermilk**
- **Orange Glaze**

Mix 2 cups flour and baking soda together. Toss the pecans and dates with ¼ cup flour in a bowl until coated. Beat the butter and sugar in a mixer bowl until light and fluffy. Add the eggs 1 at a time, beating well after each addition. Add the orange peel. Add the flour mixture alternately with the buttermilk, beating well after each addition. Stir in the floured pecans and dates. Spoon into a greased and floured tube pan. Bake at 350 degrees for 1 hour or until the cake tests done. Pour the Orange Glaze over the hot cake. Let stand until cool. Remove to a cake plate.

Orange Glaze

- **½ cup sugar**
- **½ cup orange juice**
- **1 tablespoon minced orange peel**

Heat the sugar, orange juice and orange peel in a small saucepan until the sugar dissolves, stirring constantly.

YIELD: 10 TO 12 SERVINGS

Chocolate Torte Royale

- **1 cup semisweet chocolate chips**
- **Cinnamon Meringue Shell**
- **2 egg yolks, beaten**
- **¼ cup water**
- **1 cup whipping cream**
- **¼ cup sugar**
- **1¼ teaspoons ground cinnamon**

Melt the chocolate chips in a double boiler over hot water. Let stand until slightly cool. Spread 2 tablespoons of the chocolate in the bottom of the Cinnamon Meringue Shell. Blend the egg yolks and water into the remaining chocolate. Chill in the refrigerator until thick. Beat the whipping cream, sugar and cinnamon in a mixer bowl until stiff peaks form. Spread ½ of the whipped cream over the chocolate in the shell. Fold the remaining whipped cream into the chocolate mixture. Spread over the whipped cream layer. Garnish with whipped cream and pecan halves.

Cinnamon Meringue Shell

- **½ cup sugar**
- **¼ teaspoon ground cinnamon**
- **2 egg whites**
- **½ teaspoon vinegar**
- **¼ teaspoon salt**

Line a baking sheet with a piece of parchment paper. Draw an 8-inch circle in the center. Mix the sugar and cinnamon in a bowl. Beat the remaining ingredients in a bowl until soft peaks form. Beat in the sugar mixture gradually until stiff peaks form. Spread the meringue in the 8-inch circle to form a shell, making the bottom ½ inch thick and the side 1¾ inches high. Bake at 275 degrees for 1 hour. Turn off the oven. Let stand in the oven with the door closed until cool.

YIELD: 8 TO 10 SERVINGS

To make Strawberry Fans to garnish desserts, place each firm ripe strawberry green cap side down on a cutting board. Cut into slices to but not through the cap. Spread the slices into a fan. Cut the hull out of the strawberry with a knife if the hull is not attractive and replace with a sprig of fresh mint.

White Chocolate Cake with Strawberries

2	cups flour
1	teaspoon baking powder
	Pinch of salt
4	ounces white chocolate, chopped
½	cup whipping cream
1	tablespoon rum
½	cup milk
½	cup unsalted butter, softened
¾	cup sugar
3	eggs
1½	pounds fresh strawberries, sliced
2	cups whipping cream, chilled
2	tablespoons rum
¼	cup sugar
	White Chocolate Mousse Filling
	Strawberry fans

Grease and flour two 9-inch cake pans. Line the bottom with parchment paper. Mix the flour, baking powder and salt together. Heat the white chocolate and ½ cup whipping cream in a double boiler over low heat until melted, stirring constantly. Stir in 1 tablespoon rum and milk. Let stand until cool. Beat the butter and ¾ cup sugar in a large mixer bowl for 3 to 5 minutes or until light and fluffy. Add the eggs 1 at a time, beating well after each addition. Add the flour mixture and white chocolate mixture alternately, beating just until blended after each addition. Spoon evenly into the prepared pans. Bake at 350 degrees for 20 to 25 minutes or until the layers test done. Cool in the pans on wire racks for 10 minutes. Invert the layers onto wire racks to cool completely. Cut the cake layers into halves horizontally to form 4 layers. Place 1 layer on a cake plate. Layer White Chocolate Mousse Filling, strawberry slices and remaining cake layers ⅓ at a time over the cake layer. Beat 2 cups whipping cream and 2 tablespoons rum in a mixer bowl until soft peaks form. Add ¼ cup sugar gradually, beating until stiff peaks form. Spread over the top and side of the cake. Arrange strawberry fans on the top of the cake.

White Chocolate Mousse Filling

9	ounces white chocolate, chopped
1½	cups whipping cream
2	tablespoons strawberry liqueur or rum

Melt the white chocolate in the whipping cream in a medium saucepan over low heat, stirring frequently. Stir in the liqueur. Pour into a bowl. Chill until set. Whip with a wire whisk until light and fluffy and of a mousse consistency.

YIELD: 10 SERVINGS

Coconut Chocolate Delight

¾   cup mashed cooked potatoes
1   (16-ounce) package shredded coconut
1   (16-ounce) package confectioners' sugar, sifted
1   teaspoon almond extract
1   cup chocolate chips
4   (1-ounce) squares semisweet chocolate
⅓   paraffin bar

Combine the potatoes, coconut, confectioners' sugar and almond extract in a large bowl and mix well. Chill, covered, in the refrigerator. Roll into 1-inch balls. Place on a tray lined with waxed paper. Chill in the refrigerator. Melt the chocolate chips, semisweet chocolate and paraffin in a double boiler over hot water, stirring occasionally. Dip the coconut balls into the chocolate mixture. Place on a tray lined with waxed paper. Chill until firm.

YIELD: 4 DOZEN

Make Grapefruit Baskets by cutting a thin strip around a grapefruit half, leaving 1 inch uncut on each side. Bring the thin strip up over the basket and fasten with a wooden pick. Spear a cherry or an olive on each end of the wooden pick. Use Grapefruit Baskets as containers for appetizers or desserts.

Freezer Brownies

2   cups sugar
1   cup margarine, softened
4   eggs
2   teaspoons vanilla extract
1¼ cups flour
¾   cup baking cocoa
      Chocolate Frosting for Brownies
1   cup chopped pecans

Cream the sugar and margarine in a mixer bowl until light and fluffy. Add the eggs and vanilla and beat well. Add the flour and cocoa and mix well. Spread in a 9x13-inch baking pan lined with foil. Bake at 325 degrees for 20 to 25 minutes. The brownies should be dense and look slightly undercooked. Cool. Cover the top with waxed paper. Freeze until firm. Invert onto a tray and remove the foil. Spread with Chocolate Frosting for Brownies. Sprinkle with the pecans and press gently into the frosting. Cut into small bars while still partially frozen. Store in an airtight container in the freezer.

Chocolate Frosting for Brownies

2   tablespoons butter
2   tablespoons baking cocoa
2   tablespoons warm water
1½ cups confectioners' sugar

Melt the butter and baking cocoa in a small saucepan. Stir in the warm water. Remove from the heat. Add the confectioners' sugar and mix well.

YIELD: 12 TO 16 SERVINGS

Chocolate Surprise Cookies

2½ cups flour
¾ cup baking cocoa
1 teaspoon baking soda
1 cup sugar
1 cup packed brown sugar
1 cup butter or margarine, softened
2 teaspoons vanilla extract
2 eggs
1½ cups chopped pecans
1 tablespoon sugar
50 Rolo candies, unwrapped

Mix the flour, baking cocoa and baking soda in a small bowl. Beat 1 cup sugar, brown sugar and butter in a large mixer bowl until light and fluffy. Add the vanilla and mix well. Add the eggs 1 at a time, beating well after each addition. Add the flour mixture and mix well. Stir in 1 cup of the pecans. Chill, covered, for 30 minutes. Mix the remaining pecans and 1 tablespoon sugar in a small bowl. Shape 1 tablespoon of the dough around each candy and roll into a ball with floured hands. Press 1 end of the ball in the pecan mixture. Place pecan-coated side up on an ungreased cookie sheet. Bake at 375 degrees for 7 to 9 minutes or until set and slightly cracked. Cool on the cookie sheet for 3 minutes. Remove to a wire rack to cool completely.

YIELD: 50 COOKIES

Chocolate Iced Bittersweets

1 cup confectioners' sugar
1 cup butter, softened
½ teaspoon salt
2 teaspoons vanilla extract
2 cups flour
1 cup confectioners' sugar
3 ounces cream cheese, softened
2 tablespoons flour
1 teaspoon vanilla extract
½ cup chopped nuts
½ cup shredded coconut
  Chocolate Icing

Beat 1 cup confectioners' sugar, butter, salt and 2 teaspoons vanilla in a mixer bowl until light and fluffy. Add 2 cups flour and mix well. Shape by teaspoonfuls into balls. Place 2 inches apart on ungreased cookie sheets. Make an indentation in the center of each. Bake at 350 degrees for 12 to 16 minutes or until light brown around the edges. Remove to wire racks to cool. Beat 1 cup confectioners' sugar, cream cheese, 2 tablespoons flour and 1 teaspoon vanilla in a small mixer bowl until smooth. Stir in the nuts and coconut. Spoon ½ teaspoon of the cream cheese mixture into each indentation. Drizzle with Chocolate Icing.

Chocolate Icing

½ cup chocolate chips
2 tablespoons butter
2 tablespoons water
½ cup confectioners' sugar

Melt the chocolate chips and butter with the water in a small saucepan, stirring constantly. Remove from the heat. Add the confectioners' sugar and mix until smooth.

YIELD: 5 DOZEN

Chocolate-Tipped Butter Cookies

1 cup butter, softened
½ cup confectioners' sugar, sifted
1 teaspoon vanilla extract
2 cups flour
1 cup semisweet chocolate chips
1 tablespoon shortening
½ cup finely chopped pecans

Cream the butter in a mixer bowl. Add the confectioners' sugar gradually, beating until light and fluffy. Add the vanilla. Add the flour gradually, beating constantly. Chill, covered, for 1 to 2 hours. Shape the dough into ½x2-inch logs. Place on a nonstick cookie sheet. Flatten ¾ of each log lengthwise with the tines of a fork. Bake at 350 degrees for 12 to 14 minutes or until golden brown. Remove to wire racks to cool. Melt the chocolate chips and shortening in a saucepan over low heat, stirring constantly. Dip the unflattened tips of the cookies in the chocolate mixture and roll the coated tips in the pecans. Place on a surface lined with waxed paper. Let stand until the chocolate is firm.

YIELD: 4 DOZEN

Chocolate Pecan Balls

1¼ cups butter, softened
⅔ cup sugar
1 teaspoon vanilla extract
2 cups flour
⅛ teaspoon salt
½ cup baking cocoa
1 cup pecans, finely chopped
   Confectioners' sugar

Cream the butter and sugar in a mixer bowl until light and fluffy. Add the vanilla, flour, salt and baking cocoa and mix well. Stir in the pecans. Chill, covered, for 1 to 10 hours. Shape the dough by teaspoonfuls into balls. Place 2 inches apart on parchment-lined cookie sheets. Bake at 325 degrees for 20 minutes. Remove to wire racks to cool. Sprinkle with confectioners' sugar.

Note: Cookies may be stored for up to 2 weeks in an airtight container.

YIELD: 4 DOZEN

Chocolate Chunk Cookies

⅔ **cup butter, softened**
⅔ **cup sugar**
½ **cup packed dark brown sugar**
1 **egg**
1 **teaspoon vanilla extract**
1½ **cups flour**
8 **ounces semisweet chocolate, chopped**
4 **ounces white chocolate, chopped**
⅔ **cup chopped pecans**

Beat the first 3 ingredients in a mixer bowl until light. Beat in the egg and vanilla. Stir in the remaining ingredients. Shape into 2-inch balls. Place in a freezer container. Freeze, covered, for 8 to 10 hours. Place on lightly greased cookie sheets. Bake at 325 degrees for 17 minutes. Cool on the cookie sheets for 5 minutes. Remove to wire racks to cool completely.

YIELD: 2 DOZEN

Cream Cheese Cookie Bars

16 **ounces cream cheese, softened**
¾ **cup sugar**
2 **eggs**
1 **teaspoon almond extract**
2 **packages refrigerated chocolate chip cookie dough**
1 **cup chopped pecans**

Beat the first 4 ingredients in a mixer bowl until smooth. Spread ½ of the dough in a buttered 9x13-inch baking pan. Layer ½ cup pecans and cream cheese mixture over the dough. Pat the remaining dough into small patties and place on top. Sprinkle with the remaining pecans. Bake at 350 degrees for 30 minutes or until brown. Cool and cut into bars. Chill.

YIELD: 2 DOZEN

Chocolate Raspberry Supremes

1 **cup flour**
¼ **cup confectioners' sugar**
½ **cup butter or margarine**
3 **ounces cream cheese, softened**
2 **tablespoons milk**
1 **cup vanilla milk chips or 4 ounces white chocolate, melted**
½ **cup raspberry jam**
4 **ounces semisweet chocolate, cut into pieces**
2 **tablespoons shortening**

Mix the flour and confectioners' sugar in a medium bowl. Cut in the butter until crumbly. Press into an ungreased 9x9-inch baking pan. Bake at 375 degrees for 15 to 17 minutes or until light brown. Beat the cream cheese and milk in a small mixer bowl until smooth. Add the melted vanilla chips and beat well. Spread the jam evenly over the baked layer. Drop the cream cheese mixture by teaspoonfuls evenly over the jam and spread carefully to cover. Chill until set. Melt the chocolate and shortening in a saucepan over low heat, stirring constantly. Spread over the cream cheese layer. Cool completely. Cut into bars. Store in the refrigerator.

YIELD: 25 SERVINGS

Super Citrus Bars

2   tablespoons flour
½   teaspoon baking powder
¼   teaspoon salt
3   egg whites
¾   cup sugar
1½   teaspoons grated lime peel
1½   teaspoons grated lemon peel
¼   cup lime juice
¼   cup lemon juice
     Orange Pastry
     Confectioners' sugar

Mix the flour, baking powder and salt in a small bowl. Beat the egg whites, sugar, lime peel and lemon peel in a mixer bowl until fluffy. Fold in the flour mixture. Fold in the lime juice and lemon juice. Spoon over the cooled Orange Pastry. Bake at 375 degrees for 15 to 20 minutes or until golden brown. Let stand until cool. Cut into bars. Sprinkle with confectioners' sugar.

Orange Pastry

1   cup flour
¾   cup sugar
6   tablespoons butter, cut into pieces
1   egg
1   teaspoon orange zest
1   to 2 tablespoons orange juice

Mix the flour and sugar in a medium bowl. Cut in the butter until crumbly. Add the egg and orange zest and mash with a fork until well mixed. Add the orange juice a small amount at a time, mixing just until moistened. Knead on a floured surface until the pastry is no longer sticky, adding additional flour if needed. Roll into a ball and place in a greased 8x8-inch baking pan. Press the dough toward the sides and corners, smoothing to make the pastry even. Prick several times with a fork. Freeze for 20 minutes. Spray a piece of foil with nonstick cooking spray. Place sprayed side down over the pastry. Place pie weights or dried beans over the top to keep the pastry from rising. Bake at 400 degrees for 15 minutes. Remove the foil and weights. Reduce the oven temperature to 375 degrees. Bake for 10 minutes longer. Let stand until cool.

YIELD: 1 ⅓ DOZEN

For Orange Marshmallow Fruit Dip, beat one 7-ounce jar marshmallow creme, 12 ounces cream cheese, softened, 3 tablespoons orange juice, ⅛ teaspoon nutmeg and ⅛ teaspoon cinnamon in a mixer bowl until smooth. Spoon into a serving bowl. Chill, covered, in the refrigerator. Serve as a dip for fresh fruit.

Cream Cheese Cookies

1 cup shortening
3 ounces cream cheese, softened
1 cup sugar
1 egg
½ teaspoon vanilla extract
2½ cups sifted flour

Beat the shortening in a mixer bowl until light and fluffy. Add the cream cheese and sugar. Beat until smooth. Add the egg, vanilla and flour and beat well. Chill, covered, for 8 to 10 hours. Roll the dough on a lightly floured surface using a floured rolling pin. Cut into desired shapes. Place on a nonstick cookie sheet. Bake at 375 degrees for 10 to 15 minutes or until golden brown. Cool on a wire rack. Decorate as desired.

Note: May substitute butter or margarine, softened, for the shortening.

YIELD: 3 DOZEN

Lemon Sour Cream Cookies

½ cup butter
⅓ cup shortening
1 cup sugar
¾ teaspoon baking powder
½ teaspoon mace
¼ teaspoon baking soda
  Dash of salt
⅓ cup sour cream
1 egg
1 teaspoon vanilla extract
2½ cups flour
2 teaspoons finely shredded lemon peel

Beat the butter and shortening at medium to high speed in a large mixer bowl for 30 seconds. Add the sugar, baking powder, mace, baking soda and salt and beat well, scraping the side of the bowl occasionally. Beat in the sour cream, egg and vanilla. Beat in as much flour as possible. Stir in the remaining flour and lemon peel using a wooden spoon. Divide the dough into 2 equal portions. Chill, covered, for 1 to 2 hours or until the dough is easy to handle. Roll each portion ⅛ to ¼ inch thick on a floured surface. Cut into desired shapes with floured 2- to 2½-inch cookie cutters. Place ½ inch apart on ungreased cookie sheets. Bake at 375 degrees for 7 to 8 minutes or until the edges are firm. Cool on wire racks. Decorate as desired.

Note: Do not substitute margarine for butter in this recipe.

YIELD: 4 DOZEN

Orange Shortbread

2 cups unsalted butter, softened
1½ cups packed light brown sugar
4 cups unbleached flour
　 Pinch of salt
　 Finely grated zest of 2 oranges
2 eggs
2 tablespoons water

Cream the butter and brown sugar in a mixer bowl until light and fluffy. Add the flour and salt gradually, beating constantly until a stiff dough forms. Stir in the orange zest. Chill, wrapped in plastic wrap, for 2 hours. Line cookie sheets with parchment paper. Roll the dough on a lightly floured surface until ½ inch thick. Cut into desired shapes with 1½- to 2-inch cookie cutters. Place on the prepared cookie sheets. Beat the eggs and water in a small bowl. Brush over the tops of the cutouts. Bake at 350 degrees for 15 to 20 minutes or until light golden brown. Cool on wire racks. Store in airtight containers.

YIELD: 5 DOZEN

Orange Koulourakia

3½ cups flour
1½ teaspoons baking powder
¼ teaspoon salt
2 eggs, separated, at room temperature
1 cup sugar
6 tablespoons orange juice
6 tablespoons butter, melted, cooled
1 tablespoon grated orange peel
1 teaspoon vanilla extract
1 egg
1 tablespoon water
　 Sesame seeds

Sift the flour, baking powder and salt together. Beat 2 egg whites in a mixer bowl until stiff peaks form. Add 2 egg yolks 1 at a time, beating well after each addition. Beat in the sugar, orange juice, butter, orange peel and vanilla. Add the flour mixture gradually, beating until the mixture forms a soft ball. Beat at low speed for 8 minutes or until the dough is shiny and elastic. Roll the dough 1 rounded tablespoonful at a time on a lightly floured surface into 6-inch ropes. Form the ropes into desired shapes: roll from opposite ends to form "S" shapes; roll from 1 end to form snail shapes; fold ropes in half and twist for spiral shapes; and/or fold and twist ropes and shape into a circle to form a wreath. Arrange 2 inches apart on cookie sheets sprayed with nonstick cooking spray. Brush with a mixture of 1 egg and water. Sprinkle with sesame seeds. Bake at 350 degrees for 8 to 10 minutes or until golden brown. Cool on wire racks.

Note: The dough may be wrapped and stored in the freezer, then thawed and brought to room temperature before shaping. Children love to roll the dough into desired shapes.

YIELD: 4 TO 5 DOZEN

Lemon Meringue Tart

½ cup cake flour
1¼ cups sugar
4 egg yolks
1½ cups water
 Grated zest of 2 lemons
⅓ cup freshly squeezed lemon juice
1 Macadamia Nut Crust
3 egg whites
½ teaspoon cream of tartar
¾ cup superfine sugar

Combine the cake flour, 1¼ cups sugar, egg yolks, water and lemon zest in a double boiler and whisk well. Cook over simmering water until thickened, stirring constantly. Remove from the heat. Whisk in the lemon juice. Cool for 15 minutes. Spoon into a cooled Macadamia Nut Crust. Beat the egg whites in a large mixer bowl until frothy. Add the cream of tartar, beating constantly until soft peaks form. Reserve 1 tablespoon of the superfine sugar. Add the remaining superfine sugar ¼ cup at a time, beating constantly until stiff peaks form. Spread the meringue over the cooled filling, sealing to the edge. Sprinkle with the reserved sugar. Bake at 300 degrees for 30 minutes or until the meringue is light brown. Cool before serving.

Macadamia Nut Crusts

10 ounces finely chopped macadamia nuts
3 cups unbleached flour
⅓ cup sugar
1 cup unsalted butter, cut into small pieces
1 egg, lightly beaten
1 teaspoon vanilla extract
 Grated zest of 1 lemon

Process the nuts, flour, sugar and butter in a food processor just until combined. Add the egg, vanilla and lemon zest and process well. Divide the pastry into 2 equal portions. Wrap 1 portion in plastic wrap and freeze for another use. Press the remaining portion into a lightly buttered 10-inch tart pan. Chill, covered, for 30 minutes or longer. Bake at 350 degrees for 20 to 25 minutes or until golden brown. Cool on a wire rack.

YIELD: 6 TO 8 SERVINGS

To make Lemon Curd Filling, melt ⅓ cup butter or margarine in a heavy saucepan. Add 1 cup sugar gradually, stirring constantly until the sugar dissolves. Stir in ⅓ cup lemon juice, ¼ cup grated lemon peel and ¼ teaspoon salt. Stir a small amount of the hot mixture into 3 beaten eggs; stir the eggs into the hot mixture. Cook over low heat until thickened, stirring constantly. Remove from the heat. Let stand until cool, stirring occasionally.

Famous Key Lime Pie

MONTY'S CONCH HARBOR

- 1½ **cups graham cracker crumbs**
- 1 **tablespoon ground cinnamon**
- 3 **tablespoons sugar**
- ¼ **cup melted unsalted butter**
- 6 **egg yolks**
- 39 **ounces sweetened condensed milk**
- 1 **teaspoon cornstarch**
- ¾ **cup Nellie and Joe's Key lime juice**

Mix the graham cracker crumbs, cinnamon, sugar and melted butter in a bowl. Press evenly over the bottom and up the side of a 10-inch deep-dish pie plate. Bake at 325 degrees for 10 minutes. Let stand until cool. Beat the egg yolks at high speed in a mixer bowl for 5 to 10 minutes or until stiff but still fluffy. Add the condensed milk. Beat at medium speed for 2 minutes. Scrape the side of the bowl. Add the cornstarch to the lime juice and mix well. Add to the egg mixture. Beat at low speed for 2 minutes. Spoon into the prepared pie shell. Bake at 275 degrees for 30 minutes or until the pie is set but not brown. Remove to a wire rack to cool. Garnish with whipped cream and lime slices. Store in the refrigerator.

YIELD: 6 TO 8 SERVINGS

Orange Dessert Pie

- ⅓ **cup flour**
- ⅓ **cup sugar**
- 1½ **cups milk**
- 2 **eggs**
- ½ **teaspoon almond extract**
  Tart Shell
- 8 **oranges, peeled, sectioned**

Mix the flour and sugar in a medium saucepan. Beat the milk and eggs in a small mixer bowl. Add to the flour mixture gradually, stirring constantly. Cook over low heat until thickened, stirring constantly. Remove from the heat. Stir in the almond extract. Place plastic wrap over the surface of the filling. Let stand until cool. Spoon the filling into the Tart Shell. Chill in the refrigerator. Arrange orange sections over the top before serving.

Tart Shell

- 1⅓ **cups flour**
- ¼ **cup sugar**
- ½ **cup butter or margarine, softened**
- 2 **egg yolks**

Mix the flour and sugar in a medium bowl. Add the butter and egg yolks. Stir with a fork until the mixture forms a ball. Press into a 9-inch tart pan with a removable bottom. Chill for 15 minutes. Bake at 400 degrees for 10 minutes. Reduce the oven temperature to 350 degrees. Bake for 10 to 15 minutes longer or until light brown. Remove to a wire rack. Let stand until cool.

YIELD: 8 SERVINGS

Basic Pie Pastry

DEAN JOHNSON, A.K.A. COMMANDER COCONUT,
THE ORLANDO SENTINEL

- 1½ **cups sifted flour**
- ½ **teaspoon salt**
- ½ **cup shortening**
- 4 **to 5 tablespoons ice water or milk**
  Sugar

Mix the flour and salt in a medium bowl. Cut in the shortening until crumbly. Add the ice water, stirring constantly until a soft ball forms. Divide into 2 equal portions. Roll each portion into a circle on a lightly floured surface. Fit each portion into an 8- or 9-inch pie plate or use 1 portion as the top of a pie, trimming and fluting edges and cutting vents. Sprinkle the top portion with a small amount of sugar.

Note: May substitute butter, margarine, lard or a combination of each for the shortening.

YIELD: TWO (8- OR 9-INCH) 1-CRUST PIE
PASTRIES OR ENOUGH PASTRY FOR
A DOUBLE-CRUSTED PIE

Orange Walnut Chocolate Tart

- 1¼ **cups flour**
- ¼ **cup confectioners' sugar**
- 1 **teaspoon salt**
- ⅓ **cup butter, chilled**
- 1 **tablespoon cold water**
- 1 **(18-ounce) jar orange marmalade**
- ¾ **cup coarsely chopped walnuts**
- 1 **cup whipping cream**
- 2 **cups chocolate chips**

Combine the flour, confectioners' sugar and salt in a food processor container. Add the butter and process until coarse crumbs form. Add the cold water and process until the pastry pulls from the side of the container. Press into a lightly greased 10-inch tart pan. Bake at 350 degrees for 15 to 20 minutes or until golden brown. Let stand until cool. Combine the marmalade and walnuts in a small bowl and mix well. Spoon into the pie crust. Bring the whipping cream to a boil in a 1-quart saucepan over medium-high heat. Remove from the heat. Add the chocolate chips. Stir until the chocolate chips have melted and the mixture is smooth. Pour over the marmalade mixture, spreading evenly to the edge. Chill for 4 hours or longer.

YIELD: 8 TO 10 SERVINGS

Orange Custard Tart

- ¾ **cup flour**
- ⅔ **cup yellow cornmeal**
- ⅔ **cup confectioners' sugar**
- 2 **teaspoons minced orange peel**
- ¼ **teaspoon salt**
- 7 **tablespoons butter, softened**
- 1 **egg yolk**
- 2 **teaspoons vanilla extract**
- 1 **cup whipping cream**
- ½ **cup fresh orange juice**
- 5 **egg yolks**
- ¼ **cup plus 1 tablespoon sugar**
- 2 **tablespoons Grand Marnier**
- 1 **tablespoon minced orange peel**
- 3 **oranges, peeled, sectioned, drained**
- 2 **cups raspberries**

Mix the flour, cornmeal, confectioners' sugar, minced orange peel and salt in a large mixer bowl. Add the butter, 1 egg yolk and vanilla. Beat until coarse crumbs form. Knead into a ball on a lightly floured surface. Pat the dough over the bottom and up the sides of a 4x13-inch tart pan, trimming the excess dough from the edges. Freeze for 20 minutes. Line the pastry with foil. Fill with pie weights or dried beans. Bake at 350 degrees for 15 minutes. Remove the foil and pie weights, pressing the crust up the sides of the pan if needed. Bake for 10 minutes longer. Let stand until cool. Combine the whipping cream, orange juice, 5 egg yolks, sugar, Grand Marnier and orange peel in a medium mixer bowl and mix well. Pour into the cooled crust. Bake at 350 degrees for 30 minutes or until barely set. Cool on a wire rack for 20 minutes. Chill for 3 hours or until firm. Arrange alternating rows of orange sections and raspberries on top of the tart.

YIELD: 8 SERVINGS

Try using grapefruit juice as a substitute for lemon juice. Sprinkle grapefruit juice over sliced fresh fruit to keep the colors bright. Try grapefruit juice in spice cake, carrot cake, and banana cake batters and frostings. Add zip to kale, collards, and mustard greens with a sprinkling of grapefruit juice. Marinate beef, pork, poultry, and other meats with grapefruit juice. The natural acidity tenderizes while it adds a refreshing light grapefruit flavor. Replace lemon juice with grapefruit juice in salad vinaigrettes. Blanch strips of grapefruit peel and use to tie asparagus or green bean bundles.

Pecan Tarts

½ cup margarine, softened
3 ounces cream cheese, softened
1 cup flour
1 egg, beaten
¾ cup packed light brown sugar
1 tablespoon melted margarine
½ teaspoon vanilla extract
   Chopped pecans

Combine ½ cup margarine, cream cheese and flour in a bowl and mix well. Roll into a ball. Chill, wrapped in plastic wrap, for 2 hours or longer. Shape the dough into 24 balls. Press into small muffin cups sprayed with nonstick cooking spray. Combine the egg, brown sugar, 1 tablespoon margarine and vanilla in a bowl and mix well. Fill each prepared muffin cup ¾ full with filling. Sprinkle with pecans. Bake at 350 degrees for 30 minutes or until the crust is light brown.

YIELD: 2 DOZEN

Citrus zest is the colored outer portion of the citrus peel. Zest that has been freshly grated from fresh citrus has more flavor than dried zest. A citrus zester has 5 tiny cutting holes that create threadlike strips of peel. Draw the zester down the skin of the fruit while pressing down firmly. Begin at 1 end of the fruit and cut in a spiral around and down for continuous strips of zest. Be sure when using a zester to remove only the colored portion of the peel, since the white pith will give a bitter flavor.

Bananas Foster for Two

¼ cup butter
¾ cup packed dark brown sugar
3 heaping teaspoons corn syrup
2 bananas, sliced
2 tablespoons banana liqueur
1 tablespoon dark rum
   French vanilla ice cream

Combine the butter, brown sugar and corn syrup in a medium sauté pan. Bring to a boil. Add the bananas. Spoon the sauce over the bananas. Add the banana liqueur. Simmer until the bananas are soft. Add the dark rum. Ignite the rum; let the flame subside. Spoon over ice cream in individual serving dishes.

YIELD: 2 SERVINGS

Berry Tart with Mascarpone Cream

Sweet Pastry Dough
1   cup mascarpone cheese, softened
⅓   cup chilled whipping cream
¼   cup sugar
1½   cups small strawberries, cut into quarters
1   cup raspberries
1   cup blueberries
1   cup blackberries
2   tablespoons sweet orange marmalade
2   tablespoons blackberry or cassis liqueur

Roll the Sweet Pastry Dough on a lightly floured surface into an 11-inch circle ⅛ inch thick. Fit into a 9-inch tart pan with a removable fluted rim. Roll the rolling pin over the top of the shell to trim the dough flush with the rim. Prick the surface of the shell with a fork. Chill for 30 minutes or until firm. Line the shell with foil and fill with pie weights or uncooked rice. Bake at 375 degrees for 20 minutes. Remove the foil and pie weights carefully. Bake for 10 minutes longer or until the shell is golden brown. Cool on a wire rack. Beat the mascarpone cheese, whipping cream and sugar in a mixer bowl until stiff peaks form. Spoon evenly into the prepared tart shell. Combine the strawberries, raspberries, blueberries and blackberries in a bowl and toss to mix well. Mix the marmalade and liqueur in a small saucepan. Simmer until reduced to about 3 tablespoons, stirring constantly. Pour over the berries. Stir the berries gently with a rubber spatula to coat. Mound the berries decoratively on the mascarpone cream. Remove the side of the pan before serving.

Note: The tart shell may be made 1 day in advance and stored, loosely covered, at room temperature. The tart may be assembled up to 2 hours before serving and chilled in the refrigerator. Bring to room temperature before serving.

Sweet Pastry Dough

1⅓   cups flour
2   tablespoons sugar
¼   teaspoon salt
½   cup cold unsalted butter, cut into ½-inch cubes
1   egg yolk
1½   tablespoons ice water

Combine the flour, sugar and salt in a bowl. Cut in the butter until crumbly. Mix the egg yolk and ice water in a bowl. Drizzle over the flour mixture, stirring gently with a fork until a ball forms. Divide into 4 portions on a floured surface. Smear each portion once in a forward motion to help distribute the butter and roll into a disk. Wrap the disk in plastic wrap. Chill for 1 hour or until firm.

YIELD: 6 TO 8 SERVINGS

Berry Tiramisù

2	packages frozen mixed berries
½	cup Chambord
½	pint fresh raspberries
1	pint fresh blueberries
1	pint fresh strawberries, sliced
¼	cup sugar
	Juice of 1 lemon
16	ounces mascarpone cheese, softened
2	cups whipping cream, whipped
2	(9-inch round) sponge cakes
2	packages ladyfingers

Thaw the berries in the refrigerator for 8 to 10 hours. Place in a colander over a bowl to drain. Let the berries stand until thawed. Mix the liqueur into the reserved juice in the bowl. Combine the raspberries, blueberries and strawberries in a medium bowl. Add the sugar and lemon juice and toss until well coated. Place the cheese in a large bowl. Fold in the whipped cream a small amount at a time until thoroughly blended. Trim ½ inch around each cake. Place 1 of the cakes in a 9-inch springform pan sprayed with nonstick cooking spray. Brush liberally with some of the reserved juice mixture. Dunk 1 side of some of the ladyfingers 1 at time into the reserved juice mixture and line vertically around the side of the pan with the juiced side facing toward the center. Layer ⅓ of the cheese mixture and ½ of the berries over the cake layer. Brush 1 side of the remaining ladyfingers with some of the juice mixture. Place over the thawed berry layer. Layer half the remaining cheese mixture, the remaining thawed berries and the remaining sponge cake over the layers. Brush the sponge cake with the remaining juice mixture. Spread the remaining cheese mixture over the cake. Top with a mixture of the fresh berries, leaving a 1-inch border around the side. Chill for 1 hour before serving.

YIELD: 12 TO 15 SERVINGS

Prepare Fuzzy Navel Tiramisù by making the following substitutions to Berry Tiramisù. Thaw 1 package frozen peach slices and drain, reserving the juice. Use the peach slices mixed with 2 cups orange sections instead of the 2 packages of frozen berries. Substitute peach liqueur for the Chambord and add to the reserved peach juice along with ½ cup orange juice. Use this mixture to brush the cake and ladyfingers. For the top, peel and slice 3 medium peaches and toss with 1 cup undrained fresh orange sections. Let stand for 10 minutes. Place the fresh fruit mixture on the top.

Cherry Hazelnut Sundaes

¼ **cup packed brown sugar**
¼ **cup butter or margarine**
3 **tablespoons light corn syrup**
1 **cup ground hazelnuts or almonds**
⅓ **cup flour**
8 **scoops vanilla ice cream**
  Dried Cherry Sauce

Line cookie sheets with foil and butter the foil. Combine the brown sugar, butter and corn syrup in a small saucepan. Cook over medium heat until smooth, stirring constantly. Remove from the heat. Stir in the hazelnuts and flour. Drop by 2 tablespoonfuls 5 inches apart on the prepared cookie sheets. Flatten slightly if necessary. Bake at 350 degrees for 8 to 9 minutes or until the edges are golden brown. Let stand on the cookie sheets for 1 to 2 minutes. Loosen carefully from the cookie sheets and press immediately over inverted ungreased 6-ounce custard cups to form a shell. Let stand for 8 to 9 minutes. Remove cookie shells to wire racks to cool. Place a scoop of ice cream in each cookie shell. Top with warm Dried Cherry Sauce.

Dried Cherry Sauce

½ **cup dried cherries**
¼ **cup packed brown sugar**
2 **tablespoons cornstarch**
1 **teaspoon finely shredded lemon peel**
¼ **teaspoon apple pie spice**
2 **cups cranberry-cherry juice**

Combine the dried cherries, brown sugar, cornstarch, lemon peel and apple pie spice in a small saucepan and mix well. Stir in the juice. Cook until thickened, stirring constantly. Cook for 2 minutes longer, stirring constantly.

YIELD: 8 SERVINGS

For Brie with Praline Sauce, place an 8-inch round of Brie cheese on a baking sheet. Bake at 275 degrees for 15 to 20 minutes or until soft. Place ½ cup coarsely chopped pecans on a baking sheet and dot with ½ cup butter. Sprinkle with 1 tablespoon sugar. Bake at 300 degrees for 30 minutes or until brown. Melt ½ cup butter in a small saucepan. Add 1 cup packed brown sugar, ⅛ teaspoon lemon juice and ¼ cup milk and bring to a boil. Boil for 3 to 5 minutes, stirring constantly. Stir in the toasted pecans. Place the Brie cheese on a serving platter and pour the praline sauce over the top, letting the sauce dribble over the side. Serve with crackers and fresh fruit, such as sliced apples, pears, strawberries and grapes.

Key Lime Cheesecake

2 cups graham cracker crumbs
½ cup packed brown sugar
2 tablespoons melted butter or margarine
32 ounces cream cheese, softened
1⅔ cups sugar
5 tablespoons sour cream
4 eggs
1 egg yolk
5 tablespoons whipping cream
1 cup flour
1 tablespoon vanilla extract
½ cup Key lime juice

Cover the outside of a 10-inch springform pan with heavy-duty foil and butter the inside of the pan. Mix the graham cracker crumbs, brown sugar and butter in a bowl. Press in the bottom of the prepared pan. Beat the cream cheese and sugar in a mixer bowl until light and fluffy; scrape the side of the bowl. Beat in the sour cream. Add the eggs and egg yolk 1 at a time, beating well after each addition and scraping the side of the bowl. Add the whipping cream, flour, vanilla and lime juice and mix well. Spoon into the prepared pan. Place the springform pan in a larger pan. Fill the larger pan with enough boiling water to come halfway up the side of the smaller pan. Bake at 325 degrees for 1 hour and 20 minutes or until a tester inserted near the center comes out clean, filling the outer pan with boiling water as needed. Remove the pan from the water bath and discard the foil. Cool on a wire rack. Place on a serving plate and remove the side of the pan.

YIELD: 12 SERVINGS

Chocolate Cheesecake

1¾ cups chocolate cookie or graham cracker crumbs
2 tablespoons sugar
⅓ cup melted butter
8 ounces German's sweet chocolate
2 eggs
⅔ cup light or dark corn syrup
⅓ cup whipping cream
1½ teaspoons vanilla extract
16 ounces cream cheese, cut into cubes

Mix the cookie crumbs, sugar and butter in a bowl. Press into a 9-inch springform pan. Melt 6 ounces of the chocolate in a double boiler over boiling water. Process the eggs, corn syrup, whipping cream and vanilla in a blender or food processor until smooth. Add the cream cheese a few cubes at a time, processing constantly until smooth. Add the melted chocolate, processing constantly. Pour into the prepared pan. Bake at 325 degrees for 45 minutes or until set. Cool on a wire rack. Melt the remaining 2 ounces chocolate in a double boiler over boiling water. Drizzle over the cheesecake. Store in the refrigerator until serving time.

YIELD: 12 TO 15 SERVINGS

Candied Orange Peel

6   large thick-peel oranges
2   cups sugar
1   cup water
½   cup light corn syrup
⅛   teaspoon salt
    Few drops of yellow food coloring (optional)
    Sugar for coating
    Melted sweet baking chocolate (optional)

Remove the zest from the oranges in quarters or sixths, reserving the pulp for another purpose. Cut into ¼- to ½-inch-wide strips. Combine with water to cover in a heavy saucepan. Bring to a boil and reduce the heat. Simmer for 10 minutes. Drain and repeat the process 4 times. Combine 2 cups sugar, 1 cup water, corn syrup, salt and food coloring in a heavy saucepan. Bring to a simmer. Add the drained orange zest. Boil until the syrup is thick and the zest is translucent. Spread on a wire rack over a jelly roll pan, foil or waxed paper to drain and cool. Roll the orange strips a few at a time in sugar to coat; dip the ends into melted chocolate. Let stand for 24 hours or until firm. Store in an airtight container.

YIELD: 1 ¼ POUNDS

To freeze Citrus Pulp for Marmalade, prepare the fruit by rinsing and quartering it and removing the seeds. Process the fruit in a food processor or blender. Pour into 3-cup freezer containers. Freeze until firm. To use, add 3 cups water per cup of pulp. Cook until thawed and continue to boil for 15 minutes. Let stand for 8 to 10 hours and use as you would fresh stock in marmalade.

The major honey varieties in Florida are orange blossom, palmetto, gallberry, and tupelo. Bees can feed on many different flowers, which means about 300 unique types of honey are available commercially. The color and flavor of honey differs, depending on the kind of blossoms the bees work. Blended honeys are best for cooking and baking. Pure honeys are best used in beverages or dips.

Baked goods made with honey stay moist longer than those made with sugar. In Florida, where the air is humid most of the time, this can cause foods to become sticky and frostings to thin out.

To substitute honey for sugar in a recipe, use ¾ cup of honey for every cup of sugar, reduce the liquid by about ¼ cup for each cup of honey used, and reduce the oven temperature by 25 degrees to prevent burning.

Orange Caramel Flan

½	tablespoon lemon juice
2	tablespoons water
1	cup sugar
8	ounces cream cheese, softened
½	teaspoon vanilla extract
2	tablespoons honey
½	cup sugar
4	eggs
2	cups orange juice
	Fresh berries
	Toasted sliced almonds
2	cups orange sections

Combine the lemon juice, water and 1 cup sugar in a saucepan. Bring to a boil and reduce the heat. Simmer until the liquid becomes pale amber in color. Remove from the heat. Spoon into six 7-ounce ramekins. Let stand at room temperature until hardened. Beat the cream cheese in a mixer bowl until smooth. Add the vanilla, honey and ½ cup sugar and beat well. Add the eggs 1 at a time, beating well after each addition. Add the orange juice gradually, beating constantly. Pour into the prepared ramekins. Place the ramekins in a larger baking pan. Fill the larger pan with enough boiling water to come halfway up the side of the ramekins. Bake at 325 degrees for 1 hour and 10 minutes or until a knife inserted in the center of the custard comes out clean. Remove to wire racks to cool. Chill in the refrigerator. Run a knife around the inside edge of each ramekin. Invert a serving plate over each ramekin; invert and remove the ramekin. Garnish with fresh berries, toasted almonds and orange sections.

YIELD: 6 SERVINGS

Raspberry Almond Pâté

1¼ cups finely ground toasted almonds
1¼ cups whipping cream
¼ cup butter
2 cups raspberry or milk chocolate chips
1 cup miniature semisweet chocolate chips
1½ teaspoons almond extract
Fresh raspberries
Sliced almonds

Line a 5x9-inch loaf pan with waxed paper. Sprinkle the ground almonds in the bottom. Simmer the whipping cream and butter in a medium saucepan over medium heat. Reduce the heat to low. Stir in the raspberry and chocolate chips. Cook until smooth, stirring constantly. Remove from the heat. Stir in the almond extract. Pour into the prepared pan. Chill for 5 hours or until set. Invert onto a serving platter to unmold. Remove the waxed paper. Cut into ½-inch slices. Top with raspberries and almonds.

YIELD: 20 SERVINGS

Lemon Ice Cream Pie

¾ cup fine vanilla wafer crumbs
2 tablespoons sugar
¼ cup melted butter
½ cup chopped pecans
1½ pints vanilla ice cream
3 tablespoons butter
2 tablespoons lemon juice
½ cup sugar
1 egg, lightly beaten

Mix the vanilla wafer crumbs, 2 tablespoons sugar, ¼ cup butter and pecans in a bowl. Press into a greased pie plate. Bake at 275 degrees for 10 minutes. Place in the freezer. Freeze until firm. Spoon the ice cream into the pie shell and return to the freezer. Melt 3 tablespoons butter in a small saucepan. Add the lemon juice and ½ cup sugar and mix well. Remove from the heat. Add a small amount of the hot mixture to the beaten egg. Stir the egg into the hot mixture. Cook until thickened, stirring constantly. Chill in the refrigerator until cool. Spread over the ice cream and return to the freezer. Freeze until firm.

YIELD: 6 TO 8 SERVINGS

Caramelized Raspberry Rice Pudding

½　cup water
¼　teaspoon salt
⅓　cup long grain white rice
1¾ cups whipping cream
¼　cup half-and-half
½　vanilla bean, split
6　egg yolks
⅓　cup sugar
36　frozen raspberries, thawed, drained
6　tablespoons sugar

Bring the water and salt to a boil in a small saucepan. Add the rice. Reduce the heat to low. Cook, covered, for 20 minutes or until all the liquid is absorbed. Remove from the heat. Fluff with a fork. Let stand until cool. Combine the whipping cream and half-and-half in a heavy medium saucepan. Scrape in the seeds from the vanilla bean. Add the bean. Bring the mixture to a simmer, stirring constantly. Whisk the egg yolks and ⅓ cup sugar in a large bowl until blended. Add the hot cream mixture gradually, whisking constantly. Remove the vanilla bean. Stir in the rice. Spoon equal amounts into six ¾-cup custard cups. Press 6 raspberries into each cup. Place the cups in a large baking pan. Pour enough hot water into the baking pan to come halfway up the sides of the cups. Bake at 300 degrees for 40 minutes or until set. Remove the cups to wire racks. Cool for 30 minutes. Chill, covered, for 2 hours or until the centers of the pudding are set. Place on a large baking sheet. Sprinkle each with 1 tablespoon sugar. Broil for 2 minutes or until the sugar melts and turns golden brown. Watch closely to avoid burning. Chill for 15 minutes or until set.

YIELD: 6 SERVINGS

Strawberry Pizza

½　cup butter
½　cup margarine
1½ cups flour
½　to ¾ cup chopped pecans
½　cup packed brown sugar
8　ounces cream cheese, softened
¾　cup confectioners' sugar
9　ounces whipped topping
1　(6-ounce) package strawberry gelatin
¼　cup cornstarch
½　cup sugar
1　cup water
2　to 4 cups sliced strawberries

Melt the butter and margarine in a small saucepan. Combine with the flour, pecans and brown sugar in a bowl and mix well. Press into a pizza pan. Bake at 400 degrees for 15 minutes. Let stand until cool. Beat the cream cheese and confectioners' sugar in a mixer bowl until smooth. Fold in the whipped topping. Spread over the cooled crust. Combine the strawberry gelatin, cornstarch, sugar and water in a saucepan. Cook over medium heat until thickened, stirring constantly. Let stand until cool. Stir in the strawberries. Spread over the cream cheese mixture. Chill for 1 hour before serving.

YIELD: 6 TO 8 SERVINGS

Champagne Sherbet

1   cup sugar
1   cup water
    Juice of 1 orange
    Juice of 2 lemons
2   cups Champagne
½   cup whipping cream, whipped

Bring the sugar and water to a boil in a saucepan. Boil for 5 minutes or until the sugar dissolves. Remove from the heat. Let stand until cool. Combine with the orange juice, lemon juice and Champagne in an airtight container. Freeze until partially firm. Fold in the whipped cream. Spoon into Champagne flutes. Freeze until firm.

Note: May substitute dry sauterne or white wine for the Champagne.

YIELD: 8 SERVINGS

Grand Marnier Soufflé with Champagne Biscuits

¼   cup sugar
5   egg yolks
¼   cup flour
1¾ cups hot milk
1   tablespoon butter
6   tablespoons Grand Marnier
4   ladyfingers
6   egg whites
    Pinch of salt
¼   cup sugar
    Confectioners' sugar

Mix ¼ cup sugar, egg yolks and flour in a 2-cup saucepan. Add the hot milk. Cook until thickened, stirring constantly. Do not boil. Stir in the butter. Pour into a large bowl and let cool slightly. Stir in 3 tablespoons of the Grand Marnier. Soak the ladyfingers in the remaining Grand Marnier in a bowl. Beat the egg whites and a pinch of salt in a mixer bowl until soft peaks form. Add ¼ cup sugar gradually, beating constantly until stiff peaks form. Fold into the egg yolk mixture. Butter and sugar 4 individual soufflé dishes. Pour ½ of the custard into the prepared dishes. Arrange 1 ladyfinger in the center of each. Pour the remaining custard over the top. Bake at 400 degrees for 10 to 12 minutes or until set. Sprinkle with confectioners' sugar through a fine sieve. Serve immediately.

YIELD: 4 SERVINGS

Strawberries with Grand Marnier Sauce

1   **egg yolk**
1   **tablespoon Grand Marnier**
¼   **cup sugar**
3   **ounces cream cheese, cut into quarters**
2   **tablespoons whipping cream**
1½ **cups thickly sliced strawberries**

Place the egg yolk in an egg coddler or other heat-proof container with a tightfitting lid; set the egg coddler in a larger pan of simmering water for 1 minute. Combine the coddled egg yolk, Grand Marnier, sugar and cream cheese in a blender container. Process just until smooth, stopping occasionally to scrape down the sides of the container. Mix in the whipping cream. Pour into a 1-cup bowl. Chill, covered, in the refrigerator. Divide the strawberries between 2 compotes. Chill, wrapped in plastic wrap, in the refrigerator. Pour the sauce over the strawberries at serving time.

YIELD: 2 SERVINGS

To make Chocolate Rum Sauce, combine 1 tablespoon light corn syrup, ⅓ cup evaporated milk, 1 cup chocolate chips and 1 tablespoon rum in a double boiler. Cook over simmering water until smooth, stirring frequently. Remove from the heat. Serve over vanilla or peppermint ice cream. Store, covered, in the refrigerator and reheat over hot water before serving.

French Strawberry Mousse

1	cup flour
½	cup packed brown sugar
1	cup chopped pecans
½	cup melted butter
2	egg whites
1	cup sugar
2	teaspoons lemon juice
1	(10-ounce) package frozen strawberries, thawed
1	cup whipping cream, whipped
3	packages ladyfingers
1	cup whipping cream
	Sugar to taste

Mix the flour, brown sugar, pecans and butter in a bowl. Spread in a 9x13-inch baking dish. Bake at 350 degrees for 20 minutes. Let stand until cool. Crumble the mixture and set aside. Beat the egg whites, 1 cup sugar, lemon juice and strawberries in a mixer bowl for 15 minutes; do not underbeat. Fold in the whipped cream. Line the bottom and side of a large trifle bowl with ladyfingers. Layer the berry mixture and crumb mixture ⅓ at a time in the prepared bowl. Beat 1 cup whipping cream with sugar to taste in a mixer bowl until soft peaks form. Spread over the layers. Garnish with fresh whole strawberries.

YIELD: 12 SERVINGS

Lemon Mousse with Raspberry Sauce

1	envelope unflavored gelatin
2	tablespoons white wine
⅓	cup lemon juice
1½	tablespoons grated lemon peel
3	eggs, separated
½	cup sugar
1	cup whipping cream, whipped

Soften the gelatin in the wine in a double boiler. Add the lemon juice and lemon peel. Cook over simmering water until the gelatin is dissolved, stirring constantly. Remove from the heat. Beat the egg yolks and 3 tablespoons of the sugar in a mixer bowl until pale yellow. Add the gelatin mixture gradually, beating constantly. Beat the egg whites in a mixer bowl until foamy. Add the remaining sugar gradually, beating until soft peaks form. Fold the whipped cream into the egg yolk mixture. Fold in the meringue. Spoon into individual serving dishes or 1 large serving dish. Chill for 2 hours or until set. Spoon Raspberry Sauce over the mousse before serving. Garnish with raspberries.

Raspberry Sauce

1	(10-ounce) package frozen raspberries, thawed
2	tablespoons sugar
1	tablespoon lemon juice
1	tablespoon kirsch

Drain the raspberries, reserving the juice. Combine the raspberries, sugar, lemon juice and liqueur in a blender or food processor container. Process until puréed. Strain the raspberry purée into a bowl, discarding the seeds. Add enough of the reserved raspberry juice to thin the sauce slightly.

YIELD: 6 TO 8 SERVINGS

Three-Berry Fruit Soup

MIKE THOMAS, *THE ORLANDO SENTINEL*

- 2 **cups raspberries**
- 2 **cups blueberries**
- 2 **cups strawberries**
- 1 **cup sugar**
- 1 **tablespoon minute tapioca**
- 2 **tablespoons butter**
  Fresh lemon juice to taste

Combine the raspberries, blueberries, strawberries, sugar, minute tapioca, butter and lemon juice in a Dutch oven. Bake, covered, at 350 degrees for 20 to 30 minutes or until of the desired consistency. Serve over vanilla ice cream.

YIELD: 2 ½ TO 3 CUPS

Elegant Bananas

- 2 **tablespoons butter**
- 4 **firm bananas**
- 1½ **teaspoons sugar**
- ½ **cup whipping cream**
- ¼ **teaspoon vanilla extract**
- 3 **ounces cream cheese, softened**

Melt the butter in a 1½-quart baking dish. Cut the bananas lengthwise into halves. Place in the baking dish. Beat the sugar, whipping cream, vanilla and cream cheese in a mixer bowl until smooth. Pour over the bananas. Bake at 375 degrees for 20 minutes. Garnish with fresh raspberries, blueberries or strawberries sprinkled with confectioners' sugar.

YIELD: 6 TO 8 SERVINGS

HOW TO FILLET GRAPEFRUIT
To fillet a grapefruit, cut a grapefruit into halves from the top of the stem mark. Cut a 2- to 3-inch section from each half. Cut along the skins, separating the fruit. Cut the sections into halves lengthwise.

White Chocolate Fettuccini

- **7** ounces white chocolate, melted
- **¼** cup light corn syrup
- **1** cup confectioners' sugar
- **24** large strawberries
- **½** cup (or more) amaretto
- **8** ounces semisweet chocolate, melted
- **24** medium strawberries

Mix the white chocolate and corn syrup in a bowl until a soft dough forms. Roll on waxed paper into a rectangle ⅛ inch thick. Chill until firm. Run through a pasta machine to cut into long strips ⅓ inch wide or cut with a sharp knife. Let the strips fall into the confectioners' sugar to prevent sticking. Chill until serving time. Inject the large strawberries with a squirt of amaretto with a cooking syringe. Dip in the melted chocolate. Place on a tray lined with waxed paper. Chill until the chocolate is firm. Purée the medium strawberries in a blender until smooth. Pour through a mesh strainer to strain. Pour the sauce onto individual serving plates. Add a few of the white chocolate fettuccini and top with chocolate-covered strawberries.

YIELD: 8 SERVINGS

Florida citrus fruit is available from October through June.
- Grapefruit is available October through June.
- Oranges are available during these months except for February. Hamlins are available October through December. Navels are available November through January; and Valencias are available March through June.
- Tangerines are available October through December. Honey Tangerines are available January through March.
- Tangelos are available November through January. Temples are available January through March.

CONTRIBUTORS LIST

• • •

The committee for *A Sunsational Encore* would like to thank
the following individuals and their families for sharing their favorite
recipes and volunteering to test new recipes.

Kelly Acree**
Mark Acree
Amy Adams*
Athena Adams
Maryan Alleman
Jill Anderson
Deborah Ansbro
Dana Anselmo
Cathy Appleton
Marci Arthur
Joy Ashlock**
Barbara Aufhammer
Gina Bacon
Julie Baird
Janice Baker
Catherine Ballinger
Andrea Balogh
Ann Quian Bargeron
Teresa Barr
Sheila Barth
Laura Bartlett
Ernestine J. Beattie
Jane Beaty
M. K. Beaty
Beth Becht
Gertrude Bell
Mrs. John Bell
Kahrina Bennett
Wayne Bennett
Dorothy Berger
Sarah Bethune
Jennifer Bishop*
Sally Blake**

Leigh Ann Blackmore*
Jane Blalock
Sally Blashfield
Jennifer Bohn*
Anne Boitano
Rose Boothby
Carrie Borho
Tam Braithwaite
Dorothy Branham
Cindy S. Brodie
Kathy Broecker
Lora Lee Brown*
Denise Bruder
Cynthia Brumback
Pamela Buckley**
Jane Bullock
Julie Burns*
Kim Burst
Laura Burst*
Marina Byington*
Lisa Bywater
Joanie Cahill
Beth Caito
Anne Campbell
Michelle Chira Carlton
Terry Carrin
Sandy Carroll
Shelly Carter**
Carole Caruso
Sammi Caruso*
Shannon Caruso*
Sharon Caruso
Rebecca Hathaway Casey

Linda Chapin
Camilla Chapman
Margaret Chapman
Tracy Duda Chapman
Georgianne Cherry
Mary Carter Christie
Joanne Clapham
Yvonne Clayton
Luci Coker
Beverly Coleman
Laura Collins
Sherry Cooper
Stacey Dickenson Cox
Ann Moore Croft
Lora Crone
Josephine Culp
Jean Cumming
Kelly Damon
Angie Dear
Jennifer Dingfelder*
Sharon Donoghue*
Shayna Dorsett
Janey Dougherty
Libby Drosdick
Jane Drummond
Betty Duda
Kristy Dunlap
Thomas Dunn
Nancy Dunne
Lynette Earley
Stephanie Earley**
Holly Eby
Ellen Edwards

Gina Edwards-Dole
Laura Eidson
Lindsay Ellison
Kelli Eshleman
Eileen Faix*
Linda Falcone
Vera Farmen**
Jennifer Gentry Fernandez
Theresa Feuger
Susan Filebark
Bonnie Fleming
Florida Department of Citrus
Jackie Floyd
Lisa Fluty
Julie Folmar**
Lisa Fonk
Sheri Ford
Cheree Foreman**
Jane Fox
Lucy Gaida
Vicki Gardner
Kathy Gatch
Dinky Gefvert
Alan Geiger
Robin Geisler
Kathy Gibbs
Carrie Gill**
Randy Gill
Betty Gilleland
Susan Gilliland*
Rebekah Gimenez
Grace Ginn
Kathy Glasser
Carolyn Phillips Glenn
Laura Goeb
May Golomb
Bonny Nickle Goodwin
Carina Graham
Teresa Grashoff*
Lisa Grzeszczak
Inevett Hahn
Christina Hall

Chris Hammond
Denise Hammond
Brandy Hand
Mike Hand
Stevie Hand
Ellen Hardgrove
Julee Harris**
Carole Henderson
Tricia Hensley**
Margaret Herod
Jessica Hew*
Julie Hey
Ann Hicks
Juliann Hickey*
Lonni Hillis
Peggy Reed Hopkins
Stephanie Howell*
Dedie Huder*
Allison Hudson*
Dottie Hughes
Mimi Bernstein Hull
Betty Jo Hurt
Kelly Isenhour
Jean A. Jackson
Martha Jennings
Barbara Jensenius
Ruth Joffrion
Dean Johnson
Nancy Johnson
Linda Jones
Patricia Jones
Laura Joslin
Susan Kaney
Nancy Kann
Ruth Kazeck
Barbara Keene
Erin Kelley*
Katherine Kelley
Ann Kelly**
Nancy King
Kristen Kinney
Mary Ann Kinser

Tyler Tilden Kirby
Catherine G. Kirkpatrick
Cary Klinger
Nancye Kobrin
Mary Catharine Kolbert
Beth Kroll
Marian Lacy
Martha Lacy
Jo-Ann Lamar
Penney Lawrence
April Lawson
Debbie Leider**
Susan Lewis
Paula Lightsey
Gwen Lindsey
Elizabeth Lippold
Ruth Littleford-Hanson**
Sarah Longino
Patty Love
Nancy Lower
Wendy Ludlow
Lynn Luzadder**
Ann Maguire
Joan Mahoney
Heidi Mangel
Kathryn Mangel
Karen Manglardi
Nan Mann
Becky Manuel
Ellen Marcopoulos
Susan-Marie Marsh
Brenda Marshall
Lillian Martin
Lisa Martin
Lurline Martin
Sarah McClane
Barbara McClenny
Elizabeth McClure
Janine McComas
Scottie McDaniell
Laura McDonald
Janna McGowan

Karen McGregor
Denise McKinney
Kathy McLain
Margaret McMillen
Stacey McNamara
Heather McPherson
Jennifer McRae*
Harriet Mead
Nancy Mele
Ann Mendenhall
Mindy Merrell
Deborah Miley
Susan Mitchell
Vicky Mixson
Sandi Moenssens
Lee-Ann Moher
Beth Moorefield
Christine Moran
Karen Moreno
Victoria Moreton
Berri Morris*
Marena Grant Morrisey
Diane Bouras Moshos
Leah Mullins
Barbie Murray
Sheila Musante**
Leigh Mycoff
Cynthia Forrester Nants**
Carol Nash
Barbara Nelson
Stephanie NeSmith
Lisa Neway
Mary Newsome*
Mary Norris
Leigh O'Donoghue
Robin Orosz
Danielle Oser*
Francie Owen
Jean M. Owen
Marcea Owen
Larken Pahlow
Lisle Pallin**

Nancy Palmer
Christine Panzo
Holli Parker**
Jennie Peluso
Dianna Perkins
Mary Alice Phelps
Cindy Phelps-Shirley**
Kitty Phillips
Rita Pierson
Jennifer Pruitt
Joanne Pryor
Lauren Quackenbush
Kelli Radcliff
Sara Raley
Jill Read
Diane Reece
Sheran Reich
Ann Reisch**
Tina Revelle*
Yvette Rhode**
Betty Robinson
Alex Robinson
Karen Roby-Winterkamp
Hope Roll
Carol Rosenfelt
Kimberly Ruffier
Kimberly Rugh*
Leslie Rugh*
Helena Ryan
Angie Salvo
Christa Santos
Doris Savalli
Sebastian Savalli
Sherry Scarboro
Susy Scarlatos*
Patti Secrist
Eugenia Sefcik
Angela Shaw*
Lisa Sheppard
Ruth Shively
Marcie Simmons
Dee Simpson

Wendy Simpson
Marcella Sims
Ellyn Siviglia
Sue Skambis
Annette Smith
Leslie Smith
Patricia Smith Moore
Suzanne Snow
Dana Solomon
Erin Sorvillo
Maureen Sredl*
Kelly Stevens
Patricia Stewart
Christine Stilwell
Laura Stoner
Mary Bell Streetman
Carol Streich
Alice Stuart
Jane Stuart
Cathy G. Sullivan
Susan Summar
Janie Sutton
Nancy Tallent
Amy Taylor*
Heather Taylor
Jane Terry
Dee Anne Thomas
Mike Thomas
Diana Thompson
Dana Thompson Gladden
Julie Tisdale-Simon
Wendy Trammell
Jane Trnka
Anna Tschetter**
Susanne Uncapher
Elizabeth Uslan
Joan Van Akin
Sarah Van Arsdel
Lori Van Dyke*
Debbie Vance
Gracie Vanness
Marianne Vanness**

Linda Vanrell
Holly Vanture
Susan Varnedoe
Mary Vilmos*
Mary Vojanec
Kristine Vorpagel-Shields
Kelly Wadsworth*
Jean Warren

Martha Weathers
Lisa Weaver
Teresa Wells
Jodie Wexelberg
Diana Wicks**
Patrice Williams
Amy Wilson
Patty Wilson

Jill Wollaston
Lynn Wollin
Louise Yergey
Mary Young
Jamey Zborowski
Gwyneth Zumft

*Mardi Gras Committee member
**A Sunsational Encore Committee member

We would also like to thank the following for their generous contributions.

Albertson's
Angelica Textile Services
Big Oaks Ranch
Busch Gardens
Capelli's Salon
Celebration Golf
Coca-Cola
Corned Beef Corner—
    St. Petersburg
Darden Restaurants
Dr. Dot Richardson
Dr. and Mrs. R. O. Van Dyke
Gooding's Supermarkets
Hard Rock Cafe

Historic New Orleans Society
Holland and Knight, LLP
House of Blues
Lagniappe Cafe
Lakeridge Winery
Let Us Frame It
Lombardi's Seafood
Moriah Brandon's Salon
Mr. B. B. Abbott, PA
Mr. and Mrs. William Bishop
Mr. and Mrs. Austin Caruso
Mr. and Mrs. Edward Gilliland
Mr. James Pontones
Mr. and Mrs. Michael Sredl

NFL Players' Grill
Pebbles Restaurants
Phoenix Home Life
Pitch Blue Jam
Premier Beverage
Red Lobster Restaurants
Royalty Foods, Inc.
Schenck Company
Sloppy Joe's
Steven Anthony's Catering
Sunshine Network
Superior Quik Print
The Coach Store
Tommy Hilfiger

BIBLIOGRAPHY

Chicone, Jerry, Jr., and Brenda Eubanks Burnette. *Florida Citrus Crate Labels: An Illustrated History*. Bartow, Fla.: Bartow Inc., 1996.

Robison, Jim, and Mark Andrews. *Flashbacks: The Story of Central Florida's Past*. Orlando, Fla.: Orange County Historical Society and *The Orlando Sentinel*, 1995.

Russell, Marilyn C., and Nancy Hardey. *The Florida Citrus Showcase: Classic Crates from Florida*. Orlando, Fla.: Southern Lithographing Inc., 1995.

INDEX

• • •

ORDER INFORMATION

• • •

Junior League of Greater Orlando
125 North Lucerne Circle, East
Orlando, Florida 32801
To order by phone (407) 422-5057
To order by fax (407) 422-1412

Please send _____ copies of A Sunsational Encore @ $21.95 each $ _____

Florida residents add 6% sales tax @ $1.32 each $ _____

Postage and handling @ $3.00 each $ _____

(Price is subject to change without notice.)   Total $ _____

Please charge my   [   ] VISA   [   ] MasterCard

Account Number _____   Expiration Date _____

Signature _____

Name _____

Address _____

City _____ State _____ Zip _____

Telephone Number   (   ) _____

How did buyer find out about A Sunsational Encore?

[   ] Friend   [   ] League member   [   ] Bookstore   [   ] Newspaper

[   ] Other _____

Please make checks payable to Junior League of Greater Orlando.

This page may be photocopied.